PRAISE FOR *THE GUIDE TO URBAN FLY FISHING*

"A genuinely exciting book about getting on the water in the cities where most of us live. Thoughtful, thorough, and full of ideas to inspire you to get out of the office and into the game."

—**DAVID COGGINS**, author of *The Optimist* and *The Believer*

"Some thirty years ago, I wrote about the joys of fishing on New York's East River. Urban anglers turned out to be as fascinating as the wilderness fly fishers of Vermont or Montana. There's no better way to truly see a city than when you're carrying a 6-weight rod through its urban canyons. In this remarkable book, Marc Fryt ventures deep into that world, recognizing both the urgent need to preserve and expand nearby nature and the joy to be found there."

—**RICHARD LOUV**, author of *Last Child in the Woods and Fly-Fishing for Sharks*

"Marc Fryt's *The Guide to Urban Fly Fishing* is an important and inspiring read. It brilliantly connects city dwellers with the vital waters in their own backyards, sparking a powerful appreciation and a fierce commitment to clean water advocacy. The book underscores the importance of protecting these vital resources by beautifully illustrating how engaging with our local waters, even in urban settings, can make us happier, healthier, and more at peace. It's a practical blueprint for anyone looking to discover, enjoy, and care for the healthy waters that every community deserves. Marc's book has also really helped me level up my skills."

—**MARC YAGGI**, chief executive officer, Waterkeeper Alliance

"*The Guide to Urban Fly Fishing* is a powerful reminder that great fishing can be found right outside your back door. It offers a thoughtful blend of fishing fundamentals—covering gear, fish behavior, and reading water—while also diving deeper into the history of urban angling, local regulations, water quality, and the importance of community. I appreciate the clear layout, inclusive content, and its recognition of many wonderful fishing organizations. This guide truly reflects the accessibility, diversity, and connection that define what fly fishing should be."

—**HEATHER HODSON**, founder, iFishiBelong, United Women on the Fly, and Fly Fish Instruct

"Equal parts instruction manual, fishing journal, philosophic treatise, and elegy to urban wilderness, *The Guide to Urban Fly Fishing* is to the modern city dweller what Izaak Walton's *The Compleat Angler* was to the 'contemplative man' of the seventeenth century. . . . Marc Fryt has created a sort of bible for the inner-city fly fisher."

—**KIRK LOMBARD**, author of *The Sea Forager's Guide to the Northern California Coast*

"Marc Fryt understands that the 'outdoors' isn't always some pristine wilderness . . . it's more likely a municipal park, public beach, or a river beneath a freeway."

—**ROSS PURNELL**, editor and publisher, *Fly Fisherman* magazine

"Marc Fryt knows that you don't have to launch a wilderness expedition to experience wildness. You can experience fly-fishing adventure in the heart of the city. This book will tell you all you need to know to get started. But it's more than a how-to guide. It's an eloquent celebration of the great fishing that can be found just a few blocks away."

—**MATTHEW L. MILLER**, author of *Fishing Through the Apocalypse*

"Marc Fryt's book is an amazing resource for new and experienced fly fishers who want to explore waters closer to home. It provides instruction on how to fish any body of water in or near urban areas. *The Guide to Urban Fly Fishing* will be one of my top three book recommendations for students taking the fly-fishing course at Penn State."

—**GEORGE DANIEL**, two-time US National Fly Fishing Champion; director, Joe Humphreys Fly Fishing Program at Penn State

"In an era marked by a growing loneliness epidemic and a widening disconnect from the natural world, *The Guide to Urban Fly Fishing* offers a clear pathway back to nature and each other, right in our own backyards. It challenges the outdated notion that fly fishing requires remote mountain streams, expensive gear, or exclusivity, instead celebrating the accessibility and vibrancy of inner-city waters accompanied by a deep sense of community. Urban fly fishing offers tangible mental, emotional, physical, and social benefits close to home. This book is a refreshing reminder that fly fishing is not only for everyone, but for everywhere."

—**LINDSAY KOCKA**, founder and facilitator, Wade Well: Fly Fishing and Functional Mobility

"Before reading *The Guide to Urban Fly Fishing*, clear your mind of any preconceptions about mountain streams and dry flies. Marc Fryt's thoroughly researched and fun-to-read guide to inner-city angling is miles away from *A River Runs Through It*. Instead, Fryt's book brings fly fishing to millions of city dwellers. A passionate angler and talented writer, Fryt not only shows us how to fish our downtown waterways but also illuminates why big-city waters are worth saving."

—**RIC BURNLEY**, editor, *Kayak Angler*

"*The Guide to Urban Fly Fishing* lowers the barriers to the sport, making it accessible to all, regardless of age, ability, race, class, or gender. Like all good guides, Marc Fryt, rather than handing you a line with a hooked fish, provides you with the tools you need and directs you toward waters that you can explore, experience, and discover on your own. Fryt fosters a new and rich relationship with our urban waters and the world around us."

—**DR. GREG GORDON**, professor of environmental studies and science, Gonzaga University; editor, *Rewilding the Urban Frontier*

"Grab your rod and fly box. If you don't live close to a city, then also pack a bag and plan a trip to one close by. After reading *The Guide to Urban Fly Fishing*, you will be ready to run out the door to explore the local city pond or the river that runs through downtown. Marc shares fantastic insights, tips, and advice on how to approach these different bodies of water, along with stories from anglers across the country. Every city has a community out there and *The Guide to Urban Fly Fishing* shows you to how to get started on this journey and find yours."

—**KATIE JOHNSTONE**, fly-fishing guide; cofounder, Ohio Women on the Fly

THE GUIDE TO URBAN FLY FISHING

THE GUIDE TO URBAN FLY FISHING

How to Explore and Enjoy Your Local Waters

MARC FRYT

Foreword by

TOM ROSENBAUER

Preface by

DR. BRANDON DALE

Chelsea Green Publishing
White River Junction, Vermont
London, UK

First published in 2026 by Chelsea Green Publishing | PO Box 4529 |
White River Junction, VT 05001 | West Wing, Somerset House, Strand |
London, WC2R 1LA, UK | www.chelseagreen.com
A Division of Rizzoli International Publications, Inc. | 49 West 27th Street |
New York, NY 10001 | www.rizzoliusa.com

Publisher: Charles Miers
Deputy Publisher: Matthew Derr
Project Manager: Natalie Wallace
Developmental Editor: Anna Bliss
Copy Editor: Buzz Poole
Proofreader: Fran Pulver
Indexer: Shana Milkie
Designer: Melissa Jacobson

ISBN 978-1-64502-317-3 (paperback) | ISBN 978-1-64502-318-0 (ebook)
Library of Congress Control Number: 2025029978 (print)

Our Commitment to Green Publishing
Chelsea Green sees publishing as a tool for cultural change and ecological stewardship. We strive to align our book manufacturing practices with our editorial mission and to reduce the impact of our business enterprise in the environment. We print our books using vegetable-based inks whenever possible. This book may cost slightly more because it was printed on paper supplied by Versa from well-managed, FSC®-certified forests and other controlled sources.

Authorized EU representative for product safety and compliance
Mondadori Libri S.p.A. | www.mondadori.it
via Gian Battista Vico 42 | Milan, Italy 20123

Printed in the United States of America.
10 9 8 7 6 5 4 3 2 1   26 27 28 29 30

To urban waters. Not just shaped, but shaping in return.

CONTENTS

Foreword by Tom Rosenbauer xi
Preface by Dr. Brandon Dale xiv

Introduction: Fly Fishing Right Outside Your Door **1**
Fishing Your City and Discovering What's Possible, 2 • Why Fly Fishing Is Ideal for Urban Waters, 5 • How to Use this Book, 8 • How's the Fishing?, 11

Chapter 1: Get Your Gear **13**
How Much Will I Have to Spend?, 14 • Getting the Most out of a Fly-fishing Setup, 14 • Tips for Buying Your Fly-fishing Setup, 15 • Recommended Setup #1: The All-Rounder, 16 • Recommended Setup #2: The Heavy Hitter, 19 • Prioritizing Casting Skills over Perfect Gear, 20 • Taking Care of Your Equipment, 22 • Choosing Fly-fishing Leaders, 22 • Tenkara Rods: A Minimalist's Approach to Urban Fly Fishing, 25 • Top Fly Patterns for Urban Waters, 26 • DIY Fly Patterns That Work for Your Needs, 31 • Modifying Tackle to Reduce Fish Injury and Mortality, 32 • Customizing Your Kit with Additional Gear and Apparel, 35

Chapter 2: Finding Spots to Fish In Your City **41**
Where to Start: Key Resources, 42 • Using Digital Mapping Tools, 43 • Know Your Rights to Fish, 53 • Trespassing, 56 • Secret Spots, 57 • Get Out There, 58

Chapter 3: Find Your Community **61**
Building Skills and Safety Through Community Fishing, 62 • Meeting Other Anglers on the Water, 66 • Connecting with Fishing Groups, 67 • Building and Promoting Angling Communities in Your City, 74 • Fishing Outside the City, 76 • Communal Waters, 77

Chapter 4: Reading the Water and Observing Fish Behavior **81**
Reading the Water: An Essential Skill for Urban Anglers, 81 • Observing Fish Behavior, 86 • Presenting Your Fly to the Fish, 90

Chapter 5: A Brief History of Urban Waters 93
The Urban Waterscape, 94 • How Our Urban Waterscapes Were Formed, 94

Chapter 6: Common Pollutants in Urban Waters 101
Resources for Local Water Quality Information, 102 • Resources for Learning About Water Quality in General, 104 • Thinking of Wading?, 105 • Thinking of Eating that Fish?, 107 • Common Pollutants and Water Quality Issues in Our Cities, 108 • Dirty Waters, 115

Chapter 7: Fish Species in Urban Waters 123
The Role of Anglers in the Sustainability of Urban Fisheries, 124 • Generalist Species, 125 • Common Freshwater Species, 126 • Other Freshwater Species, 131 • Saltwater Species, 135 • Understanding and Appreciating Urban Fish Diversity, 139 • Learning More About the Fish in Your Urban Waters, 141 • Which Species Will You Find in Your Waters?, 142

Chapter 8: Urban Waterways 145
Untamed Waterways, 145 • Waterways Reshaped by Channelization, 147 • Armored Waterways: Battling Erosion, 153 • Levees: Confining Waterways, 156 • Dams: Regulating Waterflows, 157 • Directors: Routing the Flow of Water, 164 • Alternative Water Control Infrastructure, 167

Chapter 9: Urban Shorelines 169
An Important Resource for the Saltwater Angler, 170 • Getting in the Water, 172 • Critically Important Shorelines, 174 • Urban Ponds and Small Lakes, 177 • Armored Shorelines, 179 • Marinas, Docks, and Piers, 182 • Breakwaters, 183 • Groins, 187 • Jetties, 189

Chapter 10: Changing Conditions of Urban Waters 193
Seasonal Changes, 193 • "Hoses" and "Straws", 195 • Streamgages, 200 • Water Level Fluctuations in Nonurban Waterways, 208 • Water Level Fluctuations in "Flashy" Urban Waterways, 209 • Traditional Infrastructure Under Pressure, 214 • Reenvisioning Urban Waters, 215

Conclusion: Making Your Cast 217

Acknowledgments 221
Further Resources 223
Bibliography 227
Index 231

FOREWORD

I don't have enough shopping carts in my life.

Part of the appeal of fly fishing is discovering new places to fish and new challenges. I live on a trout stream and have countless little mountain streams near my home where I can catch small wild brook, brown, and rainbow trout on dry flies. Yet what keeps me up at night, constantly looking at the clock to see if dawn is coming soon, is the anticipation of a long day chasing carp or bass or gar in the middle of a medium-sized, once-industrial city that is long past its sell-by date. I don't mind fishing among the shopping carts, drowned traffic cones, and abandoned bridge abutments. While traffic whizzes overhead, down in the river below I've seen bald eagles, white-tailed deer, herons, osprey, and even a mama raccoon with four little ones twirling on flimsy branches to reach the mulberries hanging perilously over the water. Meanwhile, a twenty-pound carp might be slurping the mulberries that have fallen into the water. The commuters charging to work on the bridge above have no idea what they are missing.

This is not what fly fishing looked like in its infancy. Prior to the twentieth century, it was a sport practiced by wealthy Europeans, almost strictly for trout and salmon, on private waters. But fly fishing has grown up. It is no longer as expensive as it used to be, there are vast tracts of public land in North America, and the demographic has become much more diverse. And we have discovered many new species outside of trout.

I constantly meet people from places like Dallas or Cincinnati or Oklahoma City who apologetically tell me they fly fish but have to drive hours from their homes to do so. Really? Many people tend to associate fly fishing with freshwater trout in remote wilderness streams. But in their urban and suburban neighborhoods, it's likely that they have the only freshwater fish that consistently pulls many yards of line from reels before slowing down, has fascinating, unpredictable feeding habits, and can survive in waters that would suffocate trout. The fish I'm talking about is carp. I once spent a week in Denver but didn't have the extra time to take advantage of the opportunity to drive a couple hours to fish for trout. So, I fished with Nic Hall, Rick Mikesell, and Davis James for carp in an apocalyptic landscape of chain-link fences, piles of trash, and giant buildings that housed nameless products being moved to unknown places with semis grinding back and forth. At one point, we fished off a bridge where we had to time our backcasts between eighteen-wheelers. Once we fished at night under floodlights. Was it fun? Was it exciting? You bet it was.

But carp can be tricky to catch and there are always panfish willing to play. Few things are more fun than an hour in an urban park seeing what's hiding in the depths, and most of these fish are willing to bite anything that looks reasonably alive. They also put a decent bend in a fly rod and can be as attractive as a native brook trout in a mountain stream. I don't think there is a more colorful and handsome fish in North America than a pumpkinseed sunfish, with its iridescent blue, orange, and green body and translucent yellow fins.

My grandson Ollie lives in a suburb of Boston and at age two was already begging me to take him fishing, as he'd seen videos of me on YouTube. Fully armed with a Snoopy rod, bobbers, and some worms, I was determined to get him hooked into at least one fish, as kids need to see action when they're fishing. A few minutes on an app called onWater Fish identified two lakes in public parks within ten minutes of their house, and a brief look on Google Earth showed some nice open areas. The first one looked a little deep close to shore, but a quick drive to the second lake followed by a walk around the pond showed me some sunfish in the shallows. It was a peaceful spot surrounded by mature hardwoods that offered enough shade on a sunny day to remain cool, but the trees were far enough from shore to host plenty of room for casting. If we hadn't been on a mission, it would have been a great place to lie in the grass and read a book.

The only problem was that the sunfish were in pockets of weeds that could have been a snagging problem with a worm and bobber. But they were perfect for a fly rod with a little popping bug because I could drop the fly into the spaces between the weeds without needing to reel the whole thing back through the salad.

I happened to have a fly rod in my truck, and although Ollie at that age was not ready for a fly rod, Grandpa was able to hook numerous sunfish for him. The first time I handed him the rod with a hooked fish, he immediately walked backward to land it, as all kids instinctively do the first time they catch fish on a fly rod. I don't know which of us was more excited, but I do know that I'll be exploring more lakes in the area as he gets older. I've already identified a half dozen potential spots nearby, and it doesn't matter that the nearest trout is probably hours away.

You are lucky to have this book in your hands. Marc Fryt has done a masterful job of introducing urban fly fishing in an inviting, accessible way and offering tips for how to find places to fly fish a lot closer to home than you could ever imagine. He's done extensive work, crisscrossing the country so that he can recommend tackle, techniques, and, most importantly, ways to find fish in urban areas no matter where you live. And he's gathered advice from some of the most enthusiastic and experienced urban fly fishers in the country. Whether you are totally new to fly fishing or a seasoned trout angler eager to give your fly rod a workout without the need to drive for hours, this book will be your complete guide.

The next time you are feeling stuck at work or at home, pining for some outdoor adventure, think about spending a couple hours before work, after dinner, or even on your lunch hour casting a fly to some fascinating creatures. There is something about an animal from the mysterious underwater world striking a fly that you've fooled them into thinking is their next meal—and the electric tension once that fish is hooked—that completely awakens the senses. I have no idea what it is. Just get out there and do it.

No need to wait until you can get to a trout stream.

TOM ROSENBAUER

PREFACE

"You can fish in this park?!"

It's the number one question I get—day in and day out—whether I'm fishing alone or guiding someone in Central Park, right in the middle of New York City. And it's a question that, unlike any other, consistently makes me smile. Not just because the answer is yes, but because every time someone asks, I get to witness a small mental shift—a door opening. It's a glimpse into the moment someone begins to imagine a new relationship with nature, a new version of themselves on the water, and the beginning of their own urban fishing journey. Whether that journey is from the past, present, or still to come, that spark is something truly special.

Often, this question unlocks a memory, like the time I met Gladis on the bus heading downtown to the water. A seventy-two-year-old retired banker, she sat next to me and gave me a perplexed but curious look out of the side of her eye, before she finally asked about my fly-fishing gear. She then smiled and reminisced about going fly fishing in the Catskills with her father every fall as a little girl. Or José—the early-season hotdog vendor who works a stand near the fountain—who excitedly told me about his annual trip to the Great South Bay to chase striped bass. Then there's Marcell, a Bronx native and retired NYPD officer who spends most mornings fishing for carp in Central Park with his son to pass fishing on to the next generation. And Carter, a fourteen-year-old fly angler and Upper West Side native whom I see almost daily after school in the spring and daily during the summers.

All these people represent just a sliver of what I think is one of the most beautiful and often overlooked aspects of urban fly fishing: the community. It's dynamic. It's growing. And it welcomes everyone. Urban fly fishing defies the stereotypes people often associate with both urban spaces and the fly-fishing world. It creates a community tapestry in which each thread is as rich and diverse as the fisheries themselves—and this adds strength to the whole. I have come to understand that every new urban fly angler represents an additional voice to advocate for the enhancement and protection of these natural spaces that are often overlooked.

One of the things I often tell people is that what makes nature so powerful isn't just the solitude or the scenery. It's the interconnectedness. Nature is a symphony of diverse species—fish, bugs, trees, birds—all relying on one another in intricate and beautiful ways. The trout can't survive without the bugs, and the trees need the squirrels just as the water needs clean banks. It's this web of interdependence that makes ecosystems function and thrive. And the same can be said of urban fly fishing. It's not just about the fish, although being able to catch a fifteen-pound carp, a twenty-five-pound striped bass, or a five-pound smallmouth bass within thirty minutes from home or the office sure doesn't hurt! It's about the people, the park staff, the locals, the passersby who ask questions, and the community that begins to form that now values and cares about this local urban ecosystem. That shared understanding—that appreciation of complexity and collaboration—is what makes this movement so powerful.

Marc's book helps us see and feel all of this clearly—the important ways in which fly fishing is evolving. It's becoming younger, more community-oriented, more conservation-minded, and more diverse. Urban fly fishing isn't the only reason for this shift, but it's helping to drive the change. *The Guide to Urban Fly Fishing* is a fantastic on-ramp for anyone curious about how to find fish in urban environments and, just as importantly, how to find their urban fly-fishing community.

One of the things that first surprised me when I started fishing urban waters—throwing bread into a local park pond in Louisiana as a middle schooler—was just how alive those ecosystems really were. That curiosity followed me through high school, college, grad school, and now well into adulthood. Now, I rarely travel anywhere without my fly rod. It's my passport to explore urban waterways, both new and familiar. I'm still sometimes surprised at what I find, and I'm always thankful. We have an astonishing abundance of fishable water—within thirty minutes of nearly every American city, big and small. Opportunities to chase diverse, resilient, and challenging species on the fly are everywhere. Most people don't realize it's even possible. But when they do, it changes them.

Take Anne, for example, a client and now friend whom I guided last season. A Brooklyn resident originally from Michigan who hadn't fly fished since she left home and moved to New York City years ago, Anne planned a father-daughter carp-on-the-fly trip for her father's visit to the city. Unfortunately, her father couldn't make it, but she decided to fish anyway. We fished hard all day, with several close calls and carp hooked but not landed. We continued to fish into the evening, with rats emerging from the bushes and concert sounds drifting in the muggy summer air . . . and, at last, just as the twilight finally turned to darkness, Anne landed a big one.

As the twenty-seven-inch fat-bellied common carp slid into the net, she screamed with joy and threw her hands into the air: "FINALLY!"

That moment was a door opening. A few days later, she reached out to me about getting involved in local conservation efforts to support and clean up our NYC fisheries. A month later, she joined me on the board of the NYC Trout Unlimited (TU) chapter, and since then, she's organized fundraisers, led watershed cleanups, and helped expand trout-in-the-classroom programs. I later received a thank-you message from Anne's father once he learned about Anne becoming our newest TU board member—and, more importantly, a new angler-conservationist. And it all started with one urban fly-fishing trip.

Urban fly fishing creates access where access has historically been limited—by geography, by finances, by lack of knowledge, or by fear of not belonging. It creates opportunities to build relationships with land and water that are right in our own backyards. And those relationships matter. When people connect with place, they begin to care. When they care, they protect. It's as simple—and powerful—as that.

Don't get me wrong, I love a remote trout stream or a quiet saltwater flat as much as the next fly-obsessed angler out there. But there's something profoundly meaningful about urban fly fishing. It brings people together. It sparks curiosity. And it inspires stewardship.

For the onlookers who stop to ask questions, who watch from the park benches and bridge crossings, who wonder if maybe they could try it too—this book is for you. I hope you get curious enough to start your own journey. This book is something I wish existed fifteen years ago. Marc is at the forefront of a movement, blending tactics, community insight, and a genuine love for urban water. This isn't just a how-to guide. It's a guide for how to see your city differently, how to find adventure and meaning close to home, and how to build a better, more expansive fly-fishing community—one cast at a time.

So, take Marc's lessons to heart. Explore your city. Fish your local waters. Share the stoke. Bring a friend, or a stranger. Become a steward. And when someone inevitably asks, "You can fish in this park?!" smile big and say, "Yes, you *can* and *should* fish in this park."

DR. BRANDON DALE

INTRODUCTION

Fly Fishing Right Outside Your Door

When you read the words *fly fishing*, what do you picture in your head? Maybe you imagine a mountain river, a solitary angler casting a loop of line through the air, and a trout jumping out of the water. If you are someone who already enjoys fly fishing, then you might have lived out this scene. For me, when I was searching for a way to decompress and get away from life in the military, these were exactly the images I had in mind. And in my first years of fly fishing, thanks to some helpful resources and friends, things unfolded just as I had hoped.

That all changed, however, when I left the army and moved from Washington state to Columbus, Ohio. It was a jolting transition going from alpine peaks to a flat midwestern city of over two million people. To escape the feeling of being trapped in the city, I would drive an hour to the nearest trout river. But standing in the water and casting a loop of line as farmers plowed fields of corn along the riverbank was not the image of fly fishing etched in my mind. Clinging to the idea that all I wanted were those mountains and clear, rocky streams and being alone and away from it all, my passion ebbed away.

Associating fly fishing only with the idyllic scenes stuck in our heads can prevent us from seeing the other wonderful possibilities around us, and when we're led to believe that "nature" is somehow separate from our cities, it further limits our imaginations. When I stumbled upon an online photo of someone fly fishing in a concrete canal with bridges and power lines crisscrossing in the background, my entire perception flipped upside down. Inspired, I started fishing urban waters I had never considered before. I became absorbed in new adventures, uncovering hidden spots,

Who Is the Angler?

The word *angler* comes from the fifteenth-century English word "angle," meaning "to fish with a hook." It's time to re-think the term's old-school roots, which is why throughout this book I use "angler" as an all-encompassing term: The modern angler is anyone who seeks connection with water and the life it holds, whether fishing for food, outdoor fun, community, advocacy, tradition, or something else entirely. Today, angling is about curiosity, care, a sense of discovery, and engagement.

and catching different species of fish, including the largest one I ever landed with a fly rod. It was all right there in my city—I couldn't get enough.

Over time, urban fishing drew me into angling communities, eventually leading me to teach people how to fish in the city and, later, to become an urban fly-fishing guide. While I still venture beyond city limits to visit other beloved waters, more often than not, I'm fishing right where I live. This journey has completely reshaped my view of urban life and what fishing means to me. Ultimately, it also led me to write this book—to share knowledge, encouragement, and inspiration so that you, too, can experience the joys of fishing in your own city.

Fishing Your City and Discovering What's Possible

In the United States, over 80 percent of us live in urban areas surrounded by rivers, streams, ponds, lakes, and ocean shorelines. These resources provide drinking water, are used by factories to produce goods and materials, and serve as avenues to transport countless products, among other uses. And these bodies of water are also right at our doorsteps, beckoning us

Analiza del Rosario enjoys an early morning of fly fishing for surfperch along Santa Monica Beach in Los Angeles, one of the busiest beaches in the United States.

to spend time outside, to play, to have fun, to enjoy moments with family and friends. And yes, to go fishing.

Urban riverbanks and shorelines are portals to outdoor adventure where growing communities of anglers are having unforgettable experiences that largely go unnoticed by everyone else. With a fishing rod in hand, you shift from being a mere observer of your environment to an active participant engaging with local waters. What once seemed like ordinary ponds, rivers, or shorelines become dynamic ecosystems and playgrounds for exploration and discovery. Fishing immerses you in your surroundings, offering a way to be present in the moment and enjoy something new. It's about being active, moving from spot to spot, decoding the habits of fish, and thinking creatively to solve the ever-changing puzzle of where they are biting.

Fishing in cities also fosters connection. It creates shared experiences with family, friends, and community, turning an ordinary day by the water into a meaningful memory. It's exciting to spend quality time on the water with others, bonding over the experience of trying to catch a fish. Whether it's a parent teaching a child how to cast, friends trading tips about the best fishing spots, or strangers striking up conversations, urban fishing has moments of camaraderie that transcend differences in backgrounds and experience levels. This helps to create safer and more social environments, ones that are vibrant and welcoming.

Urban fishing is very accessible. You can walk, bike, drive, or take public transit to your local waters, opening up miles of opportunities to explore. City parks, maintained paths, bridges, piers, and public waterfronts provide convenient entry points for anglers, and many urban waters remain fishable year-round. Fishing can also be an affordable way to enjoy the outdoors in your city. Despite common misconceptions, fly fishing doesn't have to be a major financial investment. In fact, the cost of a single visit to a professional football game or theme park, or a night out (or canceling some of those barely used

For an urban fly fisher, it's not uncommon to need both your arms to hold up a fish for a photo!

With urban waters being so close to where we live, it's easy to get outside with family and friends to share in engaging and fun experiences.

Urban fishing takes you to places you never imagined going to before, such as that creek flowing through your neighborhood, the base of a dam, or even a municipal wastewater treatment plant.

subscriptions), is comparable to a budget-friendly fly-fishing starter combo. This makes it an activity that fits more easily into a wide range of budgets. And because it's something you can do without needing to drive for hours, it can work with most people's schedules.

Why Fly Fishing Is Ideal for Urban Waters

This book focuses on fly fishing in urban waters, and there are some compelling reasons for this. But before we get into that, I just want to state that there are other effective fishing methods you can use in urban waters besides fly fishing, and much of the information within these pages is highly useful regardless of which method you prefer. So, if you already own some other fishing gear, please don't feel like you have to go buy a fly rod.

With that said, why did I choose to focus on fly fishing in this book? Let's begin by briefly defining what fly fishing is and how it differs from other methods of fishing. Fly fishing uses *fly patterns* made from materials (such as feathers, fur, foam, rubber, metal pieces, etc.) that are tied onto a hook. Unlike other forms of fishing that rely on the weight of a lure or bait to carry the line, fly fishing uses the weight of the fly line itself to propel the fly pattern to the fish. This technique allows fly fishers to cast a wide range of flies that mimic various food items, providing versatility in attracting and catching different species of fish in many different conditions.

That last sentence is really important. In your city, there are numerous bodies of water for you to discover and many species of fish to catch, and the really fun adventure is being able to experience the full range of possibilities. With just *one fly rod and one*

Fly patterns can imitate just about every food source that fish feed on in cities. They don't smell or go bad like bait, you don't need big tackle boxes or coolers to carry them around in, and they are much easier to use than trying to get a worm onto a hook. L. J. Houdyshell is a fly fisher in Los Angeles who also enjoys tying flies, a skill that adds to the sense of personal accomplishment when catching a fish.

line, you have an adaptable tool that can cast out flies mimicking all sorts of food items, from insects as tiny as ants and mosquitoes to larger prey such as crayfish and small fish. Using other fly patterns, you can even imitate things like worms, pieces of torn bread, fish eggs, small berries, and so on. Fly patterns can be floated on the surface, sunk to the bottom, or presented at any depth in between, allowing you to mimic whatever the fish are feeding on, and there is a lot of random stuff that fish are eating in urban areas! That kind of versatility is unmatched when compared to other fishing methods.

There is no single "right" way to fly fish, making it just as accessible to beginners as it is rewarding for the most dedicated anglers. It can be as simple or intricate an activity as you want. Some anglers keep it minimal by using just a fly rod, line, and handful of effective flies, and focusing on enjoying their time outside. Others take a more tailored approach, fine-tuning their gear with waders and specialized lines, studying water conditions, and selecting flies to catch a particular species of fish.

Additionally, if you're completely new to fishing, you can absolutely start with fly fishing. One of its great advantages is that many of the basics can be picked up intuitively. But here's something surprising: *You don't need any casting skills to start urban fly fishing*. In fact, there are many scenarios in urban fly fishing where making a proper fly cast is completely unnecessary. For example, there are times when fish feed so close to where you are standing that simply holding the rod out and "dapping" the fly onto the water might be all it takes to catch a fish. And dapping is actually a preferred method when fly fishing among trees, near fences, atop piers or boardwalks, or when fish are easily spooked by a fly line hitting the water.

As you spend more time on the water, you'll of course want to learn how to cast,

FISHING TIP

Releasing Fish without Having to Touch Them

If you are concerned about a fish swallowing the hook deeply, a fly rod is a great choice for you. With fly fishing, the hook often pierces only the fish's lip. This is because, once a fish bites down on a fly, it quickly realizes it isn't food and tries to spit it out. Most often it's as easy as landing the fish into a net, grabbing the fly with your fingers or needle-nose pliers, and removing the hook from the mouth of the fish. Point being, with fly fishing it is generally easier to catch and release a fish back into the water without ever having to actually touch the fish.

There are many casting techniques with fly fishing, but with urban fishing one of the most effective methods is getting close to the water, reaching out, dunking your fly into the water ("dapping"), and watching the fish for when it eats.

Urban fly fishing isn't new. In fact, it has been around for a while, but there has been so little written about it that anglers across the country, like Brandon Dale, are creatively figuring out how to fly fish in urban areas.

not only to increase your chances of catching fish but also to experience one of the truly unique, meditative joys of fly fishing. In the back of this book, I've listed several free online resources that will teach you how to cast a fly rod. Now, if you're still unsure about your potential to pick up this skill, it's helpful to consider that most fly fishers, myself included, had little to no formal instruction on how to cast when first starting out. We just went down to the water and started waving the rod and line through the air. With a bit of practice, maybe over at a local park, you, too, can figure out what more or less does and doesn't work, and then move on to the other fun parts of urban fly fishing. Don't let perfectionism hold you back from getting out there and learning on the go.

SAFETY TIP

Eating Fish Caught in Urban Waters

When first starting out with urban fishing, I recommend releasing what you catch and to fish from the shore or riverbank until you gain more experience and knowledge. While urban waters are much cleaner than they were decades ago, they still face problems with pollution. In chapter 6, I discuss the subjects of pollution, water quality, and fish consumption. That chapter also provides information to help you make more informed decisions about if and when it is safe to go wading into the water.

How to Use this Book

Whether you're a seasoned angler or someone who has never fished before, this book will give you the knowledge, resources, and confidence to go out and fish in your city. Note that most of the information and tips in these chapters can be applied to *any city, town, or suburban area in North America*. This is also a book written for the wading or shore-bound angler, offering techniques and strategies for fishing that don't require a boat.

In the first half of this book, chapters 1 through 4, you will find essential information and guidance to get you on the water. If you are more experienced with fishing, the topics covered here might be familiar but are presented through an "urban lens." Areas of focus include:

- choosing a fly rod, flies, and other tackle for urban fly fishing
- finding spots to go fishing in your city
- connecting with angling communities and fishing partners
- locating fish and determining where to cast your fly

Anglers like Minneapolis fly-fishing guide Rick Phetsavong were instrumental in helping me develop this book. Their kindness, generosity, and willingness to share their knowledge and experiences are a big part of what makes fishing in cities so amazing.

Our phones, computers, and other screens are always drawing us in, even as we make efforts to spend more time outside to disconnect from them. Fly fishing is another way to unplug, and this book is your starting point to enjoy the sport's immersive, sensory experiences.

The second half of this book is about taking your skills to the next level. This is where I delve deeper into the various structures in and around urban waters and strategic ways to fish them. I gathered much of this information by traveling to multiple cities and spending time with other urban anglers, collecting their knowledge, stories, and insights. Additionally, between travels, I did a significant amount of research into scientific papers and textbooks and talked with experts from various fields of study—all as part of my best effort to find, compile, and pass along vital information about modern urban waters and how to fish them. Topics covered in the second half of this book include:

- the history of urban waters and features of these unique ecosystems
- water quality and pollution and their effects on fishing
- behaviors and traits of fish species more commonly found in urban areas
- how to navigate through urban waters and fish around human-made infrastructure
- how to prepare for and adapt fishing tactics to changing conditions in urban waters

Throughout this book, you will also find uplifting stories from other urban anglers who are building communities, advocating for urban fisheries, and contributing to the revitalization of these shared waters. Learning more about these waters increases personal awareness of just how valuable these ecosystems are. If you've ever wanted to play a part in creating something better for your family, community, or city, I hope that, in whatever small way, this book inspires and empowers you to do so.

There is a lot to discover in this book and in your city! However,

Many urban waters are degraded and forgotten about or used as dumping grounds. But many anglers are finding out how precious these waters are and how rewarding it is to connect with the fish living in our cities with us.

RESEARCH TIP

Talk with Local Experts

While exploring cities with a fishing rod is incredibly fun, it's important to remember that urban fishing comes with its own set of risks. Whether you're wading into city waters or fishing around human-made structures, these decisions require careful consideration. Although this book aims to provide comprehensive guidance, I urge you to continue gathering information and insights along the way. Seek advice from other anglers in different cities, as local fishing conditions and advice can vary widely.

Also, while I'm an impassioned fly-fishing instructor and guide, I'm not a water-quality scientist, biologist, climatologist, ecologist, or engineer. In researching urban waters and talking with various experts for this book, I have learned a great deal and am excited to share it all with you through my own lens as an urban angler. If you wish to explore the science further, you can find my sources at the end of the book.

before we move on with this adventure, I want to address any preconceptions you might have about urban fishing.

How's the Fishing?

With a fishing rod in hand, you have unspoken access to urban waters. When you hop off the concrete path and head toward the water, people passing by might give sideways stares. Most often though, they'll just smile and say, "That looks so fun!" or "I didn't know you could do that!" For example, in Denver, I watched Nic Hall saddle a bridge beam to get a better shot at some fish. People passing by stared at him as if he had lost his mind. But as soon as he began casting, smiles appeared across everyone's faces.

These onlookers will also ask a very common question: "How's the fishing?" People will want to know if you caught a fish, and how big it was. At times, you will succeed and share in the excitement of an amazing catch. Enjoy the moment and hold on to those memorable photos and stories. But on other days, catching a fish—any fish—can be a huge accomplishment. While traveling to cities working on this book, there were days when the other talented anglers and I made a great effort to catch *anything*. But even when just one of us landed a fish, it was a success for us all.

I know that telling you to "Just stick with it!" rings very hollow when you're out there struggling to get a bite. But the reality is that catching fish in cities takes time, and it's normal to come up with an empty net, which anglers jokingly refer to as "getting skunked." That's because in urban waters the deck is stacked against us,

It takes some confidence to hop up onto a bridge like Nic Hall did. When I first started urban fly fishing, I was very self-conscious. I would wait until people weren't looking, then sneak down to the water and make a cast. I worried people would mock me, but after years of fishing in cities, I don't care if I make a fool of myself while fishing. I'm enjoying myself.

and it's really stacked against the fish. Fishing in cities is different—it requires a countercultural mindset, one that goes against unwritten rules and mainstream expectations to discover opportunities most people never see. Urban anglers persist, adapt, and turn overlooked waters into something entirely new. And believe me, the personal growth and sense of accomplishment that come with these challenges are well worth the effort!

Jennifer Hsia is an urban angler who has honed her skills to catch fish in the most unlikely of places, even in the heart of Minneapolis. Many of us who fish in cities share this same drive to uncover every opportunity that our urban waters offer.

Minneapolis angler Jennifer Hsia might never have gotten into fishing if her partner, Rick Phetsavong, hadn't suggested they try it out together. Jennifer, less than enthusiastic, said she'd go fishing no more than five times. They got skunked again and again. But, on the very last day, they started to catch fish, and she discovered a new passion. Now Jennifer fishes in many places around the world, but she loves being on the water so much that fishing outside cities is not enough. Spend time with urban anglers and you will find that we all have our own personal reasons for fishing in our cities. Somewhere along the way—navigating the concrete walls and chain-link fences and wading through oil-filmed water among the floating chunks of slime-covered plastics and sunken shopping carts, coping with the snagged hooks and broken lines and not catching a single damn thing—something inside us *clicked*. That "something" drives us to keep fishing in our cities, and it is unique to each of us, and it will be yours to discover as well.

CHAPTER 1

Get Your Gear

Urban fly fishing allows you to enjoy quality time on the water with minimal gear. Often, all you need is a fly rod, a couple of flies, and a pair of nail clippers to catch a fish. If you're new to fly fishing, some of the gear and tackle discussed in this chapter may be unfamiliar, but I'll do my best to make everything clear and accessible, no matter your level of experience.

If you already have a fly rod, anything from light gear to a heavier setup, don't feel pressured to buy a completely new rod or line to start

Many of the anglers highlighted in this book have high-quality gear because they are incredibly dedicated and passionate about fishing. But if you are just starting out or working with a limited budget, there are ways to keep urban fly fishing simple and inexpensive.

fishing in your city. Use what you have, and as you spend more time exploring urban waters, you might identify specific reasons to invest in a different rod or line. Or you might want to get waders and boots, or even treat yourself to a second fly rod or high-end gear—because fishing in cities doesn't mean we can't appreciate or benefit from top-of-the-line equipment.

In this chapter, I'll introduce and recommend essential gear for urban fly fishing:

- fly lines, rods, and reels (or "setups")
- fly-fishing leaders
- fly patterns

I'll also offer tips for making purchases and maintaining gear to help it last for years, along with practical insights into general fishing equipment and other useful items you might need while on the water. But first, let's consider your budget.

How Much Will I Have to Spend?

If you are a beginner with no gear, fly fishing will require an initial modest investment, but it's far more accessible than many people realize. Quality, mid-priced fly lines, rods, and reels are effective tools that last for years with minimal upkeep. A well-made, mid-priced package that includes a line, rod, and reel will support skill development and improved performance while providing a level of quality most anglers won't "grow out of." In other words, one purchase can set you up for the long term.

For those on a tighter budget or just testing the waters, several companies, including Orvis, WETFLY, L. L. Bean, Echo, Redington, Maxcatch, Cortland Line Company (specifically its Fairplay line of products), and Cabela's offer affordable combos (which will include the line, rod, and reel). With a little upkeep, these budget-friendly setups can also last for years, making them an excellent way to enjoy urban fly fishing without breaking the bank.

Getting the Most out of a Fly-fishing Setup

When I talk about a "fly-fishing setup," I'm referring to the combination of a fly line, rod, and reel, and in the world of fly fishing there's an overwhelming variety to choose from. To simplify things, as I traveled to different cities and spoke with other anglers for this book, one of my first questions was, "Is there an ideal fly-fishing setup for urban waters?" I wanted to know if a single setup could effectively catch fish in any North American city. To start answering that question, let's keep in mind that urban fishing presents a wide range of conditions, scenarios, and fish species. The versatility of fly fishing is a wonderful way to explore all the fishing opportunities within your city. To make the most of this versatility, aim to purchase a fly-fishing setup that's as all-around as possible. But what exactly does "all-around" mean?

While a setup is the combination of line, rod, and reel, here I want to focus on the fly line and rod because how these two components work together is key. With an all-around fly-fishing setup for urban fishing, you should be able to effectively and efficiently cast:

- a wide range of fly sizes—from fly patterns the size of a fingernail to the size of small fish or small frogs, 1–3.5 inches (2.5–9 cm)
- heavier flies that weigh about as much as a penny; in other words, you could throw the fly across a neighborhood street
- lighter and more air-resistant flies; in other words, you'd have difficulty throwing the fly even halfway across the street
- two-fly rigs consisting of both a heavier and a lighter fly

You'll also want the fly line and rod to perform various tasks efficiently, such as making a cast out to 25 feet (8 m) while your back is literally up against a wall, quickly making a short cast of 20 feet (6 m) or less, and making an accurate longer cast to about 40–50 feet (12–15 m).

All of that is a lot to ask of a fly line and rod! And yes, an all-around setup is a jack-of-all-trades. While it might not excel at any one particular task, it helps you to fish in different conditions and catch all sorts of species.

Now, before I recommend what fly line or rod to select, let's briefly discuss some tips for buying a fly-fishing setup.

Tips for Buying Your Fly-fishing Setup

Before buying anything, it's a good idea to talk with other fly fishers you encounter locally or get to know through social media. Listen to their preferences for fly lines, rods, and reels, and ask why they choose them for your local waters. They'll have valuable insights that might differ from my more general recommendations below. It's also helpful to talk with local anglers about the brands, online stores, and fly shops they prefer.

If there are any local fly shops in your area, also ask for their advice and consider purchasing directly from them. Many fly shops (and brands) give back to communities in the form of free fly-fishing clinics and financial support for local conservation efforts and angler outreach programs. So, even though you might end up paying a little extra, it's worth it when you see efforts being reinvested in the local fishing and angling community. Higher-priced gear might also be made entirely in North America, supporting local businesses and jobs, and established brand-name companies offer better return, exchange, and repair policies and customer service. Additionally, purchasing from a fly shop, or directly from a brand's website, can save you money, as they might offer discounts when you buy the line, rod, and reel together. Fly shops might even include a free fly-casting lesson with your purchase and ensure the fly line is set up appropriately on the reel.

While most fly shops have incredibly helpful staff, not every shop employee will understand why you want to fish local urban waters or target certain fish species, and this can be discouraging for new anglers entering the sport. I was fortunate early in my urban fly-fishing journey to receive encouragement from the team at Mad River Outfitters in Columbus, Ohio. Many of the shop's employees were genuinely excited to help me learn how to fish the local waters and catch unusual fish species. The encouragement I received from the staff at Mad River Outfitters was invaluable and gave me the confidence to fully embrace urban fishing. Plus, as I expanded my urban fishing experience, I wanted to purchase more gear tailored to my goals, so it turned out to be a win-win for both me and the fly shop.

Many cities don't even have a local fly shop. With that in mind, I've detailed the information below to assist those of you who may be ordering gear online. You'll notice that the information for each setup is presented in a specific order; this is intentional. First, I list considerations regarding conditions, fish species, and fly patterns. Those details determine the type of fly line needed. Once the appropriate fly line is chosen, the next step is to match it with a fly rod. Finally, the reel is selected to complete the setup. If you do end up visiting a fly shop, this sequence of information is key, as it helps shop employees guide you toward the best purchase for your fishing needs.

With all of this in mind, let's dive into the first setup I recommend for urban fly fishing.

Recommended Setup #1: The All-Rounder

If I could buy only one fly-fishing setup to use in any city, whether wading or casting from the shoreline or riverbank, this would be it. This setup excels in freshwater environments such as rivers, lakes, streams, ponds, and canals and performs well in wind-protected inshore saltwater areas such as harbors, bays, and calmer beaches—with the majority of casts being fifty feet and less in those environments. However, in windier conditions, such as along an exposed shoreline, this line-and-rod combination will struggle to deliver flies at a distance.

This setup has the capability to cast most of the flies needed to target these fish species: smallmouth bass, carp, average largemouth bass, bluegill and other sunfish, freshwater drum, trout, most gar, suckers, smaller salmon and steelhead, channel catfish, shad, flounder, sea-run trout, schoolie striped bass, surfperch, corbina, and spotted seatrout.

THE FLY LINE

In my experience, the fly line is the crucial component to get right, more so than the fly rod or reel. The line dictates what flies and tackle you can effectively cast. Quality fly lines cast better and are also more durable, making them a worthwhile investment.

First, you'll absolutely want a floating fly line, which allows you to present flies both on the surface and below the water. Specifically, the fly line in this setup is a **6-weight, weight forward (WF) floating line typically labeled "All-Around" or "All-Purpose."** Examples of specific fly lines I recommend are the Air Cel WF, Frequency MPX, and Mastery Infinity, all made by Scientific Anglers. My runner-up recommendations are the Superflo Universal Taper fly line by Airflo and the Orvis Clearwater Fly Line.

It is also important to note that temperature significantly affects the performance of fly lines. Most lines labeled "All-Around" are designed to work well in cold to moderate temperatures. However, in extreme heat and very warm water, these lines may become limp and difficult to cast. If you plan on fly fishing in hot climates, like Florida or Arizona, consult with a fly shop or other anglers to find out if they recommend a fly line with a core and coating designed for hotter temperatures, often labeled as "Tropical."

One other fly line you might consider is a 6-weight intermediate full sinking fly line for fishing deeper water. While not entirely necessary for most urban fly-fishing scenarios, this line is great to use when fishing along calmer shorelines, beaches, or around infrastructure like harbors, jetties, and breakwaters (the subject of chapter 9).

THE FLY ROD

The fly rod in this setup is a **6-weight, 9- or 9½-foot graphite rod**. I particularly like the shorter rod length for quicker casting and for casting in tighter spaces, such as below bridges, around walking paths and brushy

Nate McCord is able to gain additional leverage on a large fish by tucking the fighting butt into his torso to help pull and fight the fish away from debris in the water.

banks, or when you need to use a sidearm cast to avoid overhead obstructions like streetlights. The slightly longer 9½-foot rod performs better when dapping a fly on the water, roll casting (a technique that uses a forward motion to cast the line when there's limited space behind the angler), and mending line (a technique where the angler repositions the line on the water to control how it moves with the current). The extra length is also helpful for keeping your backcast higher, which is useful when obstacles like fences or walls are behind you, and the added length helps prevent your backcast from hitting the water while wading.

Regardless of the length you choose, a fighting butt is a valuable feature. A fighting butt is a short cork extension located at the base of the handle on certain fly rods (usually 6-weight and heavier). It is used for handling stronger fish and leveraging them away from objects and debris in the water. However, not all 9-foot, 6-weight fly rods come with a fighting butt and those that don't come with one will also perform well, so don't get overly concerned with this if you are trying to find a rod that's within your budget.

THE REEL

The reel for this setup is a standard **disc drag, mid-arbor reel**, typically labeled as "6/7" or "5-7" on the box. If you plan on only fishing in freshwater environments, you can go cheaper on the reel. However, if you plan on doing any saltwater fishing, you'll need a reel that is corrosion resistant with a sealed drag, which is generally more costly than a standard disc-drag reel.

For the reel, you'll want around 100 yards (91 m) of Dacron 20-pound (9 kg) backing. Backing is a strong, thin line spooled onto a fly reel before the fly line, providing extra line capacity and preventing the fly line from running out when fighting large or fast-moving fish. If you don't want to try to set up your own reel and fly line, then I strongly recommend finding a fly shop or online store that will set up your reel for you and put on the backing (often not charging you for the backing or the service). Also, most fly fishing "combos" or "outfits" (which include the rod, reel, and line) will be delivered with the fly line and backing already set up on the reel.

Recommended Setup #2: The Heavy Hitter

There is a second urban fly-fishing setup I recommend, specifically if you anticipate spending most of your time fishing along ocean shorelines, harbors, jetties, and beaches or surf in moderate winds, with the majority of casts being 60 feet (18 m) or less in those areas. This setup is suitable for larger urban fish such as stripers, bluefish, flounder, snook, small tarpon, leopard sharks, corbina, salmon and steelhead, pike, largemouth bass, false albacore, larger gar, bowfin, and very large carp and catfish. However, catching smaller fish like bluegill, surfperch, trout, and river smallmouth bass with this setup won't be much fun at all.

With this setup, you'll be able to cast anything needed for urban fly fishing, but casting small flies won't be delicate and casting very large flies—like 5-inch (13 cm) bass poppers and 7-inch (18 cm) streamers—will require sharpened casting skills.

THE FLY LINE

For the fly line, this setup uses an **8-weight, weight forward (WF) floating line, typically labeled "All-Around" or "All-Purpose."** Examples include the Air Cel WF, Frequency MPX, Frequency Saltwater, Mastery Infinity, and Mastery Saltwater fly lines, all by Scientific Anglers. Other examples are the Superflo Universal Taper fly line by Airflo and the Orvis Clearwater Fly Line. Some brands also offer an **"All-Around Saltwater"** line, like the Orvis Hydros Saltwater Taper Fly Line, which is better suited for casting heavier, more air-resistant flies. (Yes, you can use a "saltwater" fly line in freshwater, and vice versa. And the same goes for "saltwater" fly rods.)

Another fly line with this setup is an 8-weight shooting-taper (ST) line that has a fast-sinking head with an integrated intermediate sinking running line. The "head" of a fly line is the thick, more heavily weighted section that loads the rod during the initial casting strokes, while the "running line" is the thinner section that helps the line shoot farther on the final forward cast. This style of line is especially useful if you plan to fish frequently along beaches in the surf, off jetties, or over deeper water in urban lakes and wider rivers. A great example is Rio's OutBound Short series, particularly the intermediate/medium sink/fast sink line (I/S3/S5).

THE FLY ROD AND REEL

The rod in this setup is an **8-weight, 9- or 9½-foot with a fighting butt, graphite rod**. While higher-weight rods, such as 9- or 10-weight rods, offer more power for pulling big fish away from a structure or casting in very windy conditions, an 8-weight rod won't tire out your arm after an hour of casting.

The reel should be a large arbor model, typically labeled as "7/8" or "7-9" on the box. A large arbor design retrieves line faster, which is especially useful when a fish suddenly bolts back toward you. Given that this setup is geared toward larger fish, investing in a reel with a smooth drag is well worth it. A quality drag system provides consistent tension without sticking or surging, allowing you to maintain steady pressure as a fish runs. If you plan to fish in saltwater, opt for a **corrosion-resistant, sealed-drag reel** to prevent salt damage. Finally, be sure to pair the reel with at least 150–175 yards (137–160 m) of Dacron 20-pound (9 kg) backing.

Prioritizing Casting Skills over Perfect Gear

Now that we have gone through my two recommendations, there is one last thing I would like to mention. When shopping for a fly rod, you will come across a jumble of labels used by the industry, and it will feel like reading graffiti under a bridge—you recognize some words, but the rest are subject to wild guesses and personal interpretation. "Fast action," "moderate action," or "mid-tip flex" are just some of the vague terms that have zero industry standard for them. In fact, there is no universal standard for the "weight" of a fly rod either—so the concept of a "6-weight rod" isn't as clear-cut as it might seem (and even the industry standard for fly lines is largely defunct). Different brands assign these labels and weights, so what one brand calls a "Fast Action 5-Weight" might be considered a "Moderate Action 6-Weight" by another.

To translate this industry jargon, and provide you with the best advice to make informed purchases, I had long discussions with lead fly rod and line designers. Based on those informative talks, here are my simple suggestions to keep in mind while shopping for a fly-fishing setup.

Focus on choosing an all-around setup: For general urban fly fishing, start with setups like the ones I've recommended instead of getting caught up with trying to find a fly line and rod combination that casts "perfectly."

When choosing a fly-fishing setup for urban fishing, you'll find a wide range of products available. More specialized fly rods, such as switch, spey, and surf rods, offer many applications within urban environments. In the photo above, Josh Boeser is using his spey rod to make a long-distance cast out into the Mississippi River, even while standing with his back up against a large wall that prohibits a backcast.

Elizabeth Simpson hosting a free fly-casting clinic in downtown Spokane, Washington. Take advantage of such opportunities to learn how to cast or practice your skills. As you improve as a caster, consider volunteering to help teach others, even if it's just the basics, like the roll cast. Fly fishing is a growing sport, and there's always a need for mentors. Each of us who teaches started as a beginner, and giving back to the angling community is one of the most rewarding ways to share our passion for the sport.

Work on practicing your casting skills: Rather than stress about finding that "perfect" fly rod and line combination, focus on developing your cast; you'll become a much better fly fisher as a result and a practiced caster will be able to use a single rod to cast a wider array of fly lines, flies, and other tackle (such as bobbers and split shot, which we'll discuss below). Luckily, there is a growing number of free casting clinics offered by clubs and fly shops in our cities to help improve your casting skills.

Taking Care of Your Equipment

Reels and rods should be rinsed down after saltwater fishing. In the case of unsealed drag reels (which are not recommended for use in saltwater), they should be relubricated maybe once or twice a year (refer to the reel's manual for instructions). Fly lines used in urban settings need to be cleaned more frequently though, about every three to five outings, because city waters have a special way of coating your line in a fun layer of mystery grime. Cleaning the fly line will help it to cast better—and, for floating lines, to float better.

To clean your fly line, apply a mild soap, like hand soap (not dish soap, which can be too harsh on the line coating), to a damp cloth and run the line through it while applying moderate pressure; you'll hear the line squeak. Then rinse off the line with clean water. That's it. Additionally, be aware that some insect repellents contain DEET, which can damage and eat away at the fly line. Keep insect repellent away from your line, and if it gets on your hands, wash them or use a baby wipe before handling your line.

Choosing Fly-fishing Leaders

The fourth piece to your fly-fishing setup is the *leader*. The fly-fishing leader is the line that is between your fly line and the fly. It is typically made out of a clear monofilament (such as nylon or fluorocarbon), and you cannot go fly fishing without it. A leader serves several crucial roles, such as:

- providing a way to attach your fly, since tying a hook directly to your fly line isn't practical
- creating separation between the fly and the fly line, reducing the chance of fish being spooked by the fly line
- influencing the casting performance of your fly line and rod

That last bullet point is something fly fishers often overlook, making it a source of great frustration. Put simply, the leader transfers energy from the fly line to the fly during the cast. A leader made mostly of long, thin monofilament will dissipate more of this energy. If too much energy is lost, the leader may fail to straighten out, causing your fly to fall short. On the other hand, a short leader made from thick monofilament will transfer more energy, which can cause the fly to hit the water too forcefully, potentially frightening away fish. There's a lot to learn about leaders, and if you're interested in knowing more, I offer several in-depth instructional articles on my website.

One of the other great things about leaders, unlike fly rods and lines, is that they can be adjusted to alter casting performance, allowing you to present different flies more effectively. On my site there is an article, "How to Build Your Own Leaders for Fly Fishing," which covers choosing the right leader, repairing a damaged leader, and creating and modifying your own leaders. It's a technical article, but these are valuable skill sets to learn, and they are "hacks" that I—and many urban fly fishers—have found useful in becoming more self-reliant and adaptable on the water.

For now, if you're eager to get out on the water and need a simple recommendation, here are a few widely available leader options that

GEAR TIP

Make a Welded Loop for Swapping Leaders

Not all fly lines have a welded loop—the loop at the end of a fly line that allows you to swap out leaders. Many of the budget-friendly fly-fishing setups have the leader tied directly onto the end of the fly line. If this is the case with your line, there is a way to make your own welded loop. To do this, cut the leader about six inches from where it is tied to the end of the fly line and then tie a perfection loop onto the end of it. That will give you a loop so you can attach different leaders to your fly line. On the Orvis Fly Fishing Learning Center website, under Animated Knots, there is an animation and video giving step-by-step directions on how to tie the perfection loop. www.howtoflyfish.orvis.com

The joy of tying knots lies in the combination of skill, focus, and satisfaction that comes from creating something both functional and elegant. Sitting down with a spool of monofilament and learning to tie different knots is also a fun way to discover highly useful knots that can save you in a pinch and keep you on the water fishing. It's also much easier and less stressful to practice tying knots when you're in the comfort of your home than when you're outside distracted by feeding fish.

Lindsay Mlynarek and I pack our Tenkara rods with us and, after having dinner downtown, we'll walk to the water to enjoy an evening of relaxed fishing.

cover most urban fly fishing needs (just buy a couple to start). For **3- to 6-weight floating fly lines**, consider a 7½-foot (2 m) or 9-foot (3 m) 2X nylon leader. For **6- to 8-weight floating fly lines**, consider a 9- to 12-foot (3–4 m) nylon leader with 12- to 16-pound (5–7 kg) break strength; choose fluorocarbon if it's within your budget. For **sink tip and full sinking fly lines** use 4 feet (1 m) of fluorocarbon with a 10- to 16-pound (4–7 kg) break strength (spools of monofilament are available at any tackle or fly shop). Tie a perfection loop knot at one end to connect it to your fly line, then attach the fly to the other end. A quick internet search for "how to tie the perfection loop knot" or "perfection loop" will lead you to numerous tutorial videos.

Tenkara Rods: A Minimalist's Approach to Urban Fly Fishing

If all of this gear talk feels overwhelming and you're looking for a simpler fishing experience, then consider an alternative approach: Tenkara. This minimalist style of fly fishing offers a unique and straightforward experience, especially for those who value simplicity. Tenkara rods are telescoping and don't require a reel (the line attaches directly to the rod tip), and one of their greatest appeals is their light weight and portability, easily fitting into a backpack when collapsed. You can explore urban waters with the rod safely packed away, spot a fish, and be casting within minutes, offering instant escape from the world around you.

Tenkara rods perform well in a variety of urban conditions, from small, brushy creeks to larger bodies of water where fish often linger near the banks. Depending on the specific rod, you can cast many of the fly patterns listed later in this chapter. And yes, sturdier Tenkara rods can handle larger species like carp, teaching you valuable lessons about effectively fighting fish. A Tenkara rod provides an intimate, hands-on fishing experience where you can see and feel the action. The long length and ultra-light design give you greater control and finesse when presenting flies, improving your ability to imitate insects and other food sources. If you're interested in improving your skills with tricky species that are feeding along the bottom, Tenkara rods are sensitive enough to detect even the slightest bumps when a fish takes your fly, especially in discolored water where it's hard to see when the fish eats your fly.

Tenkara can be a less expensive alternative to a standard fly-fishing setup, but there are downsides. You won't be able to cast nearly as far as with a standard fly rod, which limits you to fishing close to riverbanks and shorelines or having to wade farther out into the water. Their longer length

CASTING TIP

Practice at a Local Park

When learning how to cast on your own, take your fly rod or Tenkara rod to the park. Practicing your casting is free and is an easy and relaxing way to spend time outside. While at the park, watch some casting videos on your phone and begin casting, either over the grass or water (without a fly tied on). It also helps to set your phone down and record yourself as you cast and then compare your casting to the videos you're watching. Another tip is to tie a small, colorful piece of yarn onto the end of your leader. Then, place some objects in the grass, at different distances, and try to land the yarn onto the objects. As you improve, this becomes a really fun game to play!

can also be unwieldy at times, especially when trying to present a fly to a fish right at your feet with no room to step back. These rods also have very thin tip sections, which require added awareness to prevent snapping when fighting larger fish or trying to break off a snagged fly.

Top Fly Patterns for Urban Waters

With the diversity of fish species and their varied food sources in urban areas, you could easily fill an entire book with fly patterns to try in a single city. Instead of offering an exhaustive list, below is a condensed selection of fly patterns that I recommend for any North American city. These flies are versatile enough to target multiple species of fish, popular among other urban fly fishers, and easily found online and at most fly shops.

The fly patterns you decide to buy depend on your casting skills and the type of fly rod, line, and leader you're using. If you're new to fly fishing, a good strategy is to keep it simple. Start by purchasing a handful of patterns in different sizes and test how well you can cast them. This approach will save you money while you discover which patterns fit with your fly-fishing setup and casting skills. To help you out, a few essential patterns are marked with an asterisk (*) to indicate they are must-haves that work well with the "all-rounder" setup discussed above. Next to each fly pattern, I've also listed a "size," which refers to the size of the hook. The higher the number, the smaller the hook—and the smaller the fly pattern. For example, a size 12 fly is smaller than a size 2. Smaller fly patterns are easier to cast than larger ones.

STREAMERS

Streamers are fly patterns used to mimic food sources like small fish, crayfish, and leeches. Despite their name (which most likely comes from their elongated, flowing design that mimics a lifelike swimming motion), streamers can be used in any body of water, not just streams. For these recommended flies, choose a mix of colors: black, white, chartreuse, brownish olive, and pink.

***Clouser Minnow, size 6:** A classic and very effective fly pattern that imitates small fish, this pattern (and the Woolly Bugger) is an excellent choice for finding fish. Casting and retrieving it back to you efficiently enables you to systematically fish across various sections of a body of water to maximize your chances of finding fish (what fly fishers often term as "covering the water"). If you have a heavier fly line, like an 8-weight, select size 2.

Lefty's Deceiver, size 2: A renowned fly pattern, especially for saltwater fly fishing, it can effectively imitate a variety of small fish, including Atlantic and Gulf killifish, which have a higher tolerance for certain pollutants and are commonly found along the shorelines of Gulf and East Coast cities.

***Woolly Bugger, sizes 6 to 10:** Both unweighted and weighted with a cone, this is a general imitation of a wide range of food items (small fish, leeches, larger aquatic insects, etc.) and has worked for years in countless conditions, with urban waters being no different.

Near-Nuff Crayfish, sizes 4 to 8: Crayfish can inhabit urban waters and are a food item for many fish species. They are a keystone species

A well-rounded fly box lined with a variety of streamers, egg patterns, worms, nymphs, and bottom dwellers—all great options for urban fly fishing. If you want to keep things simple, you don't need a fly box this large. A small foam box, like the Orvis Ultralight Foam Box, is packable and durable—and, if you happen to drop it in the water, it floats.

and biological indicator (bioindicator) of a healthier food web because, among other reasons, their broad diet and size can cause them to accumulate pollutants in their tissues. So, coming across a body of water with crayfish could be a sign of better water quality and fishing. When you encounter a crayfish, give it a nudge and watch how it swims through the water tail-first and with its claws folded together. The Near-Nuff Crayfish, when pulled (retrieved) through the water, does a great job at mimicking that swimming motion.

***Jig Streamers, sizes 6 to 12:** This broad style of fly patterns uses jig hooks with heavy tungsten beads. These streamers drop through the water quickly and then you impart a jigging (up and down) motion, which imitates wounded fish or vulnerable crayfish. Two examples of this style of fly are George Daniel's UV Polar Jig and Spark Plug.

FLOATING FLIES: DRY FLIES, POPPERS, AND SLIDERS

These flies are meant to float on top of the water to entice fish up to the surface. For many urban fly fishers, watching a fish rise to the surface, especially a large carp or bass, and grab your fly is one of the most thrilling moments of fly fishing.

Dry flies are designed to imitate any number of insects, such as grasshoppers, crickets, flying ants, and adult aquatic insects like dragonflies and mayflies. Poppers are flies with a concave or flat face that make splashes and noise when pulled through the water, mimicking frogs or small, distressed fish. Sliders are similar to poppers but have a more tapered or rounded head to move more subtly across the surface, imitating small fish or frogs slipping through the water.

***Chubby Chernobyl, sizes 8 to 12 in black and brown-olive:** What does this fly pattern imitate? Who knows? But since it looks like so many things floating around in urban waters, fish find it hard to resist when it lands on the surface.

***Foam Beetle, sizes 10 to 14 in black, orange, and white:** A white beetle can double as a piece of bread, perfect for those times when you find yourself trailing behind a parkgoer who's generously chumming the water with an entire loaf of Wonder Bread.

***Popper, sizes 6 to 12 in yellow, green, black, or white:** These are just plain fun to fish and kids love popping them across the water. When a fish finally charges down the fly, the take can be explosive! If you have a heavier fly line, like an 8-weight, select larger poppers.

Sneaky Pete, sizes 4 to 10 in yellow, green, black, or white: When commotion-causing poppers aren't working, try switching to one of these.

Parachute Adams, sizes 12 to 14: This versatile pattern imitates a variety of adult aquatic insects, particularly chironomids (often referred to as "midges" by anglers). Adult (winged) chironomids resemble mosquitoes, though they don't bite (nonbiting midges). Chironomids are more resilient than most other aquatic insects, so you'll often find fish feeding on them in waters that are ecologically disrupted (such as dammed rivers) or polluted waters (such as downstream of an industrial factory or concentrated animal feed lot). While chironomids in some habitats can grow relatively large, most are small and difficult to notice on the water. If you see fish feeding on the surface but can't quite identify what they're eating, they may be feeding on chironomids.

NYMPHS, EMERGERS, AND WET FLIES

These fly patterns are used under the surface of the water where fish are feeding much of the time. In entomology (the study of insects), a *nymph* is the immature life stage of certain aquatic insects living underwater, such as mayflies, dragonflies, and caddisflies. Fly fishers use "nymph patterns" to imitate these immature insects as they crawl along the rocks and mud or are picked up and swept through the current. "Emergers" is a nonscientific label given to fly patterns that mimic aquatic insects ascending through the water to break (emerge) through the surface film when transitioning into winged adults to take flight and mate. Wet flies (also commonly called "soft hackles") also imitate aquatic insects, or even tiny fish and drowned terrestrial insects, moving through the water.

If you want to learn more about aquatic insects and their life cycles (including other fun details about other insects that have larval and pupal stages), see the Further Resources section on page 223.

Soft Hackle, sizes 10 to 12: These fly patterns come in many styles and colors, so grab a couple, both unweighted and weighted with a bead, to start.

Prince Nymph, sizes 8 to 12: This is an effective pattern to use when fishing ponds that are also favorite spots for other anglers.

***Clouser Swimming Nymph, sizes 8 to 10:** In "clearer" urban waters, this pattern can draw the attention of all sorts of fish. There is an unweighted version, but with the weighted version (beadhead) you can let the fly drop to the water and then twitch it to get a fish to bite.

***Hare's Ear Nymph, sizes 10 to 12:** This is another great pattern to use, either unweighted or weighted with a bead, when fishing ponds that are popular with other anglers.

Perdigons, sizes 10 to 14: For this fly pattern, select both very bright colors and darker ones (black, olive, and purple); this is also a great fly to use when you see a fish feeding along the bottom that has rejected most other patterns you have tried.

BOTTOM DWELLERS

These fly patterns sink fast for the purpose of being used on the substrate (the bottom of a river, pond, lake, ocean, etc.). These patterns imitate larger critters commonly found scurrying along the bottom in both freshwater and saltwater environments, such as crayfish, crabs, and even small fish (like sculpins). Many fish species, including carp, freshwater drum, suckers, and multiple saltwater species, will take many or all of these flies. Choose both muted colors (rusty orange, olive, brown, etc.) and ones that have red, pink, or wine color incorporated into the pattern.

***Backstabber, sizes 4 to 10:** This pattern is highly useful for many fish, especially common carp. It can also double as a streamer to catch smallmouth and largemouth bass when fishing around municipal wastewater treatment plants and for saltwater species along beaches.

***The Hybrid, sizes 8 to 10:** Nobody really knows what this fly mimics. A worm? A clam? A mutant sewer creature? Some urban anglers swear it looks like a chunk of discarded fast food, while others think it resembles the mysterious gunk that collects in storm drains. Whatever it is, fish love it—and that's what matters!

Barry's Carp Fly, size 6: Like the Backstabber, this pattern can be used in both freshwater and along ocean shorelines while dragging it along the sand or muck.

Carp Nasty, sizes 6 to 10: Not just for carp, this pattern can seal the deal with sunfish, bass, catfish, and various saltwater species. If you are in a spot watching fish feed along the bottom, this pattern sinks quickly and can be subtly twitched to convince something to bite.

WORMS AND EGGS

When no other fly patterns seem to do the job, worm and egg patterns can connect you to fish.

***San Juan Worm or any worm pattern weighted with a bead, sizes 8 to 12 in red, pink, and olive:** The olive color is a good pattern for catching plant- and algae-eating fish species. Just like chironomids, oligochaetes (worms) tend to become more abundant relative to other aquatic organisms in waters that are ecologically disrupted or polluted.

***Egg Pattern, sizes 8 to 12 in white, chartreuse, olive, and pink:** With so many different options, select one pattern that looks buoyant and one

GEAR TIP

Work with the Fly Patterns You Own

The fly patterns recommended in this chapter are grouped by their typical uses in mimicking various food items, but these categories are meant to be flexible. Don't let labels like "floating" or "dry" limit your creativity; and just because a fly is described as effective for a particular species doesn't mean it won't work for others. Before buying more flies, experiment with the ones you already own by:

- varying the speed; move the fly faster or slower through the water
- pausing and twitching; let it sit completely still, or keep it still and then give it a few twitches
- exploring depth; if the fly sinks, let it drop deeper before you start moving it

The key is to experiment and observe because sometimes the smallest adjustment can make all the difference. If your initial fly choice doesn't catch a fish after you've experimented with it, you may need to dig a little deeper. Often, it takes observing the fish's behavior and knowing a bit about its diet and habitat—topics we'll delve into later in the book.

that will sink more easily. From coast to coast, almost every urban fly fisher I've met has had at least a few different egg patterns in their fly box because they are great attractor flies for fish.

DIY Fly Patterns That Work for Your Needs

Tying your own fly patterns is completely optional, but one of the joys of fly fishing is using fly patterns that you've created. The world of fly tying is expansive, with thousands of online video tutorials offering step-by-step instructions for tying a wide range of fly patterns, including ones you might already love using. Fly tying does require an initial investment in some essential materials and tools—primarily thread, fine-pointed scissors, and a fly-tying vise (a specialized clamp that securely holds a hook in place, allowing you to attach and wrap materials around it). But once you have your fly-tying tools and essential materials, you can create all sorts of fly patterns.

Fly tying is an excellent way to enhance your fishing skills. By observing fish behavior and their food sources, you can channel those invaluable insights into creating fly patterns tailored to help you catch specific fish. It's a rewarding way to connect more deeply with local ecosystems and food webs, and the more you observe while fishing, the more practical knowledge you can bring to the tying vise. Who knows? You might invent a fly pattern as highly effective and adapted to urban waters as Lino Jubilado's "Green Eggs and Ham."

Lino, a Los Angeles fly fisher and mentor, developed Green Eggs and Ham to help himself, and many others, catch common carp. While fishing around the city, Lino noticed small leeches and worms that would affix themselves to submerged items like rocks, shopping carts, and even pieces of discarded clothing. He figured the carp might also be eating these critters, so he took an egg pattern and enhanced its effectiveness by adding a small strip of chenille to mimic those small leeches and worms. The combination has proven to be a fly pattern that carp go absolutely crazy for! So, next time you hook a soggy sock, don't be disappointed, because it may be your epiphany for the next great urban fly pattern.

Modifying Tackle to Reduce Fish Injury and Mortality

Fly fishing is not a bloodless sport, and at times you will severely injure and unintentionally kill fish. After all, we are driving a hook through their mouths and playing them on the line. To reduce fish mortality (if you don't plan on eating it) and additional harm, consider using a pair

Brandon Dale tying up a couple patterns in his apartment before walking to the park. Tying your own flies, watching how fish react to them on the water, and then going back to the vise and modifying your patterns is such a fun and engaging addition to the fly-fishing experience.

of pliers to pinch down the barbs on your hooks. Needle-nose pliers or forceps are also useful for removing hooks from fish that have sharp teeth. A curved hemostat (small, curved pliers commonly used as a surgical tool) is great for removing flies from fish with smaller mouths, such as bluegill and other sunfish.

In some places, using barbless hooks might even be required by fishing regulations. Many anglers worry

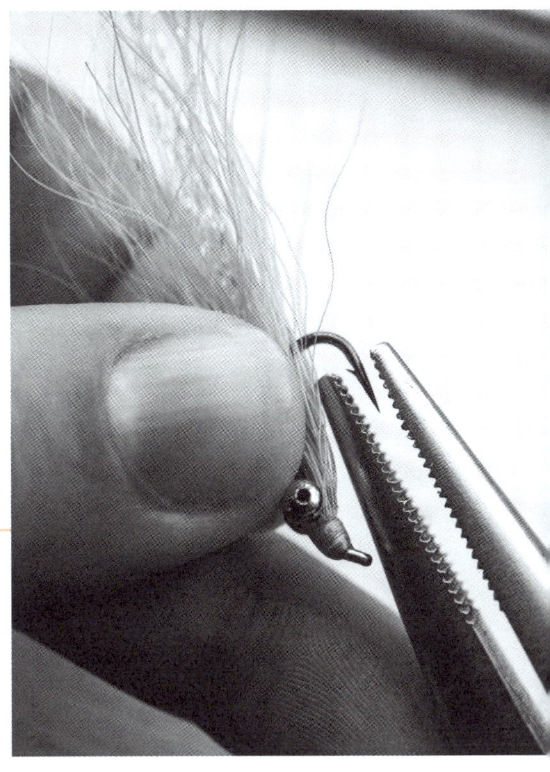

To pinch down the barb on a hook, firmly grip the hook's shank with one hand and position the jaws of a pair of needle-nose pliers over the barb. Apply steady pressure to flatten the barb against the hook, ensuring it is as smooth as possible. Hemostats can work as well, but I think a standard pair of needle-nose pliers flatten the barb better.

Northern pike, despite its harmless appearance, have sharp teeth and you don't want to go sticking your fingers into their mouths to remove a hook. Other fish, such as largemouth and smallmouth bass and crappie, have mouths that are safe to reach into to unhook a fly.

Taking Photos and Handling Fish

Simply fishing and exploring your urban waters brings attention to these places and the fish living in them. When you catch a fish, capture the moment with a photo and enjoy the experience—it's a celebration of the fact that fish still live alongside us in our cities. Sharing those photos and videos with family and friends is an impactful way to directly advocate for your local waters, their fish, and our deep, unbreakable connection with both. The presence of fish in urban waters is a powerful testament to life's resilience. However, it's crucial that our cities stop pushing the limits of that resilience.

As anglers, how we handle fish is something to take into consideration when thinking about the sustainability of urban fisheries and the well-being of individual fish. In fishing, we are driving a hook through a fish's lip and playing it on a line, but once the fish is in hand or in the net, we have another choice: to minimize any additional harm before releasing the fish or to dispatch it as quickly and respectfully as possible if we plan to eat it. Refer to www.ikijime.com for guidance on effective, humane methods for killing fish.

For tips about how to handle fish and take photos when catch-and-release fishing, visit www.keepfishwet.org. This is also a great website to help you update your fishing practices as new research emerges about fish behavior, water quality, and the best catch-and-release techniques. Many anglers are deeply passionate about responsible fish handling, and if you share this commitment, I encourage you to politely and constructively communicate these values with fellow anglers in your city.

Capturing photos for this book brought its own challenges. At times, I asked anglers to hold fish higher out of the water or for longer periods than desirable to capture photos that would inspire readers and prove that fish can be caught in highly urbanized areas. While these decisions may have stressed the fish, they were made with the goal of fulfilling a larger purpose: encouraging people to explore and advocate for local urban waters and the fish living in them.

that pinching down the barbs on their hooks will cause them to lose more fish. However, from my experience as a fly-fishing guide, I've found that losing fish is most often due to allowing the rod to straighten out when fighting a fish (this can happen even with barbed hooks). When a fish is on the line, maintain a bend in the rod while focusing on trying to point the butt of the rod toward the fish; this technique acts as both a shock absorber and an effective lever, increasing the chances of the fish staying on the hook.

When you do unintentionally kill a fish, return it to the water or surrounding habitat. Returning the fish to its habitat will allow other organisms to consume the fish and continue the life cycle.

Customizing Your Kit with Additional Gear and Apparel

Now that we've worked through the essential gear, let's briefly discuss some other pieces of equipment that can be useful for urban anglers. Again, hold off on buying some of this stuff until you've explored the local urban waters and talked with other anglers to save yourself from purchasing anything you don't really want or need.

For those who enjoy finding and tailoring their gear, the broader fly-fishing market offers plenty of options to complement the unique experience of urban fly fishing. While there isn't yet a dedicated market for urban-specific gear, many anglers are customizing existing fly-fishing equipment to fit the demands of city fishing in a way that blends function with everyday style. Whether you prefer a minimalist setup that fits in a backpack or wading attire that transitions seamlessly from the water to the sidewalk, there's room to curate a setup that feels both practical and personal. Part of the fun of urban fly fishing is making it your own, bringing together gear that works for your environment and your style, because fly fishing in the city has a vibe all its own.

WADERS

Waders aren't just about keeping you dry; they also keep other things off you. Sure, some city waters are surprisingly clean, but others are quite polluted. Despite this, urban anglers like me choose to not wear waders all the time, especially when the heat is unbearable. Deciding to get into the water, or not, is a subject we'll talk more about in chapter 6, so you can make your own informed decision.

If you do go with waders, I'd recommend choosing either chest waders, perfect for deeper waters, or wading pants, which are waders that only go up to your waist. Additionally, waders come in breathable and nonbreathable options. Breathable waders (usually made of Gore-Tex or similar materials) are lightweight and comfortable. Nonbreathable waders (typically rubber or neoprene) are better for colder weather but can make you feel like you're marinating in your own sweat on hotter days—unless you're into that, in which case, carry on.

Whichever waders you go with, be sure to wear the wading belt they come with (most waders on the market come with a belt). Keeping the belt snug prevents water from entering and potentially filling up your waders, if you accidentally dunk yourself.

FOOTWEAR

Urban waters often contain debris, from jagged concrete blocks and rebar to broken glass and metal cables. If you're thinking about wading in with sandals, take a moment to reconsider. A sturdy pair of closed-toe footwear isn't just a good idea—it's the difference between a great fishing trip and an unplanned tetanus shot. An old pair of sneakers can get you by, but if you plan on wading frequently, investing in proper wading boots is worth every penny.

The bottoms of wading boots will have treading (rubber traction), felt, or some combination of the two. Felt-soled boots are great if you are wading in water with very slippery rocks or concrete, but since they don't have any treading, they are slick when walking on dry ground.

If you plan on wet wading, you can opt to buy a pair of wading boots and neoprene socks. You could also go with a pair of "wet wading boots" or even sneakers specifically designed for wading, which are lightweight and comfortable. These shoes are great options if you are looking for something more comfortable to walk longer distances on dry land, and their breathability is hard to beat when fishing during hotter months.

SUNGLASSES

Urban fishing can be challenging because the number of fish in urban areas is often much lower than in nonurban places. Polarized sunglasses (with amber being a favorite lens color) cut through the glare on the water and help you spot fish, especially when you are crossing over bridges or along elevated walkways. Being able to look down into the water and visually locate fish can save you from endlessly casting over barren water. Also, common carp are a primary pursuit in urban fly fishing and having a pair of polarized sunglasses is a necessity for sight casting for these fish. (Sight fishing is a technique where the angler visually spots a fish and casts the fly near it.)

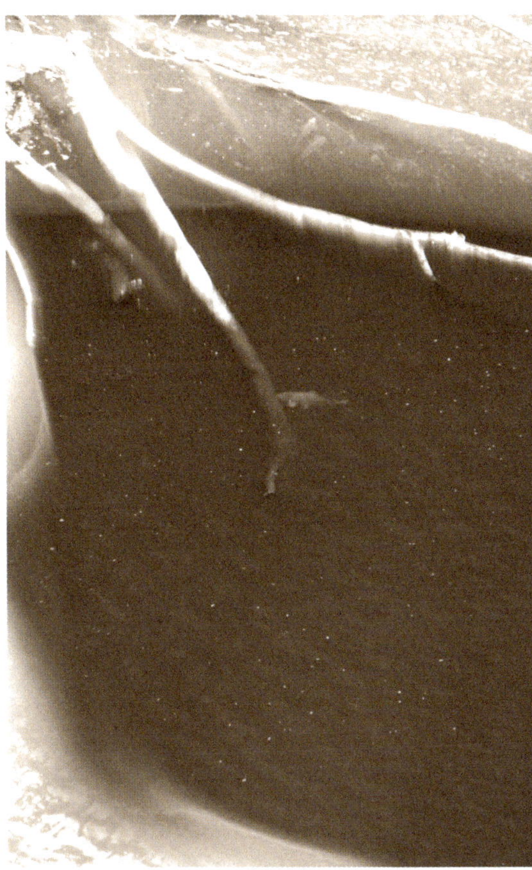

Here are two photos of a log in the water that I took while I was standing on a bridge. The photo on the left is what can be seen with the naked eye. The photo on the right is what you can see through a pair of polarized sunglasses, allowing you to easily spot the fish near the end of the sunken log.

NET

In urban waters, you'll encounter a wide variety of fish, including the rare exotic species that have been released from home aquariums. You might hook into something that looks like it swam straight out of a sci-fi movie, and in that moment you'll ask yourself, *Do I really want to touch this thing?* Having a net and a pair of pliers can make it easier and safer to remove the hook. During my travels while working on this book, another urban angler pulled a massive common pleco catfish out of the water. I had no idea what it was, and I was glad we had a net and some pliers to remove the hook (I only later found out plecos are not poisonous).

When choosing a net, opt for one with a rubber mesh, which is less likely to tangle your leader and fly and helps minimize injury to the fish by protecting their external mucus layer, which shields them from pathogens.

Some urban anglers might even use long-handle, extendable nets when fishing atop high concrete walls, docks, and smaller piers when the water level is several feet below.

BOBBERS AND SPLIT SHOT

Bobbers (often called "strike indicators" in fly fishing) and split shot might not be glamorous gear additions, but they can be absolute game changers. A bobber floats on the surface to suspend a fly (or flies) underneath and helps you detect subtle takes from fish that sip flies rather than smash them, essential for fishing slow-moving urban waters where fish can be extra picky. And let's be honest, watching a bobber suddenly dunk below the surface is just plain fun. Bobbers come in all shapes and sizes and can be bought in tackle shops. "Indicators" are bobbers that are tailor-made for fly fishing. One of my favorites is the Oros indicator because it is easy to

Using a net allows you to make that final reach to land a fish without having to get into the water.

Using a stripping basket in many situations, such as fly fishing in the surf, helps you maneuver around and make casts without damaging or tripping over your fly line.

attach or remove, less likely to cause tangles, and easier to cast. Oros indicators are not the cheapest option, but they last for multiple seasons.

Split shot, on the other hand, is weight that is attached to the leader in order to get a fly deeper in the water. Need to get your fly down fast in a current? Split shot. Trying to keep a worm pattern bouncing along the bottom where fish are lurking? Split shot. Want to snag that sunken refrigerator you keep casting over for fun? Okay, maybe don't, but you get the idea. There are all sorts of options when purchasing split shot at tackle and fly shops, so grab a variety container and experiment.

STRIPPING BASKET

In saltwater fly fishing, stripping baskets are commonly used when casting in the surf along beaches. Stripping baskets help to keep the fly line from falling into the water and being swept around by the tide, making managing and casting the fly line much easier. Stripping baskets are also very useful in other urban spots where you want to keep your fly line from falling into the water or onto the ground. For example, many urban rivers are lined with riprap (large concrete blocks and boulders) and letting your fly line drape down into the riprap may snag and abrade your line if you're not careful.

Nate McCord scans a stretch of water from the bank. Scouting and searching urban waters for great fishing spots is its own adventure.

CHAPTER 2

Finding Spots to Fish in Your City

Viewing a city from above, it might feel like you're searching for a fishing spot in the middle of a concrete maze. This is because, well, you are. But between the endless asphalt, towering glass-and-steel buildings, and network of roads, there are plenty of fishable waters. You just need to know where to look.

Even when urban waters are in plain sight, we often assume they're off-limits or simply not meant for fishing. In fact, this assumption leads people to believe fishing isn't even allowed in cities. I experienced this firsthand while fishing in Central Park with Brandon Dale. We weren't fishing in some tucked-away spot, rather we were right in the heart of New York City, surrounded by others also enjoying the lake. As we took turns trying to outsmart and catch large carp, a boathouse employee noticed our fly rods and told us that fishing wasn't allowed. Brandon, fully aware of the city's fishing regulations, explained that fishing in the park is indeed legal. In fact, New York City has hundreds of miles of shoreline, offering plenty of fishing access.

In certain limited spots, fishing will be prohibited mainly for safety reasons, such as around low-head dams (a piece of infrastructure we'll talk more about in chapter 8). These spots are regularly designated with legitimate "No Fishing" signs. However, beyond these few restricted areas, there is a surprising amount of urban water bodies that are open to fishing. We just need the right resources to find those waters and to give us the confidence to fish them. In this chapter, we'll talk about those resources and tools. While some of the fishing spots you'll find will already be known to other anglers, my hope is that this chapter will help you uncover a few

Even New York City, the most densely populated city in the United States, holds many fun and accessible fishing opportunities.

lesser-known places that, once discovered, will keep you returning to the water again and again.

Where to Start: Key Resources

The first resource to familiarize yourself with is the website of your state's fisheries management agency (such as Massachusetts Department of Fish and Game, Tennessee Wildlife Resources Agency, etc.). Here, you can obtain a fishing license and find contact information for local fisheries managers and game wardens who provide helpful information about local fishing. You will also find details on local fishing seasons, regulations, and guidelines, much of which is available in downloadable booklets. Additionally, check the website for information on kids' fishing derbies or free fishing days, when a license isn't required. These sites might also provide details on fish-stocking programs, including where hatchery-raised fish are released, frequently in small, local ponds, which can be easy spots to catch your first fish or help others catch theirs. Stocked ponds are popular with other anglers, so visiting midweek or early or late in the day can help you avoid the bulk of the crowds.

Some state agencies also offer helpful apps. For example, Washington State has a fishing app with a map displaying all bodies of water in the state. When clicking on a water body, the app displays fishing seasons, target species, and permitted tackle. If your state's agency doesn't offer a similar app, there could be interactive maps on the website. For instance, Arizona Fish and Game has an excellent "community fishing" website with a map of urban ponds, information on the fish species you might encounter, park rules, amenities, and other helpful details for anglers, such as the size (acreage) of the pond and the maximum depth of the water.

City and park websites are also valuable resources, offering additional maps of fishing locations. These sites might also feature "fishing in the city" programs, where you can attend free clinics to learn about urban fishing, techniques for specific species, and local bodies of water to try. In cities, there might be special fishing regulations, such as catch-and-release rules or restrictions on certain tackle like lead weights and barbed hooks. It's a good idea to check your city and park websites, or look for informational signs and kiosks at the park, to stay informed about any additional regulations.

Become familiar with your state's fishing regulations and fishing seasons so you can go cast a line without worrying about the legalities. Now, it's time to find exact spots to go fishing in your city.

Using Digital Mapping Tools

A handful of free online tools will help you find fishing spots in your city. While you are most likely familiar with these tools for other navigational

FISHING TIP

What's the Best Time of Day to Go Fishing?

The best time of day to go fishing depends on many factors, especially when fishing within city limits. To guide you to the best answer, start by asking yourself a few questions.

What's my daily schedule? Even if you only have a short window, fish whenever you can—time spent casting is never wasted.

What size fish am I after? Dawn, dusk, and nighttime often bring bigger fish closer to shore, but if you're not picky, midday or whenever you're free can still be productive to catch fish of all sizes.

What time of year is it? Seasonal changes affect fish behavior and feeding patterns, a subject we'll explore more in chapters 7 and 10.

What other factors are there? Boat (or car) traffic, public events or festivals along the waterfront, and park hours might all impact prime fishing times. Additionally, when fishing on urban rivers, streams, and creeks, conditions can change on a daily or weekly basis (another topic we'll discuss in chapter 10).

Ultimately, the "best" time to fish hinges on your schedule, your goals, and your local conditions. Let these considerations guide you as you learn to fish your city's waters.

needs, you can use them to create a general search strategy to locate spots to explore and fish.

First, you'll need to consider your mode of transportation. Do you have a bicycle or car? Are you going to walk, take public transit, or rent an e-scooter or e-bike? Knowing this and how much time you have available will give you an idea of how far you can travel to reach a body of water.

Next, use a mapping application like Google, Apple, Bing, or Wiki OpenStreetMap to identify bodies of water near where you live (or where you are staying, if you're visiting from out of town) that are within the range of your transportation mode and the amount of time you have. Open any one of these and start looking for and dropping pins on bodies of water or sections of those waters. Come up with a list of at least half a dozen locations. At first, I suggest not ruling out too many places, including bodies of water in the heart of downtown, and especially smaller urban waters. You'll refine that list of potential fishing spots as we introduce additional tools and insights in this chapter.

IDENTIFY PEDESTRIAN AND BICYCLE TRAILS

Pedestrian and bicycle trails are an excellent way to navigate a city and fish at different locations—many in the same day, if you like. You can locate these trails in Google Maps by selecting the "Layers" icon, which is located in the top right-hand corner on the phone app or in the bottom left-hand corner on the desktop version. Then, select the "Biking" layer. Four types of green lines can appear on the map, but the two most useful are the solid dark-green line for "Trails," and the dashed dark-green line denoting "Dirt/unpaved trails." Being familiar with these mixed-used paths and trails in your area will allow you to journey more easily to your fishing spots.

Fly-fishing guide Josh Boeser remembers to pay the parking meter before going to fish a stretch of the Mississippi River in downtown Minneapolis.

FISHING TIP

Exploring Smaller Urban Waters

When you fish smaller urban waters like creeks, ponds, or canals, you can cover most of the water while wading or fishing from the bank. This gets your flies or lures in front of fish, improving your chances of catching something. This is especially helpful if you are new to fly fishing or learning to catch a new species. Larger bodies of urban water are lots of fun, but they are more challenging to fish because there is so much water to cover; the majority of fish might be located around certain structures or deeper depths based on the season, leading you to believe there aren't any fish living there.

Being familiar with these smaller waters will give you the option of fishing before or after work or when spending time with family and friends who might not be into fishing. If you only have an hour to fish and want to hook into something, it's easy to head over to a nearby creek, pond, or canal. Lastly, smaller waters, especially ponds, can hold some massive fish species, which could be your chance to land a personal best record.

There are lots of urban ponds in the very hearts of our cities. While these waters can be popular spots for many anglers, and other people enjoying the outdoors, they are absolutely worth fishing, and the results can really surprise you.

Brandon Dale keeps an eye on a fish as Quincy Milton wades into the water for a better shot. Using trails, like this bike path in Providence, Rhode Island, offers easier access when moving up and down a section of water in search of fish, especially in areas with thicker foliage.

In many cities, trails that run close to rivers, canals, lakes, and coastlines are the product of thoughtful urban planning. Enjoy a day of strolling to two or three locations along such a trail, spending an hour or so fishing each one. While traveling along the trail, you may uncover other accessible fishing spots, and you can either fish them or take notes and come back during a future outing.

In Denver, there is an extensive pedestrian path that parallels much of the South Platte River. I'm not sure how many miles Nic Hall, Nate McCord, Rick Mikesell, and I put in as we walked from spot to spot along the river looking for carp, rainbow trout, smallmouth bass, and white suckers (species we'll learn more about in chapter 7). As we fished, we would spread out at times and whenever someone found actively feeding fish they'd call or text letting the rest of us know. We would then head their way to join in or help net a hooked fish.

MAP OUT PUBLIC TRANSPORTATION ROUTES

Another "Layers" option in Google Maps is "Transit." This map layer displays subway and rail lines, along with bus stations. This is especially convenient for East Coast anglers who live in cities with more robust subway lines that can shuttle you to and from ponds, rivers, and saltwater coasts. In Boston, for example, the combination of subway lines, bus routes, and the Harborwalk is a convenient, low-cost way to travel around

When fishing in the city, there can be entire stretches of water that hold very few fish. Experienced urban anglers like Nic Hall and Nate McCord understand that it takes time getting to know the local waters and figuring out which spots are worth moving past.

the city fishing for both fresh and saltwater species, such as bluegill, carp, flounder, and stripers. When I met up with Ben Carmichael in Boston, I started with fly fishing for stripers in one part of the city, then hopped on the subway, transferred to a bus, and made it over to a beach where I linked up with Ben. Along the way, I grabbed a bite to eat and answered a couple questions from fellow subway riders as to why my pant legs were soaked.

Brandon Dale takes a quick bus ride to one of his favorite fishing spots in New York City. If you look closely, you'll notice that his fly rods are all rigged up. To make traveling with a fly rod easier, he disconnects the rod in the middle, folds it over, and straps a rubber band or hair tie around the two rod sections to make it more portable—all without having to unstring the line or cut off the fly.

TAKE A LOOK AT THE TOPOGRAPHY

A third layer to be found in Google Maps "Layers" is "Terrain," which shows changes in elevation, giving a better three-dimensional representation of the landscape (or topography) to help you identify small creeks, not only along rivers and lakes, but along the coastline as well. Small creeks—especially intermittent creeks that only flow with water during part of the year—typically don't always appear on the map as blue lines. The Terrain layer can help display these features as small serpentine canyons or gorges. At spots where these small creeks meet a larger body of water, fish can be drawn into those creeks when water levels rise, such as after a rainstorm.

The Terrain layer can also help you identify fishing spots along the periphery of lakes and larger ponds. Analyzing the surrounding terrain around part of a lake clues you in to potential underwater features. If the land bordering a lakeshore is steep, then that steep gradient might continue under the surface of the water, forming deep underwater cliffs (drop-offs) that fish cruise along. If the land gently slopes into the water, you may find an extensive shallow area of the lake that's good for wading.

USE SATELLITE IMAGERY

Satellite imagery is where you can find surprising fishing spots in your city. When looking at the normal view on a mapping application, even when using the Terrain layer, it only shows part of the story. It helps to regularly

toggle back and forth between the regular map view and satellite view to get the full picture.

As one example, the Los Angeles River's illustrious carp fishery resembles a featureless canal when seen on a normal map; its straight lines seem to offer little in the way of fish habitat. Even when you switch over to the satellite view, sections of this river are truly nothing more than concrete walls and traces of water offering little to no fishing opportunities. However, continue to scan up and down the river and, before long, a unique fishery is unveiled. You'll discover a very contrasting river, one that is full of islands, riffles, trees and vegetation, boulders, and other structures, all forming a wonderful section of river prime for catching carp, bass, and catfish.

Smaller features can also be picked up on satellite imagery, such as pieces of old bridges, sunken pillars, and concrete slabs left in the water after removal of urban structures like railway bridges, roads, and docks. These urban structures, and a variety of others, shape habitats by acting like artificial reefs where fish can hunt for food, find protection from predators, or simply congregate.

Along lakes, ponds, and coastal zones, the satellite view reveals further interesting features as well. In clearer bodies of water, you could potentially see underwater structures, giving you targets to cast at once you arrive at the water. An example of this is the immediate coastline around Seattle, where you can easily see deeper troughs of water, piles of rock, and shallow sandbars.

GOOGLE EARTH PRO

In the free desktop Google Earth Pro, you can adjust the date of the satellite imagery you're viewing. Changing the date shows you what bodies of water look like at different times of the year. In Google Earth Pro, click the clock icon in the top toolbar to open a timeline with a slider bar. Moving the timeline slider takes the date forward or backward in time.

The timeline changes the imagery by either a few months or a year or two, depending on the image data available. By going through the timeline, you can glean some interesting insights. For example, go to the confluence of the Olentangy and Scioto Rivers near downtown Columbus, Ohio, and slide the timeline forward and back. You'll notice that, at certain times, the water is high and discolored, making it difficult to wade in or fish from the bank. However, if you keep scrolling throughout the

Urban fly fisher Caroline Craven points out a fishing spot on the Los Angeles River. Using satellite imagery, talking with other anglers, and studying bodies of water in person will help you become skilled at finding fishing spots in your city.

Ryan Birringer makes a bow-and-arrow cast underneath a bridge. The urban stream he is fishing has regularly run dry during previous years, but a very wet spring surged water levels and brought a lot of fish back into the area.

timeline, you'll see dates when the river looks vastly altered: clearer water, riffles, sandy flats, side channels, and exposed islands or urban objects all readily available to cast at.

Keep in mind that water conditions in urban areas will change quite frequently throughout the year, or even on a daily basis. If you do arrive at a spot where the water is high and the fishing tough, don't write off that location. If you go back a few days or weeks later, the water could be lower, potentially clearer, and the fishing better. Many urban anglers will return to a particular spot again and again under different conditions when the water is higher or lower, or when the weather has changed. It's all part of building a more complete picture and understanding how and why conditions change so much in urban waters, a subject we'll explore in greater depth in chapter 10.

STREET VIEW

Street view, offered in Bing, Apple, and Google Maps, offers you a further look at a body of water before heading out to fish it. To access street view, click on the layer called "Street View" in Google Maps or "Streetside" in Bing Maps (in Apple Maps there is an icon near the bottom of the screen

FISHING TIP

Encountering Fenced-Off Water

If you encounter fences while fishing, it doesn't necessarily mean that fishing is off-limits or access to the water is prohibited. Often, the fencing is there simply to prevent pedestrians from accidentally falling into the water. In Minneapolis, Jennifer Hsia was walking on top of a high wall with a fence when she spotted a large fish down below. Thinking quickly, Jennifer came up with a plan. She made a short cast, sliding the fly close to the fish's mouth. The fish quickly took the fly, and then she handed me the rod with the fish still fighting on the line. She climbed over the fence and down the wall, then I tossed the rod down to her, and she landed the fish. Whew! A cheer erupted from some onlookers nearby, which we thought was for Jennifer's impressive catch, but it turned out they were celebrating a couple getting engaged right next to us. You could say there were two great catches that day!

Try not to get dismayed when you struggle to fly fish around fences, walls, and other barriers between you and the water. These barriers can make you think outside the box and come up with creative solutions to catch a fish. Plus, the fish in these harder-to-reach spots might never have encountered a fly or lure, making them more likely to bite and reward your extra effort.

called "Look Around"). After clicking this layer, certain roads, bike paths, and trails will become highlighted, and you can then select any of those highlighted roads or paths near the area you are interested in. Look around and see what the water offers. A very useful place to use Street View is atop bridges that span lakes, rivers, and coastal zones. You might find a clear view down to the water beneath a bridge, and you might even spot the first place to make a cast when you get there.

Street View isn't available everywhere on the map, but being an urban angler has its perks because our cities are covered in Street View options. Additionally, Street View isn't limited to streets. More and more water views are becoming available from the vantage points of boats, canoes, and ferries. You may also notice other important details like "No Trespassing" or "No Fishing" signs.

LOOK UP PARKS IN AND AROUND YOUR CITY

Using a mapping app, zoom in on your selected area to find spaces shaded green to denote city and state parks. The aquatic habitat in these green spaces is usually more intact, offering potentially better fishing opportunities. Clicking on any city or state park will bring up links to informative websites, phone numbers, and user reviews. You may also find information about fishing piers or bodies of water designated only for kids, senior anglers, and those with disabilities. Often, these linked websites will provide quick information on fishing rules, available fish species to catch, and permitted gear and tackle. For example, in Google Maps, clicking on "Fairgrounds Park Lake" in Saint Louis, Missouri, will provide a link to a city website with information about fishing rules and regulations, when fish stocking occurs, and a link to other local parks with lakes.

If a website isn't listed, or isn't helpful, you can sometimes find additional information by checking uploaded user photos in the reviews. People often take and upload pictures of informational kiosks located in the park. If the photo quality is high enough, you can

FISHING TIP

Taking Kids Fishing

If you are planning an outing with young kids, it is a good idea to pick a park that not only has a fishing pier on a pond but also a bathroom, playground, and convenient parking or nearby public transportation. If the kids lose interest in fishing after about twenty minutes, they can scamper off to the nearby playground and enjoy more time outside . . . and maybe even circle back later for more fishing!

zoom in and read the information listed on the kiosk, which may include fishing regulations for that location. Checking user reviews can also lead to insights. Click the "Reviews" tab and type keywords like "fishing" in the search bar to see if other anglers have shared their thoughts and experiences, along with any uploaded photos of fish they caught. Some user photos might show the body of water itself, giving you a glimpse of what to expect. You can also search for keywords and photos indicating wheelchair-accessible or kid-friendly fishing spots. Users sometimes upload drone footage as well, which can provide an invaluable bird's-eye view of where you plan on fishing.

OTHER DIGITAL RESOURCES

Google, Apple, and Bing are not the only mapping applications available. Two very useful apps are onWater Fish and onX Hunt, which are scouting tools that urban anglers use too. A free version of onWater Fish provides views of public land parcels, but onX requires a paid subscription for full access to view both private and public land. If you want to discover less trafficked pieces of public land and avoid trespassing, applications like these are fantastic options.

Know Your Rights to Fish

Every state has laws that protect your rights to fish and access public waters, and you may encounter people who challenge these rights. These individuals might not be aware that fishing is allowed in cities or they mistakenly believe you are trespassing or they are simply unhappy that someone is fishing near their home or workplace. These interactions can range from polite discussions to tense confrontations. Educating yourself on your state's water access laws and becoming familiar with your state's fishing regulations equips you with powerful tools when it comes to defending your rights to fish in public urban waters.

WATER ACCESS LAWS

Each state has its own specific water access laws that define an individual's right to access streams, rivers, and shorelines—to fish and wade in, and enjoy various other recreational activities. It's crucial for urban anglers to be aware of these laws. Water access laws can be confusing, but the nonprofit group American Whitewater provides a helpful resource that breaks down these laws into something we can all read and understand. Simply search online for "American Whitewater's Navigability Toolbox" and then select your state on the website. This will provide you with a summary of the access laws and links or references to official state publications. If the access laws in your city and state are angler friendly, you can have access to a lot of water and fishing opportunities.

The free onWater Fish app also provides water access laws whenever you click on a body of water (along with links to state fishing regulations). Another option is to call or email your county or district game warden to ask if you are allowed to fish a specific body of water. A quick internet search will locate the contact information. Additionally, Backcountry Hunters & Anglers (BHA) offers information on stream access and defending the public's rights to access these waters (yes, the public access issues that BHA focuses on also apply to fishing in urban areas). www.backcountryhunters.org/accessourwaters

Depending on your state, water access laws can offer ample opportunities to fish in your city. In states with favorable regulations, simply finding a small public entry point is all it takes to wade or move along an entire shoreline or riverbank, potentially leading you into some interesting fishing locations.

ANGLER HARASSMENT LAWS

Every state has laws that protect the rights of anglers (and hunters), and a quick internet search will inform you of your state's exact laws. If someone is disrupting your legal angling activities, the law is on your side. Remain calm and rational, and then:

- get an accurate description of the person, and any other information like license plate number, vehicle model, the building they came out of, etc.
- report the incident to authorities; call your local game warden or conservation officer, as they are better trained to handle these incidents than other local law enforcement
- be prepared to file harassment charges if necessary

Efforts by anglers to keep urban waters open to public fishing go a long way in helping other anglers, families, and kids enjoy these outdoor experiences as well.

Many urban anglers have successfully asserted their rights because they were well-informed about these laws and regulations. These anglers treat their public urban waters as their own, because they are—just as they are yours. For example, Rafael Del Razo, a Boston fly fisher, was once challenged by an employee of a newly built apartment complex. The employee was upset to see people fishing near the building, despite the fact that fishing was permitted in this publicly accessible area. Rafael calmly explained the regulations and brought the issue to the attention of the apartment manager and informed

Most "No Trespassing" signs are legitimate, like the one in this photo. However, on rare occasions, I have seen and heard about "No Trespassing" or "No Fishing" signs posted next to a body of water that the public had full legal rights to access and fish. If you do come across such questionable signs in your city, you can reach out to your state's department that manages fisheries, or to local game wardens, to ask for clarification and notify them of such signs.

them that more anglers, and Massachusetts's Division of Fish and Game, would be involved if necessary. The manager agreed with Rafael and public fishing access was successfully defended.

Trespassing

There are many gray areas when it comes to urban fishing, and no, I'm not talking about all the concrete. Cities are a confusing mix of public and private areas, and it won't always be clear if you are trespassing, even when using the resources I've suggested. I've talked with anglers who double- or triple-check to ensure they are fishing in public waters and won't fish if there is any confusion, especially when the potential consequences of trespassing can vary greatly depending on factors such as race, gender, what you're wearing, who you're with, etc. I've also spent time with other anglers who will less cautiously pursue fishing opportunities as they are presented to them. Ultimately, with urban fishing, the decision to fish in "gray areas" is a personal choice.

Fortunately, in most cities, there are lots of public areas and public waters to explore and fish. For example, next to downtown Fort Worth, Texas, near the former site of Douglass and McGar Parks, there are 383 acres (155 hectares) of public land (that's roughly the size of 290 American football fields). In the heart of the city, this public land offers free, ample opportunities to create meaningful connections to local waters and to rediscover the urban landscape through fishing.

In the United States, urban waters are arguably the most publicly accessible places where we can all have lasting experiences that connect us to where we live and with the communities that share them. Public land and public waters are something we should never take for granted, and really good people fight hard to protect them.

Secret Spots

There are no truly "secret" fishing spots in cities. Urban environments are too densely populated. Yes, there are places that are more challenging to access, but they are not unknown to other urban anglers.

When fishing urban waters, it's reasonable to expect that you'll be sharing the water with other anglers. In fact, many of us are glad to see other anglers taking an interest in urban fishing. We desperately need more advocates who are willing to help promote urban fisheries, better water quality, and public access.

Of course, there are special spots that you might want to keep to yourself—the little slices of fishing bliss. It's perfectly fine to keep some of your discoveries private. However, don't be upset if you encounter

Even though rivers like the South Platte in Denver are burdened with pollution problems, you, too, might catch an urban fish that will have you pulling out the tape measure.

another angler at your favorite spot or if they post an image on social media later because they're excited to share their experience. This is bound to happen in your urban angling adventures.

Get Out There

After pinpointing a few spots on the map, it's time to check out things in person, because you don't need to read the rest of this book to start fishing your local urban waters. Use whatever fishing setup you currently have, whether it's a fly rod, a spinning rod, or anything else. If you don't have a fishing setup, see if any friends or family members have one you can borrow (maybe some are gathering dust and need to be reacquainted with the water). Some fishing clubs and communities might also provide fishing gear you can borrow or rent.

If you're wondering, "Don't I need to know about the fish in my local waters first?" the short answer is, the basics are all you really need to get started. If you are going to a local pond or small stream, you will most likely come across largemouth or smallmouth bass and some sort of

sunfish (like bluegill, pumpkinseed, green sunfish, etc.). These species are frequently found in urban waters and are a blast to catch; some of them are amazingly colorful. An effective fly to use for these fish is a black Woolly Bugger (size 10). If you are fishing with a spinning rod, then try a gold or black micro spoon—a small, lightweight metal lure designed to mimic tiny fish. Even easier, if bait is allowed, just place a piece of worm, hot dog, or bologna on a hook about three feet below a bobber (and yes, that works with a fly rod, too). For now, just have fun getting out onto the water. Later, in chapter 7, we'll look more closely at fish species commonly found in urban waters.

While I was in Denver, I talked with Emma Brown, a rancher, wrangler, and fly-fishing guide who takes people into the Colorado Rockies backcountry. The Rocky Mountains are a world away from urban fishing, but Emma started fly fishing in downtown Boulder. Considering her spectrum of experiences, I asked what insights she'd like to share with people who are new to fishing or urban fishing and are hesitant about getting on the water. Here's her advice.

Get into it slowly: Set your limits and be comfortable with where you want to go fishing. Maybe it's just heading to a park with some family or friends to check out the water, or finding a nice wide-open, grassy area to practice casting (without a fly tied on).

The more you do, the more you will want to do: With outdoor experiences like urban fishing, the more you get outside and around the water, the more you'll want to keep doing it and expanding those experiences.

It doesn't have to be all about fishing: Enjoy the experience beyond fishing. It can be frustrating, and it may take several outings before you catch a fish. So, make it more than just about fishing. If you have a dog, take it for a walk to a nearby pond, or bring the fishing rod as part of a fun date activity.

Be ready for questions: People will want to talk with you. They'll want to know what you're doing and why, and they might be just as interested in fishing local urban waters as you are. Sometimes, you might even get tips about where and when they've seen fish.

If you don't have any fishing gear, haven't bought a license, the weather is really cold, or you just aren't ready to start exploring your city with a

Emma Brown fishing the South Platte River in Denver, enjoying a little time away from the Rocky Mountains.

Anglers like Lino Jubilado and Jane Miller spend a lot of their personal time helping other people to catch their first fish with a fly rod.

fishing rod yet, no worries. I'd still encourage you to visit the fishing spots you've pinpointed. Go for a stroll, take a look around, cross a bridge, peer into the water, and see if you can spot any fish down below. While you're out there, you might even come across someone fishing, maybe even fly fishing. If you feel comfortable, strike up a conversation; you might learn something or even get a chance to cast a line. In every city I visited while working on this book, there was always someone who talked with the anglers I was with. Some of the people who came up to us even got the chance to catch their first fish on a fly rod.

CHAPTER 3

Find Your Community

"I love the people and communities I've met through urban fishing."

I heard this sentiment echoed in all the cities I traveled to while working on this book, and it never got old. Fishing in urban areas connects you with communities of like-minded people who share a passion for the outdoors, advocate for their local urban waters, and encourage and support experienced anglers and newcomers alike. While we all need and enjoy our own moments on the water, it's also about the people we meet along the way.

Urban fishing will create unforgettable memories, and having a friend or family member there makes those moments even more special. Some urban fishing moments can feel downright ridiculous when you're by yourself, like renting a swan boat on a pond and fly fishing from it. But with a group of anglers, it instantly becomes a floating party! Even the mishaps turn into comedy gold. One minute you're frustrated by snagging yet another piece of trash, only to discover it's the third pair of pants you've hooked in a row, and everyone gets a good laugh over your unexpected fashion catch.

If you're new to the sport, fly fishing—urban or not—can be intimidating to try out alone. Social support and

The celebration of a birthday and a shared love of fishing!

mentorship from fellow anglers make all the difference. In this chapter, we'll explore ways to connect with established urban angling communities and ideas for building your very own local angling network.

Building Skills and Safety Through Community Fishing

If you're new to urban fishing or looking to improve your fly-fishing skills, spending time with other anglers is an invaluable way to practice your casting, learn to tie fly patterns and knots, experiment with new techniques, and make the most of your time on the water. For example, when fishing with a partner, you can rig two fly rods with different setups. One angler might use a streamer, which is a great choice for covering water when you're not sure where the fish are. (By "covering water" I mean

Fishing with someone else is a perfect way to bounce ideas off each other, and when a fish is finally in the net, it's high fives all around.

systematically casting and retrieving the streamer across different areas of a water body to search for active fish, effectively maximizing the chances of triggering a fish to bite.) The other angler can then use a setup with an indicator and nymph suspended a few feet below, which is perfect for when you locate fish under the surface. As you both fish, you may find that one setup is working better than the other. After catching a fish or two, swapping rods gives both of you a chance to benefit from each approach.

Exploring urban fishing areas with other anglers is not only more fun but also much safer, especially when you venture beyond familiar city and neighborhood parks into uncharted territory. These urban backwaters can be industrial, gritty, and seemingly isolated from the rest of the city. Yet, many of these areas are public waters filled with untapped opportunities and fish waiting to be caught. And remember, urban fishing doesn't stop when the sun goes down; some of your best chances at landing a giant fish

Within an hour of landing in Denver, I went into urban backwaters with Nic Hall, Nate McCord, and Rick Mikesell and found myself crawling under bridges and around barbed wire. It was my first time meeting them, but I knew they would look after a fellow urban angler.

Nate McCord directs a fish into shallow water where his son, Colton, is ready with the net.

might be at night. So, if you're planning to fly fish in these unconventional spots or explore them after dark, it's wise to go as a group for both safety and the added bonus of shared adventure.

In busy public areas filled with cyclists, joggers, kids, and dog walkers, having a fishing partner by your side is also very practical. You can watch each other's backs to help prevent the accidental snagging of a bystander (another reason to pinch down the barbs on your hooks, for easy removal in that unlucky circumstance) and alert each other when the coast is clear to cast, letting you focus on that fish you're trying to catch. Plus, your partner will be there when you need a hand. For instance, Jane Miller, a Los Angeles fly fisher, was once battling a hefty carp that was proving tough to reel in. As the fish made another run across the lake, her phone alarm went off, a reminder that her parking meter was about to expire. With a parking enforcement officer approaching her car, Jane quickly handed the fly rod (still attached to the fish) to her friend and dashed off to pay the meter. She then returned to the water, retrieved her rod, and ultimately landed the fish.

Colton McCord holds a hefty white sucker as his dad looks on with pride.

Urban areas are filled with fences, walls, bridges, steep banks, poles, and countless obstacles that can stand between you and the fish you want to catch. With a partner, or partners, before making a cast, you can work together to develop a strategy. This is where ingenuity, creativity, and quick thinking come into play! One of the coolest moments I witnessed involved Nate McCord and his son, Colton, collaborating to catch a fish two stories below them. Standing atop a footbridge, Nate hooked a large fish and, on cue, his son raced down into the river. Nate tossed a net to Colton and guided the fish toward his waiting son, who swooped it up—a truly amazing father-son moment!

Meeting Other Anglers on the Water

Fishing in cities is inherently social, and you'll find other anglers and potential fishing partners as you travel around your urban waters. The anglers you meet won't be using just fly-fishing gear; you'll encounter people using other methods to catch fish. Fishing in urban areas brings together people of diverse fishing backgrounds and knowledge, and oftentimes other anglers will show you their techniques and tactics, even if they can't help you with the specifics of fly fishing. You might even find ways to creatively adapt their approaches to suit your own style of fishing. In fact, many fish species are particularly challenging to hook with fly patterns, making it a fun and rewarding challenge. Sometimes, first catching these fish using other methods provides valuable insights that help you figure out how to successfully catch them using just a fly.

Occasionally, you'll come across other anglers who want their alone time on the water. If they're wearing

Many of the insights Shuhei "Shu" Kamata gave me are included throughout this book because he was happy to have me pass them on to help you, too.

headphones, it's probably a good indication that they want their space. I encountered one such angler at an urban lake in Los Angeles; he was skillfully and methodically fishing for largemouth bass using multiple rods. Despite his headphones (and going against my own advice), I decided to strike up a conversation, knowing I could learn a lot from him. Fortunately, Shuhei "Shu" Kamata was very friendly and didn't tell me to scram. He's a sushi chef, surfer, and, yes, competition bass angler. He knew how to fish that urban lake so well he could do it blindfolded. Shu was an open book, generously sharing valuable fishing tips, and he mentioned that he's always willing to do the same for anyone who wants to listen.

Connecting with Fishing Groups

There are numerous community groups that offer opportunities to meet other anglers, gain social support while learning about fishing and fly fishing, find fishing partners, and take part in advocacy and stewardship events. Listed below are a handful of communities found across the country with local chapters. Perhaps there are ones close to you.

AMERICAN CARP SOCIETY

The American Carp Society promotes and educates the public on the common carp, one of the most cunning freshwater fish in the world. The American Carp Society is membership-based and responsibly promotes the sport of fishing for carp; the organization focuses on bait fishing, but they also provide tips and techniques for catching carp with a fly rod. www.americancarpsociety.com/flyfishing-for-carp

BROWN FOLKS FISHING AND HUNTERS OF COLOR

Brown Folks Fishing and Hunters of Color are two community-driven organizations supporting Black, Indigenous, and People of Color (BIPOC) in the outdoors. Brown Folks Fishing fosters a sense of belonging among BIPOC anglers by creating spaces for connection, collaboration, and expanding opportunities within the fishing industry. Instagram @brownfolksfishing

Similarly, Hunters of Color (HOC) increases participation in the outdoors while promoting conservation, food sovereignty, and the preservation of ancestral traditions. While primarily focused on hunting, many HOC members are also avid anglers in urban areas. The organization offers a growing mentorship program with engaging events, networking opportunities, and pathways for involvement in conservation and outreach. There

Quincy Milton combines his love for fishing and the outdoors with his expertise as a biologist to provide environmental education and share stories that inspire an appreciation for the mysteries and beauty of aquatic life.

Events like this clean-up of the Spokane River in Washington bring together people who share a love for their local waters. Seeing the number of volunteers grow is truly encouraging. Organizations like the Spokane Riverkeeper can always use any help you are able to provide. Photograph courtesy of Spokane Riverkeeper

are low-cost and free membership options, and anyone can join. www.huntersofcolor.org

CITIZEN-BASED GROUPS

Across the country, there are citizen-based groups that advocate for local waters. These groups host clean-up events and volunteer opportunities to get involved in restoration projects and water-quality monitoring programs. Examples of such citizen-based groups are the Waterkeeper Alliance and Surfrider Foundation, which have local chapters or affiliates in many cities, such as the Spokane Riverkeeper, the Pearl Riverkeeper in Jackson, Mississippi, and the Surfrider Foundation New York City.

A quick internet search will inform you of other citizen-based groups in your city, such as the Friends of the Lower Olentangy Watershed in Columbus, Ohio, and Save the Harbor in Boston. Going to events hosted by a citizen-based group is a fantastic way to meet other local anglers. In the words of Los Angeles angler Lino Jubilado, "These beautiful urban destinations are a big part of my life, so participating in cleanup and conservation events with Friends of the Los Angeles River is important to me. And simply bringing awareness will hopefully translate to more efforts. Once you fall in love with something, you'll want to do everything you can to protect it."

Before getting involved with any citizen-based group, such as a nonprofit or "river steward," I encourage you to take a closer look at the organization and the people behind it. A little research goes a long way in helping you to determine if their values align with yours and whether or not to attend events, volunteer your time, support their initiatives, or donate any money. For example, a mission statement such as "protect, enhance, and celebrate our river" rings differently when it comes from a nonprofit led by a team of property managers, real estate developers, private wealth investors, and commercial bankers—they likely don't need your donation to continue their work.

FLY SHOPS AND GUIDE SERVICES

Fly shops are hubs for meeting other people who share an interest in local fishing. At these shops, experienced local anglers might also collaborate and provide free seminars about how to fish urban waters. Fly shops might also regularly publish fishing reports about local urban waters, including helpful tips and fly pattern recommendations, and many conduct fly-fishing classes and instructional lessons that you can sign up for.

Guided urban fishing continues to grow each year, with talented guides providing unique experiences and educational lessons right in the heart of cities. Examples include Rick Mikesell's Colorado Carp (www.coloradocarp.com) in Denver and Josh Boeser's Larry the Lunker (www.larrythelunker.com) in Minneapolis–Saint Paul.

Evan Griggs, owner and head guide at Fishing For All (www.fishing-for-all.com) in Minneapolis, emphasizes accessibility, education, and community. "I believe fishing and guiding should be fun, educational, and inclusive," says Evan. "There's plenty of guides and retail shops out there, as well as programs for people to first try out fishing. But there wasn't a great way for people to keep learning more about it after taking the intro course or buying their first fishing rod. I started Fishing For All to fill a gap in our fishing community—to teach fishing, grow a community of anglers, and advocate for our home waters."

Similarly, Brandon Dale of Carp In The Park NYC (www.carpintheparknyc.com) is bringing a fresh perspective to guided fishing. "Re-wilding New Yorkers is a personal calling. It's something I love doing. To show people that anywhere, even here in the concrete jungle, you can live intentionally with nature is really powerful. Helping New Yorkers learn that they

Rick Phetsavong, a guide with Fishing For All, ensures that whomever he guides or instructs gets the most out of their time on the water, and tailors every trip to meet the needs and skill level of the angler.

Spending time on the water with Brandon Dale will elevate your carp fly-fishing skills, especially by learning strategies for catching fish in very murky water.

Bob Bartlett, one of the founders of Ubuntu, has spent years dedicating his time and energy advocating for the Spokane River.

can find and engage with nature in an incredibly meaningful and fulfilling way is something that really pushed me to open Carp In The Park NYC."

IFISHIBELONG

iFishiBelong is about helping people get into all types of fishing. The organization values individuals from diverse backgrounds, recognizing the personal and meaningful connections people have with water and the fish they pursue. Through various programs and events, iFishiBelong fosters an empowering community where everyone feels included and inspired by their shared love of angling. Beyond fishing, the organization focuses on cultivating leaders within the community and providing tools and building confidence to make a lasting, positive impact in the fishing world and beyond. www.ifishibelong.org

UBUNTU FLY ANGLERS NETWORK

Ubuntu Fly Anglers Network, an affiliate of iFishiBelong, is a community that emphasizes collectivism over individualism and is working to cultivate new fly anglers and environmental advocates who reflect the diversity of the growing fishing community. By fostering relationships with others who can benefit from angling, whether as a hobby or a profession, they strive to make the often-overlooked contributions of anglers of color more visible and valued. www.ifishibelong.org/ubuntuflyanglers

While talking with Jane Miller about the Mayfly Project, she expressed a great passion for providing young people a sense of community and belonging through fly fishing.

UNITED WOMEN ON THE FLY

United Women on the Fly, another affiliate of iFishiBelong, is a supportive and inclusive community where women connect, grow, and thrive, both within fly fishing and beyond. Across the country, women's fly-fishing groups, like Ohio Women on the Fly and Spokane Women on the Fly, provide opportunities to meet up on the water, learn together, and participate in a variety of fun activities. These local groups create spaces where women can enjoy the camaraderie and joy of fly fishing while fostering a sense of belonging and shared adventure. www.uwott.com/connect

THE MAYFLY PROJECT AND OTHER COMMUNITY-BASED GROUPS

The Mayfly Project is dedicated to mentoring children in foster care through fly fishing. By introducing them to the art of fly fishing and their local waters, the organization creates opportunities for children to engage in a fulfilling pastime, build confidence through support, and form meaningful connections and a sense of belonging in the outdoors.

Jane Miller, the Lead Mentor for the Los Angeles Mayfly Project, along with many other LA fly fishers, volunteers tirelessly to demystify fly fishing for groups of kids each year. This includes providing gear and food, matching mentors to kids, teaching about advocacy and conservation, and continuously re-engaging with families once a month to provide additional support when needed. These mentors also hold fly-tying events where they "tie one, give one" so kids and families who don't have the means can have a box of useful fly patterns for where they go fishing. www.themayflyproject.com

Beyond the Mayfly Project, there are other uplifting and supportive groups of anglers that are volunteering to teach people how to fish and connect with the outdoors. For instance, Community Fly Fishing in Denver (www.communityflyfishing.com) is an organization that "creates access for people who are looking to experience the outdoors through free community-based events, taught by those who reflect our country's demographics." A quick internet search might yield similar groups in your city.

TROUT UNLIMITED

Trout Unlimited (TU) is a nationwide nonprofit with a focus on cold-water conservation. With over three hundred thousand members and many TU chapters throughout the country, it is also a social network where anglers can meet one another, learn how to fly fish, inspire others to get into urban fishing, and take part in conservation efforts. TU envisions communities across the United States coming together to revitalize the rivers, streams, and waterways that sustain us all. www.tu.org

Building and Promoting Angling Communities in Your City

Currently, there are many cities that don't yet have well-established angling communities. In fact, it's downright impressive that so much creativity and ingenuity are coming from an overall community of urban anglers that is still quite small. Right now, if I had to guess, there might be around a thousand people who are very passionate about urban fly fishing and actively building local angling communities. But the numbers are increasing as word continues getting out.

If you're interested in joining communities of anglers like the ones we've discussed, you might find yourself building or helping to create one in your city. There are many ways to get started, and even if you're completely new to fishing, you can create the social support groups you want to see and invite others to join you on the water. Take Los Angeles angler Analiza del Rosario's story as an example:

> *In 2013, I was conducting research on fly fishing to create a fly-fishing guide service website for my boss. Upon watching so many fly-fishing videos, I became curious, and I told my boss that there was a beginner's fly-fishing class I wanted to take. He said, "Don't take*

the class, I can teach you." We were on the East Coast for a work trip, so he decided to teach me on the Batten Kill River in Vermont. By the third day, I hooked my first fish, and I've been hooked ever since.

As soon as I got back to Los Angeles, I immediately looked for places to go fly fishing. As a woman angler, it wasn't always easy getting started. I remember going to different clubs around Southern California and while some of them gave me a friendly welcome, I also saw a few raised eyebrows, and some of the men thought I was lost. However, this didn't stop me from coming back to attend all the events happening locally because I wanted to keep learning how to fly fish and find people I could go fishing with.

Back then, I fished mostly with men because it was hard to find women to go fishing with me. That's why I made it a mission to help get more women and kids into fly fishing. With SoCal Fly Gals and SoCal Women on the Fly, I organized women's fly-fishing outings to the Los Angeles River, MacArthur Park, various beaches for surf fishing, and over to the San Gabriel River. I also became a mentor for the Mayfly Project.

Some community fishing groups, such as iFishiBelong and Hunters of Color, can give you advice about creating a local fishing group for your city. Simply reach out to them. Most importantly though, being out on your local waters will draw the attention of people who never knew it was possible to fish in the city. Even if some of the basics of fishing and casting are all you know, you can still invite them to fish with you to learn these skills together.

Social media is another way to promote your city and the fishing opportunities within it. Lino Jubilado has fostered a vibrant urban fly-fishing community in Los Angeles,

Lino Jubilado is an instrumental leader in the LA fly-fishing community and a positive force within the broader fly-fishing culture. Many cities, where urban fly fishing has yet to blossom, could use more people like Lino.

and social media has been pivotal for meeting other anglers and introducing people to urban fly fishing.

I also encourage you to reach out to nonlocal anglers on social media when seeking further fishing tips or safety advice. Urban anglers are spread across the country, and while they might not be able to meet up with you on the water, it's still great to connect and possibly find a remote fishing mentor. Many of the urban anglers have very informative videos and posts about strategies and techniques they use to catch fish in their city, which you can apply to your local waters. There are also many insightful viewpoints, conversations, and ideas that speak to other topics, such as specific safety tips for women and anglers of color when exploring urban waters.

One other creative way to help people get interested in fishing in your city is through fishing tournaments or "scavenger hunts." Fishing competitions, especially ones that are beginner-friendly, offer a chance to test skills and boost confidence. These events are also great places to build social connections, find mentorship programs, promote urban fisheries, and discuss stewardship projects to look after local waters.

The Denver Carp Slam and Sucker Slam and the Minneapolis Carp Angler's Potluck and Fly Fishing Tournament were started by impassioned anglers who wanted to showcase their local waters, share their local fly-fishing experiences, and bring together their angling community. To run tournaments like these, where prizes are awarded, there might be bureaucratic red tape, such as the requirement to obtain a permit from the government agency that manages your state's fisheries. However, there's nothing to stop you from gathering anglers and having a fun, low-key fishing challenge. Lino's "Surf and Turf Slam" is a great example; fly fishers meet up and try to catch saltwater species from Santa Monica Beach and then race over to the Los Angeles River or one of the local urban lakes to catch a carp—all in the same morning!

Fishing Outside the City

Fishing outside of cities provides its own unique and thrilling experiences, and you'll want to take the opportunity to venture to mountains, remote beaches, forests, and valleys when you can. Recreating in places minimally impacted by people is rewarding and refreshing, but these trips can

Learning to fly fish in the surf is a book unto itself. Heading out to less crowded beaches cuts down the learning curve by allowing you to cover greater expanses of water without worrying about other people getting in the way. Fly fishers like Carl Crawford are invaluable mentors who can coach you along the way.

be expensive and inaccessible for many urban residents. However, meeting experienced anglers in your city is a great way to offset the expense. Many of the urban anglers you meet in community fishing groups are also experienced with fishing in more remote places and can advise where to go, how to get there, and where to stay. They might help coordinate these trips and even join you.

For example, Carl Crawford graciously offered to drive me to a beach outside Los Angeles for the day when I was visiting the city. I've always wanted to improve my own fly-fishing skills in the surf, so I jumped at the chance to watch and learn from Carl, who has taught many anglers the art of surfcasting.

Communal Waters

Urban waters and the surrounding areas are shared by many different nonangling communities and groups, highlighting our common need and desire to be near water. When Brandon Dale first started fly fishing in Central Park, a friend would join to bird watch while Brandon fished, a partnership that proved to be very fortunate. Working as a team, Brandon's friend used his binoculars to help spot fish, and if Brandon needed to make a long cast, his friend would tell him when the fly landed within casting range.

Check out nonangling outdoor groups online, many of which have websites with useful information about accessing urban waters. For

example, the Spokane River Forum (www.spokaneriver.net/watertrail) includes maps and information for enjoying the local river that anglers also use to plan fishing outings. If you are going to an event or meetup with an outdoor group, consider bringing your rod in case a fishing opportunity presents itself. Someone else at the meetup might then become interested and want to know how to get into urban fishing, too.

ALL THE PICTURE TAKING

If you are fishing on your local urban waters, maybe with a fly rod, it is not uncommon for onlookers to snap photos of you. As distracting and awkward as that can be, it can also be a moment of positive impact. Seeing someone on the water fishing begins to change a person's idea of what these urban waters represent, opening their mind to new possibilities.

In Los Angeles, Caroline Craven was fighting a hefty carp that wasn't giving up. Along a path above us, a crowd formed and watched Caroline reel in the carp closer and closer, and many phones were out capturing the moment. Once the carp started to relent, Analiza del Rosario waded out and tucked the fish into the net, and the crowd cheered. It was a great moment for Caroline, for all of us in the river, and for everyone watching from above. But one person from the group of onlookers needed to know

Nothing better than hanging out with such a rad group of anglers!

more. He jumped over the railing, ran down the concrete bank, and asked what we were doing and how he could be a part of it. Before that day, that person had never imagined urban waters as a place where they could fish. In an instant, a new world of possibility opened up. I witnessed similar moments in other cities I visited, where all sorts of people reacted to our fishing pursuits with genuine interest and excitement.

COMMUNITIES LIVING ALONG THE WATER

While it is fun and exciting to talk about building a supportive community of anglers in the name of personal growth and shared enjoyment, it's necessary to recognize the broader social and environmental issues that impact our urban waters and the communities surrounding them. One such issue is homelessness.

In the United States, over 650,000 people experience homelessness on any given night—that's roughly the population size of Washington, D. C. This crisis affects everyone, especially in urban areas, where the challenges show up in our shared urban waters through trash, unsanitary conditions, mental health and addiction struggles, and even fish poaching. And while homelessness has many root causes, the most significant is the widespread lack of affordable housing.

As someone who is passionate about urban fishing, and who supports accessibility to this activity, the complex issue of homelessness has made me reflect more on personal safety, compassion for others, personal autonomy, and the shared need to care for our public waters. Navigating these principles isn't easy; it's a delicate line to walk, much like wading through murky urban waters, sliding one foot cautiously forward as I strive to reach a better place, and occasionally stumbling at times.

I'm fortunate to live in a city with local organizations and programs where I can engage in meaningful conversations and actions. These connections help me better understand the challenges and offer ways to contribute as I work toward doing what feels right for both my community and the local waters I care about deeply.

Urban waters are more than fishing spots; they are shared spaces that reflect both the best and worst of our society. These spaces test our values as well as our commitment to addressing complex issues. If you are someone who wants to meet these challenges head-on, I encourage you to seek out community members, fellow anglers, and local organizers who foster meaningful dialogue and constructive conversations, not divisive shouting matches. By working together in a spirit of compromise and collaboration, we can create solutions that actually work to uplift individuals and communities while making urban waters safer and cleaner for all of us.

Nic Hall netted a hefty fish, demonstrating the rewards of learning how to read the water and observe fish behavior. Before making his catch, Nic was on the bank and noticed rings appearing on the surface of the water. In this instance, it happened to be rainbow trout rising up to feed on small adult aquatic insects.

CHAPTER 4

Reading the Water and Observing Fish Behavior

Over the last few chapters, we've discussed resources to help you select useful gear for urban fly fishing, find places to go fishing in your city, and connect with other anglers. Hopefully, you've had the chance to get out on the water—and maybe you even caught a beautiful bluegill, a bulldog of a bass, or another species in a local pond or urban stream. If so, congratulations!

However, if you've been out fishing and haven't managed to hook a fish yet, try not to get discouraged. As I mentioned previously, it takes time on the water to start catching fish, and every urban angler goes days without catching anything. Some waters are very popular with other anglers, which can make the fish more cautious, skittish, and tougher to catch. In other cases, the fish simply might not be biting where you are. But if the fish aren't biting in one spot, that doesn't mean they're not active somewhere else. In this chapter, we are going to work on developing two skills to increase your chances of finding and catching those active fish.

Reading the Water: An Essential Skill for Urban Anglers

Finding a spot where the fish are consistently biting feels like a game of luck, especially in urban environments where conditions are often unpredictable. However, successful anglers don't cast blindly into the water and hope for the best; they actively observe their surroundings, assess the conditions, and interpret the features of the water to guide them to the fish. This skill is known as "reading the water" and it makes the difference between a fish in the net or getting skunked. This skill also determines whether a spot is worth revisiting and reduces the time and frustration spent casting over barren waters. By regularly observing and interpreting water conditions, you shift the odds to your favor, turning what might seem like a game of chance into a more predictable, productive pursuit.

Let's explore how you, too, can read the water to find where the fish are feeding. There's a lot to unpack here, so we'll start with the basics and build from there. The next time you are on or near the water, with or without a fishing rod, take the time to observe and watch for these important clues and features.

LOOK FOR SEAMS

Begin by observing any moving water, which can be caused by currents or wind creating ripples or small waves on the surface. Focus your attention on areas where faster-moving water meets slower or calmer water, which are

The fish that Nate hooked into, seen near the bottom right corner of the photo, was sitting right at the seam where the faster current met slower water. Nate placed his indicator (bobber), with a fly suspended a few feet below it, right on the seam. Once the bobber either twitched or went down, Nate swiftly lifted the rod while pinching the fly line to the cork handle (which tightens the line and keeps it from slipping), setting the hook on the fish.

known as *seams*. Fish often position themselves in the slower water, conserving energy while waiting for food to be carried to them by the faster current. For example, in this photo, Nate McCord saw a seam between the calm water near where he was standing and the faster current passing under the bridge. He never physically saw the fish, but by reading the water and noticing the seam, he was able to correctly determine that a fish might be in that spot.

LOOK BEYOND THE TURBULENCE

If you are observing turbulent water, with waves, bubbles, and foam all over the place, look for calmer spots or areas where the water changes direction or slowly circulates in an eddy. These locations can be prime spots for fish to hang out, waiting for food. In the photo, Nate is fishing an area with significant turbulence, but within the chaos there is an eddy where fish are likely located. Foam collecting on top of the water is a great indication of calmer water.

The calm, foamy water in this photo is wedged between two sections of fast, turbulent water, making it a great spot for fish; a streamer is a great fly to use in such a situation. After making a short cast, Nate extended his arm and twitched the rod tip up and down to jig the streamer (mimicking a wounded fish). He is also pinching the fly line to the cork handle with one or two fingers from his rod hand to keep the line tight when a fish bites. If a fish eats the fly, all Nate has to do is raise the rod swiftly while keeping the line pinched to the cork.

WHEN THE WATER IS COMPLETELY CALM

In completely calm water, such as a pond on a windless day or a really slow river, look for rings or splashes that signal fish feeding on insects, smaller fish, or other food items on top of the water. You can also watch for small wakes on the surface that could indicate fish swimming right below the surface. As an example, the photo below shows Brandon Dale at a lake in Central Park when the water was very calm. I was surprised when he pointed out small wakes on the surface created by carp racing toward a nearby restaurant at lunchtime, swarming around the scraps of food tossed over the railing by the waitstaff.

SEARCH FOR CHANGES IN WATER DEPTH

Another feature to look for is where shallow and deeper waters meet. These areas of convergence are ideal for fish seeking safety in deeper water or moving into the shallows to feed. If you can't see the bottom, darker water typically indicates greater depth. Pay special attention to *drop-offs*, where the water depth changes drastically. Rick Phetsavong brought me to a very industrial section of the Mississippi River in Minneapolis near one of the lock and dams. The river was calm in this spot, but just beyond the shoreline were drop-offs into deeper water. While standing on a concrete wall, Rick made several casts over the drop-off and got a couple of fish to bite.

FIND STRUCTURE AND COVER

Bridges and dock pilings, the corners of concrete walls, rocky areas, moored boats, sunken trees, or debris provide places for fish to hunt, forage, or seek

Urban lakes like this one can be very opaque, making it tough to spot fish in the water. If you find yourself in a similar situation, remain in one spot for a minute or two, steady your eyes, and try to pick up any movement of the water that stand outs. Pay particular attention to areas where tree branches or bushes touch the water.

While fishing this spot, Rick Phetsavong would land a weighted streamer into the deeper water, wait a couple moments for the fly to sink, and then start his retrieve back toward shallow water. Those big, circular structures in the background are mooring cells that barges and other vessels secure themselves to when loading and unloading cargo. Fish gravitate toward mooring cells to avoid predators or to ambush prey.

Here's how to make a bow-and-arrow cast like Brandon Dale in this photo: With your free hand, pinch the bend of the hook between your thumb and forefinger (with the fly upside down to avoid the hook stabbing your fingers). Next, pinch the fly line against the cork handle with your rod hand to maintain tension. Now, pull the fly back like drawing a bowstring while keeping the rod tip pointed at your target. The rod should now be curved back like a loaded bow and all you need to do is let go of the fly (like releasing an arrow) to send it toward your target. This short-distance cast works great in tight spots.

protection. Shadows over the water created by tree branches, bridges, and buildings also offer cover and a sense of security for fish. The photo on the bottom of page 85 shows Brandon Dale at a lake in Central Park. It was very early in the morning, and he headed to a dock where rowboats are rented. The place wasn't open yet, so everything was calm and quiet. The rowboats provided excellent structure for carp, and they cruised slowly around the boats, feeding both on the surface and just below.

WHEN YOU FIND A PRIME SPOT

When you find a spot with some combination of moving water with seams, changes in depth, and some sort of structure, you've likely found a prime location to catch a fish. If I were to choose one fly for such a prime spot, to catch any number of fish species, it would be a beadhead (weighted) black Woolly Bugger, which imitates various food sources in both freshwater and saltwater. For saltwater, a Clouser Minnow in a mix of white and some other color is also a great choice. For freshwater, another option would be a two-fly rig: a foam beetle with an egg pattern or weighted nymph suspended a foot or more beneath it. This two-fly rig is commonly called a "dry-dropper"—the "dry" is a floating fly and the "dropper" is a sinking fly suspended beneath. On my site, there is an article titled "Fly Fishing How To: 3 Ways to Create a Dry-Dropper Rig," which gives step-by-step instructions on setting up this rig.

Observing Fish Behavior

Reading the water isn't the only essential skill that you'll want to develop. Experienced anglers also know the importance of watching the fish in the water when it's possible to make them out. Watch how they move, notice what they're feeding on, and see how they respond when a fly or lure is presented to them. This is all part of observing the behaviors of fish, and it's another universal skill to help you catch all sorts of species. Observing fish in the water, really taking the time to watch and learn from the fish themselves, improves your chances of selecting the right fly and boosting your fishing success.

Observing fish behavior is something you can do anytime you're near the water, with or without a fishing rod in hand. Just like reading the water, reading fish behavior is a developed skill. There's a lot to learn here, so I'll cover the essentials to get you started. While each species of fish (and even individual fish) has its own unique behaviors, there are general patterns shared among all fish, so the advice below is useful for whatever fish you encounter.

TIPS FOR SPOTTING FISH

The first step is to spot fish, or signs of fish, in the water.

Clear Skies, Low Wind, and Plenty of Light: Finding clear or shallow water helps, but even in murky conditions, you'll have a better chance of spotting fish when the sky is clear, the wind is low, and the sun is high. If you're out at night, streetlights can provide enough illumination. Higher vantage points, like bridges or overlooks, also allow you to look straight down and reduce glare on the water's surface.

Leaping Fish: Fish may leap out of the water for various reasons, such as to catch a bug or escape a predator. Although jumping fish aren't always actively feeding, seeing them can give you a good idea of where fish might be congregating; such an area is worth exploring further. One species you might see jumping out of the water is the common carp. Although this behavior isn't fully understood, it often occurs during spawning season.

Surface Activity: Ripples, splashes, or other surface disturbances can indicate fish feeding on insects or other floating food. In rough water, look for spots where fish might be corralling smaller prey toward the surface, causing visible turbulence. You might also notice birds flying just above the water, which could mean they are also feeding on flying insects or diving into the water to nab smaller fish pushed to the surface by larger fish.

Tailing Fish: In shallow water, you might see fish tails poking above the surface. Many fish tilt their heads down in the shallows to forage, causing their tails to rise up. This "tailing" behavior is a strong indicator of actively feeding fish. For fly fishers targeting species like common carp and suckers, seeing a tailing fish is especially exciting

DETERMINE IF THE FISH IS FEEDING

Once you've spotted a fish or signs of fish, take a moment to really observe. Watch how the fish moves and try to get a sense of its behavior. A feeding fish is often more likely to take your fly, and it may be so focused on feeding that you can get closer for a well-placed cast. But if you're new to reading fish behavior, it can be hard to tell when a fish is feeding. Be sure to keep an eye out for the following cues.

Surface Feeding: Fish like bluegill, trout, and bass often rise to grab food on or just below the surface. Look for rings, ripples, or swirling water as these often indicate fish feeding on floating items. The best-case scenario is finding a "steady riser," in other words a fish that repeatedly

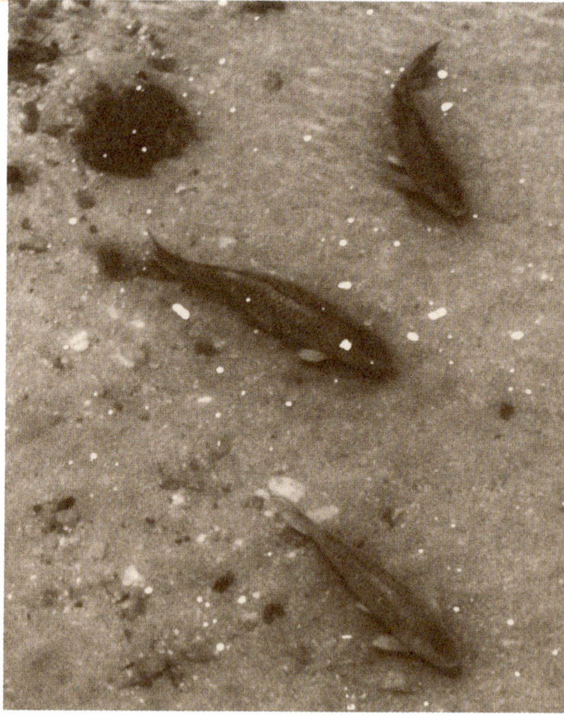

Even if you don't have a fishing rod with you when you spot a fish, take a moment to observe the fish in the water. Watch its behavior and see if it prefers to stay near a certain structure or depth of water. This photo shows three common carp slowly swimming close to the bottom. Occasionally, one of the carp would pause, dip its head down, and start plucking food from off the bottom. At the same time, its tail would rise up and start wagging, signaling a very happy feeding fish!

rises, almost like clockwork, allowing you to time your cast.

Mid-Column Feeding: Some fish feed in the mid-column, the zone between the surface and the bottom. In moving water, these fish might hold their position—tipping upward or swiping side to side—as food drifts by. In calmer water, they often cruise around, occasionally changing their direction to feed on something.

Bottom Feeding: Some fish, like carp, suckers, freshwater drum, redfish, and corbina, feed off the bottom, sifting through rocks, gravel, or sand. They'll often have their heads down, tails up. Species like smallmouth bass might also prowl along the bottom, especially near rocks where they hunt for crayfish.

Flashes: When keeping your eyes fixed on the water, you might notice a flash. If you see a flash in the water, it could be a fish turning or moving quickly to eat something on the surface, the bottom, or somewhere mid-column. Several species, such as trout and largemouth bass, are known for having white linings inside their mouths, which become visible when they open wide—either when striking prey or interacting with other fish. This "white flash" is subtle, but it'll become more noticeable as you keep watching.

FIGURE OUT WHAT THE FISH IS EATING

Once you've determined that the fish is likely feeding, the next step is to figure out what it's eating. Watching the fish and the water closely may reveal clues about its diet, helping you choose the right fly pattern to

Rick Mikesell spotted a carp feeding at the surface in very foamy water. The fish in the center of this photo was just a couple feet off the bank, allowing Rick to reach the rod out and dap a fly into the foam. You can see the fly dangling in the water near the top of the photo with the carp heading right for it. Even though the carp wasn't feeding on food that was the size of the fly Rick was using, it still took the pattern.

mimic its food. Sometimes you'll know exactly what a fish is eating, like a beetle or cricket, small fish, or food scraps tossed into the water by others. Quite often though, it's less obvious because urban waters offer diverse food sources. This is where your curiosity comes into play. Here are some tips to help you investigate further.

Get into the Weeds: It's worth combing through vegetation lining the shorelines and banks for different types of insects. Caterpillars, beetles, grasshoppers, ants, and plenty of other bugs climb along grasses, shrubs, and trees and fall into the water below. Aquatic vegetation (plants growing directly in both fresh and salt water) harbor creatures like crustaceans and schools of juvenile fish that are food items for larger fish. Aquatic vegetation in fresh water is also great habitat for a multitude of aquatic insects on which fish of all sizes feed. If you can get into the water, move slowly through these plants to see what is stirring below.

Use an Aquarium Net: If you see that a fish is feeding on the surface or mid-column, you can dip a small (and cheap) aquarium net into the water to scoop up the likely food source.

Dig in the Dirt: Along the bottom of a body of water, you'll often find a mix of rocks, shells, decaying vegetation, and urban debris. Nudging your boot, or poking a stick, to disturb the bottom can kick up critters like crayfish, crabs, and dragonfly nymphs. Observing how these creatures move through the water also gives you valuable insights into how to mimic their motion with your fly pattern, helping you attract more fish.

These types of investigations will narrow down your options. Once you have a good guess at what the fish are eating, select a fly pattern from your fly box that resembles the fish's food source as closely as possible. But don't overthink it. However, after trying all these methods, if you're still not sure what the fish are eating, or what fly pattern to select, try using one of the essential patterns I recommend in chapter 1.

Presenting Your Fly to the Fish

Once you've spotted a fish, observed its behavior, and selected a fly pattern, the next step is to make your cast. This is where the excitement of fly fishing heats up, in an art known as "presenting the fly to the fish." Few aspects of fly fishing are as rewarding, or as challenging, as getting your fly in front of a fish and convincing it to bite. It's an encounter that can have you shouting with joy or dropping your head into your hands wondering why the fish treated your fly like an unwanted pop-up ad.

The topic of presenting flies to fish is vast, with entire books, videos, and podcasts dedicated to it, often tailored to specific species. It's far too broad to cover adequately in this book, but there is one technique that I saw anglers consistently use from city to city that I'd like to share with you: the "drag and drop."

The drag and drop is particularly effective when using a floating fly line paired with a fly that sinks (nymphs, bottom dwellers, streamers, wet flies, egg patterns, etc.), and it works well for many different fish species. Additionally, it's very useful with fish feeding in shallow water—a depth less than 3 feet (1 m)—as this increases the chances of the fish noticing and reacting to your fly.

First, you'll want to identify the direction the fish is facing. Ideally, the fish will be broadside (sideways) to you, which reduces the chances of the fly line landing over the fish and potentially spooking it off; or what fly fishers call "lining the fish." First, cast your fly ahead and slightly beyond the fish. Then, gently pull your line to drag the fly closer to the fish's head. When the fly is about a foot from the fish's mouth, pause the movement of the fly, which allows the fly to sink down toward the fish. In a perfect scenario, the fly will be a few inches in front of the fish's mouth.

At this point, observe closely to see how the fish reacts. It may take the fly, not see it, or approach and turn away (in which case, you might want to try a different pattern). This method does require patience and focus on your part, but when it all finally comes together, it is an electrifying moment!

Finally, when you see or catch a fish, or even feel a tug on the end of your line, ask yourself this one valuable question: "Why was that fish there?" Take note of your surroundings, think about the conditions, and consider what might have attracted the fish to that spot. Each observation helps you build a mental map of what attracts fish to certain areas, making you a more insightful and successful angler. The more you observe, analyze, and reflect on these moments, the better your instincts will become, and that can be the difference between falling short and landing your next catch.

Reading the water and observing fish behavior are universal skills for any angler. Not only do they increase your chances of catching fish, but they also expand your understanding of local waters. As we venture into the second half of this book, we'll delve deeper into urban ecosystems, the unique habitats they create, and advanced strategies to fish them more effectively.

Denver fly fisher Mike Medina was at a pond filled with common carp feeding at and just below the surface. On the left side of the photo, the ring of water with a black dot is a carp feeding near the surface (the tip of its mouth is barely poking through the surface). The carp is also slowly swimming to the right. Toward the top of the photo, there's another small ripple, where Mike just landed an unweighted egg pattern. Notice how Mike landed the fly in front of and slightly beyond the fish. Next, he dragged the fly, by pulling in some fly line, until the egg was suspended right in front of the fish's mouth. Without a doubt, sight fishing like this really gets your heart rate going, even when you're only observing!

For urban anglers, part of the allure of fishing in cities is exploring new and different waters and the challenges they present, following curiosities wherever they lead.

CHAPTER 5

A Brief History of Urban Waters

Now it's time to dive deeper into the art and science of urban fishing. To help take your skills to the next level, we will explore what makes these environments so interesting, fun, and unique for fishing. We'll peer beyond the murky surface and plumb the mysteries of urban waters, the aquatic habitats they form, and how and where the fish live within these ecosystems.

Wading deeper into urban waters and bringing complex subjects to the surface will occasionally get gross—but hey, I never said urban fishing is glamorous. We'll push through some gritty details and step into some thicker topics, but I'll try my best to keep us from going in over our waders and getting our boots sucked into the muck. In the end, this deeper exploration will help us to read urban waters better and make smarter, more successful casts.

Part of the joy of urban fishing is its simplicity, and another part is pulling further on the line, getting into a few tangles, and seeing what comes up out of the water. These puzzles and challenges set urban fishing apart. Every city presents opportunities

Caroline Craven catching a first glimpse of the fish she is hooked into.

that lead to moments of genuine discovery, and catching fish in the most unlikely of places. Embracing these experiences will enhance your fishing skills. You will discover new species, net larger catches, elevate your confidence, and, potentially, get more involved in caring for these waters.

The Urban Waterscape

Crossing the bridge into the second half of this book, it helps to pause, look down, and get a glimpse of urban waters before we make our way into them. With a mapping application, zoom out and observe your city from above. You'll notice the familiar grid of roads, parking lots, buildings, and green spaces. As you look around, you'll also see bodies of water, perhaps an ocean coastline, ponds, streams, or wide rivers. Switching between map view and satellite imagery can show you these water features more clearly. But there's more to discover when you zoom in closer. You might spot dams, concrete-covered riverbanks, buildings rising straight from the water, and other structures that most certainly did not grow out of the earth, like factories, refineries, and large circular tanks holding water in a municipal wastewater treatment plant. All these elements are part of what's known as the *urban waterscape*.

Urban waterscapes are relatively new environments, having only developed significantly over the past century and a half. This makes them unfamiliar not only to anglers but also to the fish that inhabit them. As anglers, the more we understand these urban waterscapes, the better equipped we are to navigate them, locate fish, and recognize the significant impacts these environments have on the health and quality of our fisheries.

To build this understanding, we need to look back at how and why these waterscapes were designed and constructed. This historical perspective will also lay the groundwork for the topics we'll explore in the upcoming chapters.

How Our Urban Waterscapes Were Formed

Broadly speaking, there are three major ways in which humans have shaped and formed the urban waterscapes we fish. The first, and perhaps most foundational, is the development of water control infrastructure.

ANCIENT WATER CONTROL INFRASTRUCTURE

Cities need water for many purposes, and throughout history, humans have attempted to control and manage the watery world. Ancient civilizations such as Egypt, Rome, and those in the Indus Valley and Lower

Mekong Basin endeavored to control water by engineering and building *water control infrastructure,* such as dams, seawalls, canals, and aqueducts. Even here in North America, the Hohokam people in present-day Phoenix, Arizona, built around 500 miles (804 km) of canals that transformed the desert into fertile farmland. All of these marvels of human engineering allowed societies to thrive in hazardous, dynamically shifting landscapes formed by rivers, coastlines, deserts, and swamps.

Controlling water brought significant benefits, including reliable drinking water, irrigation for agriculture, energy for mills, land development, and improved navigation for trade and commerce. However, when these engineering feats failed, or couldn't adapt to changing climatic conditions, the consequences were severe, resulting in floods, coastal erosion, droughts, significant loss of life, and even the abandonment of entire cities. Despite these challenges, humans eventually developed water control infrastructure on a massive scale in attempts to dominate the watery world.

WATER CONTROL INFRASTRUCTURE IN MODERN TIMES

Fast-forward to the United States over the last century and a half, when the human population surged from around 38 million to over 330 million. This extraordinary growth was unprecedented in history and was partly enabled by the construction of dams, canals, seawalls, levees, and more—some of the very same water control infrastructure that humans have built for thousands of years. However, what changed this time was the scale and speed of construction. Throughout the nineteenth and twentieth centuries, the United States built an immense network of water control infrastructure at a pace and magnitude unmatched in human history up to that point. To put this into perspective, according to the National Levee Database and the National Inventory of Dams, there are 24,000 miles (38,624 km) of levees and over 91,000 dams across the country, and those are just the ones we know about; another estimate for the number of levees is closer to 40,000 miles (64,373 km). By building so extensively, the United States emerged as a powerhouse of water control infrastructure, with these unprecedented engineering projects rapidly transforming its rivers and coastlines in barely a blink of the eye, geologically speaking.

The United States and its cities are covered with water control infrastructure. When fishing beside or within these structures, look around and reflect on the amount of human labor this required. Then imagine what these waters must have been like before this colossal network was built. Yet water control infrastructure is not the only force shaping aquatic habitats in urban areas. In many ways, it enabled further development of the

The Los Angeles River, a once free-flowing, sinuous river home to steelhead, has been locked into a concrete channel for decades. But even in such austere environments, some fish species have found a way to survive.

roads, parking lots, bridges, and buildings that now cover our landscapes and continue to alter these aquatic environments.

THE LAYERS OF CONCRETE

Before massive urbanization and suburban sprawl, the landscape was filled with vegetation like trees, bushes, and grasses, as well as plenty of soil. All of this vegetation and soil absorbed water that fell across the landscape, soaking it up like a giant sponge, then slowly released that water into rivers, streams, lakes, and, eventually, the ocean. This giant sponge helped to regulate the flow of water, buffering and reducing how often catastrophic flooding occurred. This giant sponge also helped to filter and purify the water, removing harmful contaminants before the water ended up in bodies of water.

Now, in the twenty-first century, the extensive water control infrastructure built over the past two hundred years has allowed our societies to develop vast networks of roads, buildings, parking lots, and sidewalks with reduced concern about damages due to flooding. These are known as *impervious surfaces;* collectively, they act like a giant waterproof tarp that is covering the landscape.

Now, instead of the landscape being like a giant sponge, impervious surfaces like roads and buildings cause water to rush off all at once into our streams, rivers, lakes, and coastal areas. This results in extreme conditions in urban waters, where fast-moving, high, discolored water in rivers and sunny-day flooding along ocean shorelines have become regular occurrences throughout the year. As humans covered over these landscapes with impervious surfaces, they also removed many of the beneficial features that soil, plants, bushes, grasses, and other vegetation perform to purify and cleanse water.

CLEANING UP OUR WASTE

A third, and equally profound, impact on the health of our waters and fish has been pollution. In the nineteenth and twentieth centuries, as the US population surged, sewer systems in cities were expanded to address the health challenges of increasingly urbanized areas. Human and animal waste, alongside industrial by-products, were channeled into rivers, lakes, and oceans via networks of pipes and open trenches. Although these systems removed waste from city streets, they failed to treat it before discharging it into the water. This transformed waters into literal toxic wastelands that endangered and killed both humans and fish. Something had to be done to stop this.

In 1972, the Clean Water Act was enacted to address the environmental and health impacts on waters in the United States. This legislation made it unlawful to discharge any pollutant (without a permit) through a single, identifiable source such as factories, wastewater treatment plants, construction projects, and oil refineries.

Despite limitations of the Clean Water Act, this legislation marked a significant advancement toward ensuring clean water throughout the country. The importance of the Clean Water Act for all Americans cannot be overstated—it laid the groundwork for discussions and initiatives on water cleanliness that continue today. Without this key piece of legislation, exploring urban fishing as an enjoyable pastime wouldn't even be possible.

THE HISTORY OF YOUR URBAN WATERSCAPE

The rapid development of water control infrastructure and the expansion of cities have forever altered the bodies of water we rely on. These changes have not only reshaped the ecosystems within our cities but have also transformed how we approach fishing in these environments. Of course, there's much more to this history than what can be covered in a few paragraphs, and I urge you to explore the origins of your local waterscape. Often, you can find pieces of this history as you fish. For example, you might come across informational signs along pathways and or near buildings that offer clues about why certain urban waters behave the way they do.

For example, in Minneapolis, there are signs detailing the history of what was once the largest flour mill operated by Pillsbury. The mill is no longer in use and has been converted into an apartment complex. However, beneath the building runs a tunnel that once channeled water to power the mill. Today, that same tunnel channels water to power a hydroelectric turbine, providing energy for the building.

I had the opportunity to watch Evan Griggs fish around this old Pillsbury mill. We were there at midday and it was quite hot. The residents in the apartment complex must have been using their air conditioners, as water was flowing out of the tunnel at a good pace. This flow of water, acting as a conveyor belt carrying all sorts of food items, also attracted quite a few fish, giving Evan several opportunities to cast as they swam in and out of the tunnel.

With the water flowing from that tunnel only at certain times, I might not have puzzled it out if Evan had not explained it all to me, and if the informational signs nearby hadn't also provided clues. Fishing opportunities like this are scattered around urban waters, and you'll undoubtedly encounter similar scenarios in your own city. With a little detective work, and historical knowledge of your local waterscape, you can start to understand how these unusual features and their current uses influence fish behavior.

BY-PRODUCTS OF PROGRESS AND BURIED HISTORIES

Fishing in urban waterscapes provides plenty of adventures, and these built environments have greatly contributed to the growth of our cities and industries. But they also have profound impacts on the health and quality of our urban fisheries. Additionally, their development has buried histories that are seldom acknowledged by the historical markers in our cities. For anglers, that makes it important to look beyond the visible structures and consider the broader implications of urban development.

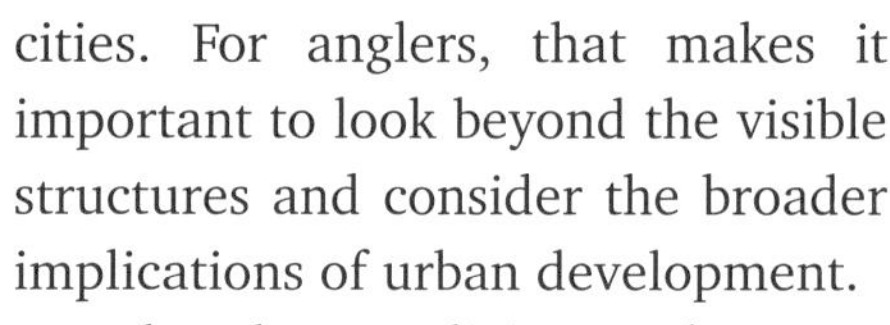

The plans, policies, and visions used to build water control infrastructure, cover our landscape with impervious surfaces, and continue to pollute our waters have rarely considered the health of fish populations and other aquatic life. Much of the

Evan Griggs fishes the tunnel at the base of the old Pillsbury Mill. Urban waters like this hold many artifacts that are slowly decaying, being grown over and eroded away, and these structures are part of what make up aquatic habitats. Take the time to observe these artifacts and how fish use them for shelter and feeding grounds. Also notice where currents converge or diverge around these structures, to read the water and predict fish behavior.

During my time in Denver, I had a chance encounter with William Tall Bull, a member of the Cheyenne, who is dedicated to preserving his tribe's history and fostering awareness of our connections to the landscape and local waters.

infrastructure developed over the past century and a half was designed with narrow objectives, such as flood control, irrigation, establishing shipping channels, controlling water supply, and hydroelectric power generation. The fish that remain in these altered waters are essentially byproducts, swimming around structures that were not designed with their well-being in mind. It's why fishing in urban areas can be so tough—because urban fish are survivors in environments and habitats that aren't suited for most species of fish. Our waters once thrived with aquatic biodiversity, but we have lost vast quantities of fish and entire species of aquatic life to urban life and industry.

More troublingly, these plans and policies have often lacked holistic vision, transparency, meaningful involvement from diverse communities, and long-term considerations. Fishing in urban areas means being surrounded by layers of history, much of it buried beneath concrete. Cultures and communities have been profoundly harmed, and traditions that once connected people to their local waters have been severed. More of that history is gradually being lost. One example is the historic area along the West Fork of the Trinity River in Fort Worth, Texas, where Douglass and McGar Parks once served as vibrant gathering and recreational spaces for Black communities during the era of Jim Crow segregation. While the landscape continues to change through ongoing development, it remains uncertain whether that cultural legacy will be acknowledged and meaningfully carried forward. These waters, like so many across our cities, hold the potential not only to sustain life, but to reconnect people to place, to one another, and to the deeper histories that still flow beneath the surface.

Evan Griggs fishes downstream of a bypass channel for a hydroelectric dam; the bypass channel is a controlled release point to regulate water levels when the main turbines aren't in operation. Fishing in urban areas comes with questions about where the water comes from and what *exactly* is in it.

CHAPTER 6

Common Pollutants in Urban Waters

Fishing urban waters offers thrilling experiences and moments of discovery, but it's crucial to be informed when we venture out into them. We all have to face the fact of polluted waters, but if we were to just sit around hoping for the situation to change, we would probably never go out fishing in our cities. With some knowledge and common sense, we can fish safely in our urban waters.

Water quality is a measure of how clean and safe water is for its intended use, such as fishing or swimming. Questions like "Should I get into the water?" and "Can I eat this fish?" are important to ask. In this chapter, I'll help you find the answers by recommending resources for learning about local water quality, offering insights about wading and eating fish, and providing an overview of common pollutants in our urban waters.

Broadly speaking, the quality of our urban waters is far better than it was decades ago. As mentioned in the last chapter, the 1972 Clean Water Act has played a monumental role in cleaning up waters in our cities. Without it, we wouldn't have wastewater treatment plants, meaning our urban waters would be utterly toxic and deadly to both humans and animals.

While fly fishing in Los Angeles, I waded through the Los Angeles River alongside Analiza del Rosario, searching for fish. As we crossed the river, she pointed out the water flowing between our boots. It was clear. Aquatic plants swayed in the current, rooted to the riverbed and fish were not only surviving but reproducing. Some of us even experienced the thrill of netting those fish. What were we not wading through? A canal oozing with oily sludge and feces.

Jennifer Hsia with a smallmouth buffalo, a species notoriously difficult to catch using fly patterns. Restoring amazing fish like the smallmouth buffalo depends on cleaner urban waters.

Resourceful species like common carp and largemouth bass (species we'll talk about more in the next chapter) have been able to adapt to many urban waters throughout the country. Several other incredible species are still persevering, and even coming back. Buffalo Bayou in Houston, once severely impacted by pollution, has seen noticeable improvements in water clarity and fish diversity, thanks to large-scale cleanup and habitat restoration efforts. Areas once thought to be dead zones now are home to many different species, including some really cool ones like freshwater drum and alligator gar. The bayou's ongoing recovery highlights the resilience of urban waters and the impact of revitalization efforts in bringing back fish.

We have come a long way from using oceans, rivers, and lakes as dumping grounds for a city's worth of raw human, industrial, and animal waste—and we should not lose sight of those historical gains. Yet, as much as the Clean Water Act has done to protect our health, it only addresses some of the problems. We continue to pollute our waters in myriad ways, impacting the health and quality of our drinking water, aquatic habitats, and fish populations.

Resources for Local Water Quality Information

Urban water quality varies from city to city due to local climate, geography, industrial use, and water management practices. The urban waters you are interested in exploring might have relatively good water quality or they might have concerning pollution problems. Given such a wide spectrum, it is impossible for me to provide specific details about your local waters. However, the answers are available if you know where to find them.

One vital resource is the How's My Waterway page on the Environmental Protection Agency (EPA) website (www.mywaterway.epa.gov). This website provides details about:

- whether a body of water is deemed safe for swimming or other recreational activities such as wading
- overall status of aquatic life, fish consumption advisories, and any pollution problems existing in the water
- any efforts currently underway to rejuvenate or protect ecosystems
- overall water quality based on physical, chemical, and biological factors

For more specific and current information on local water quality, a quick internet search for state and city environmental or health agency websites provides further guidance. As one example, the Denver Department of Public Health & Environment samples the city's public waters, provides that

SAFETY TIP

Hand Washing

When fishing, wash your hands before touching your food. Also, when tying knots, spit on the monofilament, or dunk it in the water (lubrication helps tighten and seat knots into place, improving their strength). Don't lick it. Spare your taste buds and avoid an upset stomach.

Keep an eye out for signs along your urban waters that give information about the health of local waters. The sign might include websites where you can find additional resources and contact information to speak directly with experts such as local water quality specialists.

data on the city's website, and notifies water users about when to avoid swimming or wading.

Local advocacy groups that monitor water quality issues are another resource that might be available in your city. For instance, the Pearl Riverkeeper, in Jackson, Mississippi, conducts weekly *E. coli* bacteria testing during summer months, letting the public know whether it's safe to get in the water; their website shows a map of where those monitoring tests are conducted.

Resources for Learning About Water Quality in General

For information beyond the common pollutants and water quality issues that we'll discuss in this chapter, check out the following free resources to deepen your understanding of water quality.

The Environmental Protection Agency's Watershed Academy: This online library of learning modules and webinars is designed to bring you up to speed on water quality. www.epa.gov/watershedacademy

DataStream's Learning Centre: This Canadian organization provides an excellent, easy-to-read, water quality guidebook with information applicable to all cities. www.datastream.org

Creek Critters App: This Izaak Walton League of America app gives step-by-step instructions for collecting and identifying bioindicators—bugs and organisms that reveal freshwater

Jule Schultz from the Spokane Riverkeeper and I were leading a water quality class for a group of high school students. At two local waterways, we guided the students in collecting aquatic organisms that serve as indicators of water and habitat health. In one waterway, we found a stonefly (pictured in the top-left corner of the ice cube tray) and cased caddisflies (in the bottom two corners), which indicate better water quality. In contrast, the second waterway yielded leeches (top-right corner), which can signal degraded water quality when they are found in greater abundance compared to other aquatic organisms.

health (and hint at fly patterns to try). The League also runs the only nationwide volunteer program to protect waterways and monitor water quality. www.iwla.org/water/stream-monitoring

Equity in Every Drop: This Waterkeeper Alliance podcast explores issues and solutions surrounding water quality through the voices of various experts and community members. www.waterkeeper.org/equity-in-every-drop-series-one

Thinking of Wading?

Many fly fishers wade in urban waters, but given the uncertainties of water quality, why would we ever choose to go in? Wading puts you closer to the fish, helps you cast more accurately, and reduces the chance of snagging obstacles on the bank. Once in the water, you notice details better, like crayfish crawling around or insects floating on the surface, helping you to choose the right fly pattern. Plus, you get away from banks that are sometimes crowded.

Wading also connects you more intimately with local waters. My friend Robert Bartlett is adamant about getting in the water. To him, fly fishing and wading are inseparable; having the water around you deepens

Wading into the water can also make it easier to pursue larger fish if they take off on a run, requiring you to maneuver to keep it on the line, especially if the banks or shoreline are covered in foliage or urban obstacles.

your experience and furthers your bond with the water. There is also something mentally healing about being in the water. As you cross into another world, the noise and bustle of the city fade, your mind clears, and you are in a space all your own.

Be sure to use the resources found earlier in this chapter to help make an informed decision about getting in the water. After reviewing those sites, if you're still unsure about the water quality but want to go in, consider wearing waders as a protective measure. While many urban anglers "wet wade" (wade without waders), especially in the peak of summer, it's best done with knowledge of local waters and acceptance of additional risk. Don't plan to wet wade if you have any open cuts, wounds, or sores that could get infected. Wet wading is something I also prefer when the weather is hot and I don't want to deal with the sweaty hassle of wearing waders. But when fishing unfamiliar city waters, I take the time to visit the relevant websites and consult with local anglers before making the decision to wet wade.

If you come across water that has an oily film or thick layer of green muck, or you see lots of dead fish, use common sense and stay out. Though uncommon in most urban waters, such conditions do occur. Report them using the EPA's online form (www.echo.epa.gov/report-environmental-violations) or through state, city, or local environmental groups. Increased

Even if you could get down into the water at this spot, this is a clear example of when it's best to stay on dry land. The floating fish (barely visible near the bottom of the frame) came from a small channel that was isolated from the main river flow due to barriers used in a construction project. With no fresh water exchange, oxygen levels dropped, leading the fish to suffocate. When workers removed the barriers, the stagnant, low-oxygen water—along with the dead fish—drained back into the main stem of the river.

reports lead to cleanup and better monitoring, and as anglers, reporting pollution is one way to demand improved water quality.

Thinking of Eating that Fish?

For those of us who include fish in our diets, cooking and eating a fish we have caught and killed is a deeply impactful experience. People in urban areas should have access to this experience and the nutritional benefits of healthy fish. Even if we do it infrequently, harvesting our own catch builds a direct connection between us and the living world around us and grounds us in the reality of what it means to take an animal's life to sustain ours. It also encourages mindfulness, often leading to more intentional eating habits, such as reducing food waste or deciding to eat fish more sparingly.

Before eating a fish, you need to be aware of local fish consumption advisories because many urban waters are currently too polluted to even consider harvesting fish from them. To make a more informed decision, refer to the resources I've mentioned, as well as the Food & Drug Administration's advice (www.fda.gov/food/consumers/advice-about-eating-fish).

Unfortunately, fish consumption advisories don't cover every pollutant accumulated by fish, adding risk if you decide to eat your catch. Urban waters are contaminated by a range of pollutants and testing for them year-round is challenging. As a result, agencies often recommend only eating fish caught beyond city limits or full-grown fish that were raised in hatcheries and stocked in specific waters, such as designated city ponds. There are many good intentions to fish stocking (including some reasons we'll touch upon in the next chapter) but this solution is flawed.

Ideally, our urban waters would support healthy local fish populations. At the same time, whether from urban or nonurban waters (or lab-grown alternatives), city dwellers would have access to nutritious fish without the need for off-site farming facilities and hatchery trucks. And if you've ever cut open a stocked fish—often pale, softer-fleshed, and pellet-fed—and compared it to a fish raised and nurtured in a healthy ecosystem, where a varied diet produces brighter flesh and firmer texture, you've seen firsthand what nutritious really looks like. As urban anglers, we know how much there is to gain by advocating for our local waters through policies and outcomes that reconnect us to our ecosystems in mutually beneficial ways.

Despite advisories and regulations, some urban communities and individuals continue to rely on fish as a food source because other options are neither affordable nor accessible—highlighting a public health issue for marginalized city dwellers. Urban fishing attracts people of diverse socioeconomic backgrounds. What connects us all is a heightened appreciation for our local waters.

FISHING TIP

Killing and Cooking Fish

Check out www.ikijime.com for guidance on effective humane methods for dispatching fish to reduce suffering and ensure their quality for eating. For information on how to cook fish, I recommend *Hook, Line, and Supper* by Hank Shaw. In his book, Hank walks you through the entire process of cleaning, storing, and cooking fish with pages and pages of delicious recipes for both freshwater and saltwater species.

Common Pollutants and Water Quality Issues in Our Cities

It would be both impractical and impossible to offer a complete list of pollutants and water quality issues lurking in our cities. Instead, let's get to know some of the usual suspects within city waters and consider their impact on fish and aquatic habitats. Be forewarned, it's going to get a bit grimy.

Before we wade in, I want to reiterate that urban waters aren't hazardous waste barrels. Each city faces its own pollution challenges—some minor, others more severe. The good news is that I've met angler advocates in the thick of it, giving their time to make a difference.

Take Nic Hall, president of Denver's Trout Unlimited. This organization, along with other advocacy groups, is taking legal action against a local oil refinery that is discharging effluent containing high levels of chemicals known to cause cancer when ingested. The refinery's discharge flows into waterways that run through predominantly low-income communities, raising serious concerns about both public health risks and aquatic habitat degradation. In Nic's inspiring words, "We firmly believe that no river is beyond repair. Abandoning this section of river or conceding that it should not meet current water quality standards is simply unacceptable. Together, we can restore the health and vitality of the Denver South Platte for the benefit of our community and future generations."

So, don't lose hope. There are anglers out there who are using the available information to not only fish better, but to advocate for the fundamental right to clean water—for both people and the fish that depend on it.

THE IMPACT OF WATER TEMPERATURE ON URBAN FISHING

The first issue to start with is how rising water temperatures can impact water quality. Generally speaking, water bodies in urban areas warm up much faster and reach hotter temperatures than those in nonurban areas due to factors like water control infrastructure and the "heat island effect," which is a fancy way of saying, "We've paved over everything, and now it's hot as hell."

When water temperatures rise, water quality issues are amplified. Warmer water creates more favorable conditions for pathogens like *E. coli* to grow and spread, and it also increases the concentration of certain pollutants, like ammonia, which can be deadly to fish and harmful to humans if ingested. For these reasons, it's best to avoid wading into very warm, stagnant water, which is most common during late summer.

Human-induced changes to water temperature can also negatively impact aquatic organisms and habitats. Such changes can disrupt the migratory and spawning habits of fish, alter their feeding behaviors and metabolism, and lower oxygen levels in the water, causing fish to suffocate and die. This is important for anglers to understand: As water temperatures increase, dissolved oxygen levels decrease, making it harder for fish to "breathe."

The upper limit of the water temperature a fish can survive in depends on the species. Some are a bit sensitive, while others seem nearly indestructible. For example, rainbow trout begin to suffocate and die when water temperatures are above 70°F (21°C) for prolonged periods. Smallmouth bass face lethal temperatures in water that is warmer than 95°F (35°C), and, incredibly, common carp have been observed surviving for short durations in water up to 106°F (41°C), basically one step away from becoming poached fish.

Water temperatures in urban areas change abruptly due to human activity, and many urban anglers find it helpful to carry a thermometer. Fish are cold blooded, and their feeding habits and activity levels are determined by water temperature. In the next chapter, we'll discuss water temperatures at which certain species are more active. Having a thermometer will quickly clue you in to what species you may or may not find in certain bodies of water, as well as whether the fish might be actively feeding. It is a simple tool that can help you piece together some of the puzzles of urban fishing.

URBAN RUNOFF: THE IMPACTS OF IMPERVIOUS SURFACES

In the last chapter, I briefly covered the roads, parking lots, sidewalks, rooftops, and the like throughout cities, referred to as *impervious surfaces*. These impervious surfaces repel water like a nonstick frying pan. When it rains, snow melts, or sprinklers turn on, the water hitting these impervious surfaces slides off and that is called *runoff*.

As runoff flows across these impervious surfaces, it picks up a variety of contaminants, such as pesticides, fertilizers, oil, microplastics, bacteria, and road salts, among other things. Runoff, with its cocktail of contaminants, is a massive problem for cities. It has profound negative and long-lasting effects on fish and other aquatic organisms, and at times is a considerable health concern for humans.

There are two significant ways cities try to deal with the problem of runoff: *combined sewer overflows* (CSOs) and *municipal separate storm sewer systems* (MS4s).

COMBINED SEWER OVERFLOWS

Most cities in the Northeast, Midwest, and Pacific Northwest of the United States, and many cities throughout Canada, have CSOs, which sounds fancy until you realize it's a polite way of saying, "We put rainwater and raw sewage in the same pipe, sometimes discharge that liquid into your local lake or river, and hope for the best."

CSOs collect runoff through street drains and send it into underground pipes, which are also carrying industrial waste and municipal sewage. Ideally, this mystery slurry gets sent to a municipal treatment plant where it is properly cleaned before being released into local waters.

But when the system gets overwhelmed (such as during a heavy rainstorm), it takes the express route straight to the nearest river, lake, or ocean shoreline, often with zero treatment. And here's the kicker: This is a totally legal form of pollution that is permitted and regulated under the Clean Water Act—because, apparently, the best solution many cities have come up with is crossing their fingers and hoping it doesn't rain too much.

The liquid discharging out of CSO pipes during times when the system is being overwhelmed carries bacteria like *E. coli* and other hazardous substances. In cities that have CSO systems, there can be many CSO pipes, making them difficult to avoid. For example, in Chicago, there are about three hundred CSO discharge points up and down the Chicago and Little Calumet Rivers.

The more you fish in your city, the more you'll see storm drains from a completely different perspective.

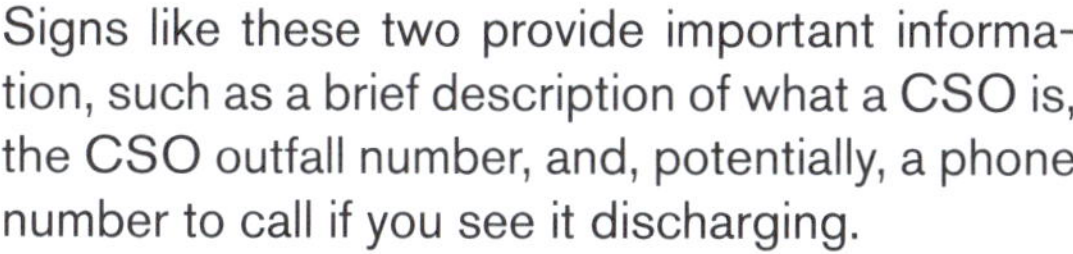
Signs like these two provide important information, such as a brief description of what a CSO is, the CSO outfall number, and, potentially, a phone number to call if you see it discharging.

Since CSOs are ubiquitous in many cities, we need to look after ourselves when fishing in or along urban waters, which we can do by keeping the following in mind:

- CSO outfalls are designated with signage along bodies of water, so you know what they are; a CSO *outfall* is the discharge point, often looking like a large pipe sticking out toward the water
- many states and cities advise waiting seventy-two hours after a rainstorm before going into the water, as this is when CSOs are likely to be used
- fishing from the bank can be safer than wading along bodies of water that have numerous CSO outfalls that discharge during wet weather; when in doubt stay out
- if you are wading and a CSO outfall starts discharging liquid, fish elsewhere

Report any instances of an outfall discharging during dry weather (which signals a problem in the sewer system) by calling the number on a

Ryan Birringer uses a streamer to target smallmouth bass near a combined sewer overflow (CSO) in Minneapolis. Notice how Ryan keeps the rod tip pointed down at the water while pinching the fly line against his cork handle with one hand and pulling the line with the other. This smooth move—aptly called "stripping streamers"—retrieves the streamer while keeping slack to a minimum. And if he gets a bite, he delivers one aggressive strip to set the hook.

CSO sign or contact your state environmental agency or the EPA (echo.epa.gov/report-environmental-violations).

Now, do I still fish along stretches of water that have CSO outfalls? Yes, because I pay attention to the weather, and I know the locations of CSO outfalls along the waters I fish. For example, when I lived in Columbus, Ohio, if a large rainstorm was approaching the city, I would not go wading in areas where CSOs were located. But once the storm passed and things settled, I'd be right back out there. One of my favorite places to wet wade and fish for carp had six CSO outfalls along just a 2-mile (3 km) stretch of river. Only once during dry weather did I see one of those "sewage geysers" burp out foul sludge, and when that happened, I did what any reasonable angler would do: I took my fly rod and went somewhere else. The carp fishing was world-class along that stretch of river, where I racked up so many fun memories catching and releasing personal records. And guess what? I'm still alive and in good health.

For further information on CSOs, along with a map of their locations, visit the EPA's website here: www.epa.gov/npdes/combined-sewer-overflow-basics. Just be aware that not all CSOs in the country are listed on that map. For example, Toledo, Ohio, has over two dozen CSOs, but none are displayed on that federal EPA map. So, you'll want to also check with your state EPA (or similar environmental or health agency) and city website for information on where CSOs are located in your local waters.

As more people become aware of the health risks that CSOs pose to both humans and animals, concern is growing that the problem might actually be getting worse in some cities. And it's not just a hunch—climate data backs up this claim. Weather patterns are shifting, and extreme rainstorms are expected to become more frequent across the country. More powerful storms mean more frequent sewer overloads, unless changes are made. The good news is that some cities, like Toledo, Minneapolis, and Spokane are stepping up and making major investments to reduce or eliminate CSO discharges.

In other cities, there might not even be any CSOs, or very few of them. These cities most likely have a separate system that manages runoff in a different way but often still sends pollution straight into our urban waters.

MUNICIPAL SEPARATE STORM SEWER SYSTEMS

MS4s are a second major way cities deal with runoff. When it rains, this system collects runoff through street drains and carries it in separate pipes, keeping it away from municipal sewage and industrial wastewater (which, admittedly, is a slight upgrade from CSOs). However, once collected, it's uncommon for this runoff to undergo any sort of treatment before being delivered straight into bodies of water. This results in pollution entering our urban waters, and it's also permitted under the Clean Water Act.

You've likely seen this system before. Those "Drains to Stream" or "Drains to River" labels on street drains mean that anything dumped in there goes straight into local waters.

Rick Phetsavong fishes on top of a MS4 outfall discharging into a local river. During large rainstorms, these outfalls turn from benign waterfalls into raging torrents that fish could either be attracted to or completely avoid. Fish will avoid these outfalls if the water being discharged is low in oxygen, due to factors like excessively warm water, decomposing organic material, and chemical runoff from roads.

MS4 outfalls, unlike CSOs, usually don't have advisory signs, so unless you know what you're looking for, you might just assume it's a nice little urban waterfall and not a drainage pipe delivering unfiltered runoff. Again, many states and cities recommend waiting at least seventy-two hours after a storm before getting into the water due to the spike in pollutants from runoff.

FISHING DURING RUNOFF EVENTS

Many urban anglers choose to fish during runoff events. While this might seem counterintuitive, there are good reasons why anglers go fishing when water levels spike. Rainstorms and high-water events often put larger fish on the hunt for food because they feed on smaller fish and prey swept through the current. Rising water also brings fish into creeks and smaller channels, creating new fishing opportunities that wouldn't exist in normal, drier conditions. Choosing not to fish during high-water events is completely valid, but in many cities, urban waters are constantly influenced by storms and runoff, meaning you could be waiting weeks for conditions to fully stabilize.

For those of us who fish during runoff events, we take precautions—like washing our hands before eating and wearing waders or staying out of the water—to minimize risks while still making the most of these conditions. I told you urban fishing isn't exactly glamorous, but let's be honest, are we really supposed to just sit around and not fish when the bite is on?

Whether you heed the advice to stay out of the water during a runoff event is up to you, but if you do decide to cast a line, then I might as well pass along some fly-fishing tips for when waters are high and discolored.

Use Darker Streamers: Use black or dark-colored streamer patterns or ones that have flashy material. These can contrast against the off-color water and attract fish. The larger size of streamers also increases the chances of a fish seeing your fly.

Get Your Fly Close to Structures: Some fish wait in slower water for prey to be swept by, so get your fly close to structures like bridges and rocky shorelines that are creating eddies.

Jig Your Flies: The heavier weight of jig streamers punch through high water. Once the fly is in the water, hold out your arm and fly rod and slowly jig the rod tip up and down. This is a great technique to use close to structures and in eddies. Strikes by fish can be quite intense when doing this, so hold on!

Try Nymph Patterns: When all else fails, use weighted nymph patterns a few feet under an indicator. Be sure to use patterns you don't mind

Nic Hall displays his rainbow trout, caught from a river in Denver after a rainstorm. And a special shout-out to Emma Brown for swooping in and netting the fish.

losing, and you may want to add a couple pieces of split shot to help get those flies down through the water.

During my trip to Denver, there was a day when it rained for hours. The river that Nic Hall and I had fished days prior became a raging torrent of high, discolored water. But Nic knew a spot on the river where heavy current flowed into a deeper, slower pool. The river bottom was sandy and mostly free of debris, which meant Nic could get a fly pattern close to or on the bottom without getting snagged. To do this, he placed a bobber (indicator) on his leader and then attached a dark red worm to the end of the leader several feet below the indicator. In order to get the worm pattern near the bottom, Nic pinched a couple pieces of heavy split shot onto the leader right up against the eye of the hook. Understanding his urban river, and using this nymphing technique, helped Nic to catch a hefty rainbow trout that day.

Knowing how to fish in high, murky water is a useful skill for urban anglers. Even if you choose not to fish during a runoff event, it's important to understand that impervious surfaces are just one of many factors discoloring our urban waters.

Dirty Waters

Urban waters—particularly rivers, streams, and creeks—sometimes flow with water the color of chocolate milk due to fine sediment particles like sand, silt, and clay. According to the EPA, fine sediments are among the most significant pollutants in waterways across the country. That's right, something as simple as dirt is classified as a major pollutant. There are many contributors, but agricultural runoff is the largest, particularly when fields are tilled or cleared right up to the water's edge. This practice dumps massive amounts of sediment into rivers and streams, choking aquatic habitats and washing away a farm's most valuable resource: soil.

The negative impacts of sediment on aquatic habitats and fish are wide-ranging. For example, the bottom of a body of water, called the *substrate*, can be a mix of larger sediment like boulders, smaller rocks, pebbles, and gravel. These rocks and gravel provide excellent habitat for many species of fish and their food sources. While bodies of water need some level of fine sediment, when excessive amounts of sand and silt are released into the water, called *sedimentation*, it smothers and destroys habitats.

Excessive fine sediment not only clogs up the bottom but also clouds the water, traps heat, and blocks sunlight. This disrupts plant and algae growth, smothering the foundation of the food pyramid. Healthy waterways have a mix of rocks, plants, and algae, creating diverse, complex habitats that support thriving fish populations. But when sediment takes over, the water turns into a featureless, uniform environment, much like an underwater parking lot. And like a parking lot, it's not exactly a great place to live. Urban streams overloaded with mud and sand become inhospitable

to most species of fish—except, of course, common carp, which seem to thrive in just about any conditions short of being beamed into space.

The problem of sedimentation goes beyond turning the water brown and degrading aquatic habitats. As sediment erodes from the surrounding landscape, it hitchhikes pollutants such as pesticides, herbicides, and heavy metals straight into urban water bodies, causing other damages. Among these pollutants, excessive fertilizer use is one of the most obvious culprits.

WHAT THE MUCK IS FLOATING AROUND IN THE WATER?

Fertilizer, containing nutrients like phosphorus and nitrogen, are widely used on agricultural crops, lawns, city parks, and sports fields. These nutrients help terrestrial plants grow, and when they enter bodies of water, it's no miracle they also promote the growth of aquatic plants and algae. Excessive amounts of phosphorus and nitrogen lead to dense growth of algae and aquatic plants in a process called *eutrophication*. You've likely seen eutrophic water bodies in your city, especially ponds that turn green or have a layer of brownish-green muck floating on the surface.

As algae and aquatic plants die, bacteria decompose this material, using up a lot of oxygen in the process. This decreases the overall amount of dissolved oxygen in the water, causing fish and other aquatic organisms to suffocate and die. This is one reason why you might see dead fish floating in those green ponds.

Eutrophication is harmful not only to aquatic life but also to humans. Harmful algal blooms (HABs), like red tide and cyanobacteria (blue-green algae), release high concentrations of toxins that can cause sickness in humans and pets and contaminate our drinking water. HABs occur throughout many cities, and staying out of the mucky water and not drinking it are obvious ways to avoid getting sick, but it also helps to know more about HAB events.

CDC Resources: Consult the HAB webpage, which provides information, protection tips, and links to monitoring programs. www.cdc.gov/habs/index.html

Hangman Creek in Spokane, Washington, converges with the Spokane River. In the spring, the creek is choked with sediment due to poor land-use practices along the waterway. As the sediment-laden creek water mixes with the Spokane River's clear water, beneficial aquatic habitat is smothered beneath a layer of sand and silt, reducing the population of fish and aquatic insects in the river. Photograph courtesy of Cutboard Studio

NOAA Forecasts: Check forecasts and alerts about harmful algal blooms and red tides. www.oceanservice.noaa.gov/ecoforecasting

City and State Resources: Some cities and states have in-depth, local reporting of HABs. For example, the New York State Department of Environmental Conservation notifies of any harmful algal bloom and includes an interactive map showing current HABs across ponds in New York City.

Pay Attention to Signs: Signs are often posted along waters notorious for having HABs. Read these signs for additional safety precautions.

I recommend avoiding fishing in areas experiencing intense HABs, which are often indicated by thick, green muck and numerous dead fish floating on the surface. In these conditions, it's best to report the issue and give the remaining fish a break as they are struggling to survive in low-oxygen, toxic waters.

With that said, algae and aquatic plants play crucial roles in supporting habitats and entire ecosystems, just like sediment. In urban waters where they aren't growing out of control (causing low-dissolved oxygen levels and fish kill-offs), they help create a rich and diverse food web. In such places, you could find great fishing opportunities. However, the struggle is real when you're trying to fly fish around aquatic plants and algae. One minute, you're making a perfect cast; the next, your fly is dragging back what looks like a soggy salad. To keep your sanity intact, here are a few tips when fishing around aquatic plants and bits of floating algae.

Cast to the Edges: Retrieve a small streamer, like a woolly bugger, parallel to the edges of aquatic plants or floating algae to entice fish to come out and strike.

Use Flies with Weed Guards: Weed guards are pieces of monofilament that hang over the hook point to minimize the fly snagging. When a fish bites hard, the weed guard bends out of the way, allowing the hook to penetrate the fish's lip. Certain fly patterns, like poppers, sometimes have weed guards. You can also ask a fly shop if they have any "weedless" flies.

Decode the Bubbles: Fly fishing in green-tinted ponds inhibits spotting and casting flies to individual fish (sight fishing). But you might notice bubbles appearing on the surface and then moving in a certain direction. While this could be a turtle, or just gas releasing from the bottom, it could be a fish feeding. Cast an indicator with a weighted fly beyond the bubbles and then drag the indicator toward where you guess the fish to be. Watch the indicator for any twitching, which could be the fish biting your fly.

I joined Brandon Dale for some carp fishing at a very green, murky lake in Central Park. The lake we fished often has HABs, especially in late summer. But the day we were there, casting from the bank, the algae weren't intense enough to form hazardous, thick, green muck. The carp were also actively feeding, showing us there was plenty of dissolved oxygen in the water for them.

A few of the carp were swimming under tree branches that were dropping mulberries (which look similar to blackberries) into the water. When a mulberry fell, a carp would rise up and eat it. However, if a berry sank, then there was a swirl of water as a carp feasted below the surface.

In the murky, green water, it was tough to see fish feeding below the surface, so Brandon set up a dry-dropper rig to gain an edge. His rig featured a floating foam fly mimicking a mulberry on the surface and a weighted nymph imitating a sunken mulberry below. Sometimes the carp pounced on the floating fly. But when they hesitated, Brandon kept his eyes on the floating fly, aware of the nymph hanging beneath. If the foam fly twitched—hinting at a bite—he quickly raised his rod to set the hook. Presenting flies both above and below doubled his chances of landing some plump carp that day.

You might also come across small, vibrantly blue ponds. Pond managers use blue dyes as a way to repress HABs by limiting the amount of sunlight penetration into the water (with less sunlight, photosynthesis decreases, making it harder for algae and aquatic plants to bloom). This is a common management practice with smaller ponds on golf courses and decorative ponds around business districts. The dye is not toxic to fish, but it's more of an aesthetic fix rather than a real solution. The dye doesn't remove excessive nutrients (phosphorus and nitrogen) that were introduced into the pond, and it's not effective on larger bodies of water or ponds already undergoing severe HAB events. While dyes can be a prevention tool, better pond management strategies must also include reducing fertilizer runoff, adding aeration (like fountains and bubblers), and reconnecting ponds to riparian areas in the case of concrete shorelines. Many of the fishing tips throughout this chapter on fishing in discolored water are applicable to fishing blue-tinted ponds.

TRASH

We can't talk about pollution in urban waters without mentioning the never-ending stream of trash piling up in and around them. A lot of it is petroleum-based, single-use junk such as water bottles, Styrofoam cups, food containers, and a mysterious assortment of other plastic debris. The problem doesn't stop at the visible garbage because plastics break down into tiny

A significant portion of the plastic in the ocean originates from rivers. Urban rivers, especially in cities with significant industrial and residential development, act as conveyor belts for plastic waste. Plastic enters these rivers through storm drains, illegal dumping, or runoff from streets and landfills.

particles called microplastics, which end up *in* fish, other animals, and, yes, even us. And beyond the health concerns, let's be honest, a river or shoreline covered in trash isn't exactly making it onto the cover of any fishing magazines (believe me, I've tried).

If you are one of those honorable souls who brings a bag with you to fill up with garbage after a day of fishing, I commend you. Still, there's way more trash out there than any of us can clean up on our own. Reducing garbage in our waters on a significant scale requires policy changes, shifts in values, and figuring out who's going to foot the bill—because right now, the fish are paying for it, and they don't even use plastic.

SAFETY TIP

Collecting and Disposing Sharp Objects

You'll come across broken glass bottles and other sharp objects while fishing. This isn't safe for people, and it's especially hazardous to kids and pets. My preferred method for picking up broken glass and other sharp objects is to first find a plastic bottle with a lid (there are plenty lying around). I then place the sharp objects into the container, screw the lid back on, and dispose of the container. I've seen too many barefoot kids running around along riverbanks to just leave sharp objects on the ground. While it's not my trash, I want cleaner, safer local waters for myself and others.

FACTORIES, MUNICIPAL WASTEWATER TREATMENT PLANTS, AND INDUSTRIAL PLANTS

When we think of urban fishing, many of us might imagine various factories and industrial plants flanking our urban waters. These places provide jobs and keep cities running, but they also have a habit of "sharing" their leftovers with the nearest river, lake, or stream. And the liquid waste being discharged from these places can be a mix of lead, cyanide, arsenic, bacteria, oil, mercury, PCBs, PFAS, benzene, and a whole bunch of other ingredients no one ordered.

The Clean Water Act imposes stringent environmental regulations and pollution control measures to reduce the ecological footprint of these industrial and municipal sources and other single, identifiable sources known as *point source pollution*. Admittedly, water quality has significantly improved, water treatment technologies continue to advance, and many industries strive to self-regulate and reduce pollution. However, our urban waters are still cluttered with warning signs, public health advisories, and fish tainted with toxins.

Many chemicals used in industrial processes have long-term negative impacts on water quality, habitats, and fish health. These chemicals can persist in the environment, bioaccumulate in the food chain, and cause extensive ecological harm long after factories have shut down.

Water treatment technology is much better at capturing and neutralizing harmful toxins. However, newer chemicals are constantly being developed, and their long-term effects on the health of humans, animals, and ecosystems often remain untested or poorly understood. While many regulations aim to protect local ecosystems, they can also place burdens on certain industries and livelihoods—and those with the means to exploit loopholes often continue polluting. At the same time, some of the legal safeguards that limit pollution from sources like oil refineries can also slow down, or even block, the development of alternative energy projects such as wind and solar farms.

If you are curious about the specific pollutants discharging from any of these industrial or municipal sources, you can look up that information on the EPA's Enforcement and Compliance History Online (ECHO) website (www.echo.epa.gov). ECHO is not the most straightforward site to use, but an advocacy group, River Network, provides a helpful resource called the Clean Water Act Owner's Manual (www.rivernetwork.org/connect-learn/resources/clean-water-act-owners-manual).

CHAPTER 7

Fish Species in Urban Waters

Fish are the world's oldest vertebrates, having first appeared over half a billion years ago. They've shown remarkable resilience, surviving multiple extinction events and evolving into four-legged animals to escape evaporating seas. (I can even imagine modern fish trying to grow legs again to escape certain urban waters.) In a fascinating twist, humans evolved from those four-legged fish, creating a unique bond between us and our aquatic neighbors in the city.

We share our urban waters with a lot of really cool fish species. Some are living dinosaurs that have changed very little over the last two

There are moments in urban fishing when you hook into something surprisingly big and you're not entirely sure what is pulling on the other end of the line, which is chaotic and thrilling!

hundred million years. Other species are so well camouflaged that you won't see them until they surprise you by swiping at your fly as they go by. Lots of fish are small and colorful and will readily pluck your dry fly as it floats on the surface, making for an easy and relaxing day outside. Other fish are huge, so large in fact that anglers catch state and world records in city limits.

Since you can encounter various species, it helps to do a little investigation before, during, or after your time out on the water. Knowing some facts about fish species can be very helpful when trying to catch them. Each fish species has its own behaviors, such as how they go about feeding, what they prefer to eat, where they travel to during different parts of the year, and the types of places they seek out to live their urban lives.

In this chapter, we will take a closer look at a handful of fish species that you might find in your local urban waters. To learn about other species of fish beyond the ones listed in this chapter, talk with anglers in your city about what they've learned. You can also take a screenshot of a fish identification sheet from your state's fish and wildlife department website or just snap a photo of the fish you or others catch to identify and research it later.

The Role of Anglers in the Sustainability of Urban Fisheries

As urban anglers, it's essential to think about the sustainability of local fisheries, be it a small pond, lake, or section of river or coastline. The long-term health of fish populations often hinges on how much we, as individual anglers and communities, understand the unique challenges of each local fishery, such as water pollution, degraded habitat, and increasing angling pressure. The more we try to understand these challenges the more we can make informed choices about how we interact with these environments.

In some urban waters, personal choices to limit the number of fish you catch, whether that's catch-and-release or catch-to-keep, may be necessary to support and maintain healthy fish populations and local ecosystems. That might mean avoiding fishing during sensitive spawning periods or focusing on challenging your fishing skills, landing a single fish, and calling that a great day on the water. It might also include recognizing when conditions are particularly harsh on the fish (such as intense water temperatures or harmful algal blooms) and making the decision to give the fish a rest.

That said, simply adjusting individual angling practices won't address the root causes affecting fish populations. Issues like pollution and habitat degradation often have a far greater impact on fish populations than recreational fishing or noncommercial harvest limits. Yet, these systemic problems are frequently overlooked in fisheries management discussions. Compounding this issue, many urban waters are stocked with hatchery-raised fish, which can obscure deeper environmental challenges. While fish stocking programs (which vary state by state) serve important roles in species conservation, research, and education, excessive stocking to meet recreational demands acts as a short-term solution that fails to address underlying problems. Real solutions should focus on improving water quality, revitalizing habitats, and empowering individuals and communities to help manage local fisheries in sustainable ways.

Generalist Species

While a variety of fish species inhabit urban waters, certain species are more commonly found than others due to the challenging conditions of these environments. Remember, cities function as complex ecosystems involving human activity, industrial infrastructure, pollution, bodies of water, flora, fauna, weather events, and so on. While each city has its own unique urban ecosystem, there is a common thread among these systems and the general effects that urbanization has on fish.

When I talk about "urbanization," I mean the process of expanding and concentrating human populations in specific areas, along with the development of systems to support the results of this process. This urbanization process, both past and present, acts as a giant "filter" that favors certain fish species while creating disadvantages for others, ultimately shaping which species can live in urban waters and which are unable to survive. Currently, this "urbanization filter" favors fish species that can:

- consume a broad selection of food items (such as insects, crustaceans, other fish, food scraps, etc.) and adapt their diet quickly in response to changing food availability
- seek out new habitat by migrating across large areas and between various bodies of water, especially when habitats are fragmented
- tolerate a wider range of water temperatures, especially warmer water temperatures
- tolerate reduced habitat diversity and adjust to more uniform conditions, such as water with excessive sediment (muddy water) or higher amounts of hardened structures (like concrete)

These fish species are often referred to by scientists and biologists as "generalist species." Let's begin with the generalist *freshwater* species that you are most likely to find in your city.

Common Freshwater Species

Common generalist fish species found in urban freshwater rivers, streams, ponds, lakes, and reservoirs include:

- common carp
- largemouth bass
- green sunfish
- bullhead catfish

Bluegill, channel catfish, and smallmouth bass are also generalist species commonly found in many urban waters but generally do not exhibit the same level of hardiness as the species listed above.

CARP

In urban waters, common carp (*Cyprinus carpio*) is a species that is, well, common. Most cities in the United States have carp living in diverse bodies of water. But this doesn't mean carp are easy to catch. It's one of the most fun, addicting species to pursue with a fly rod and it will test your urban-angling skills.

Carp are minnows, just very large and robust minnows, that are in the same family (Cyprinidae) as goldfish. Common carp often weigh 10 pounds (4.5 kg) and exceed 24 inches (61 cm) in length while grass carp, sometimes found in local urban ponds, can weigh over 40 pounds (18 kg). Mirror and leather carp are the same species as common carp but with very few large scales or they are almost scaleless.

Common carp—a face only a mother could love! Many urban fly fishers share in the joy of trying to catch carp, which are picky, fight hard, and get easily spooked. As a fly fisher, you could easily spend a lifetime figuring out different methods and tactics for catching common carp. The fly pinned to the carp's bottom lip is a simple egg pattern that even the pickiest of carp can find hard to resist.

Common carp have highly adapted senses of taste, hearing, and smell. Their well-developed sense of hearing is due to a structure called the Weberian apparatus inside their inner ear that acts as an amplifier of sound waves. You will often find carp feeding in shallow, calm areas in the morning or evening and they will scatter at any loud noise or ripple on the surface of the water. Their sense of smell is so highly attuned that it is a wise idea to wash your hands in water and rub them in gravel after using any sunscreen or insect repellent before handling your fly.

Carp also have better eyesight than other fish species, or at least many urban anglers believe this is the case. Often, getting within close casting range of a carp—20 feet (6 m) or less—increases your chances of catching it. However, the closer you get, the more likely you will spook the carp with your presence, which is why many urban fly fishers wear drab colors that blend in with the background where they are fishing (or bright clothing to match the vibrant graffiti on the walls).

Common carp flourish in a broad range of habitats, from tiny ponds to large rivers and lakes. They are known for their tolerance of oxygen-depleted waters and are able to endure water temperatures exceeding 90°F (32°C). They typically prefer areas with silty bottoms and plenty of aquatic plants with deeper water nearby. In silty or clay-ridden channelized canals, carp may be one of the very few species capable of surviving such harsh conditions. But carp can also easily be located in very clear, clean waters that have rocky or sandy bottoms. One of the few places that do restrict carp are habitats with increased salinity (saltier water), so you generally won't find them in brackish water along seacoasts.

Common carp really get into a feeding mood when water temperatures are above 68°F (20°C). As omnivores and primarily bottom feeders, they suck up and filter out aquatic insects, snails, clams, and crustaceans from the sand, gravel, silt, and mud. They sometimes chase down small fish and crayfish trying to scurry away. It is a thrilling sight-fishing opportunity to find carp feeding in shallow water with their tails or backs visible above the surface. You will also find them eating aquatic insects drifting through the current as well as surface feeding on aquatic and terrestrial insects, mulberries, and cottonwood seeds. They spawn in the spring when water temperatures are around 63°F (17°C), and in rivers they can migrate long distances to locate shallow, weedy areas for spawning. The spawning event is a commotion, and you'll easily come across schools of large carp thrashing around in knee-deep water. During spawning season, carp are difficult, but not impossible, to catch.

Grass carp (*Ctenopharyngodon idella*), like common carp, prefer warmer waters that have an abundance of aquatic plants, which make up the majority of their diet. In fact, many pond managers place grass carp in their ponds to help control aquatic vegetation, and it's in these ponds where you have the chance of hooking into one of these massive fish. Also, though grass carp feed primarily on aquatic plants, they occasionally eat other things like aquatic and terrestrial insects.

BASS AND SUNFISH

The Centrarchidae family of fish includes many species you can catch on a fly rod, including bluegill, pumpkinseed, green sunfish, and many species of bass typically found in urban waters such as largemouth and smallmouth bass and rock bass. Out of the Centrarchidae family, largemouth bass, bluegill, and green sunfish are particularly hardy and tolerate water with lower dissolved oxygen that normally suffocates other species. Largemouth bass and bluegill are also very common in urban waters because fishery managers routinely stock them in small impoundments (ponds) due to their reliable predator-prey dynamic.

Largemouth bass are most active in warmer waters—60°F–75°F (16°C–24°C)—and prefer silty bottoms that have plenty of cover for their prey, such as urban debris, weeds, and sunken trees. They feed on a large array of prey, including, but definitely not limited to, smaller fish (like bluegill), crayfish, frogs, dragonfly and damselfly nymphs, leeches, and small snakes. At times, their prey can be almost half their body length due in part to how wide they can open their jaw and engulf a piece of food.

Largemouth bass begin spawning in late spring in lakes, ponds, rivers, and streams when water temperatures warm up above 60°F (16°C), and you will begin to see males building and defending their nests from other bass and predators. After spawning, largemouth bass stay in shallow water until water temperatures start to reach over 75°F (24°C). Then, they seek slightly deeper and cooler waters while still staying within easy reach of shallow, vegetated hunting grounds.

Smallmouth bass, more than largemouth bass, prefer habitat that is rocky and gravelly with higher levels of dissolved oxygen. Areas with a lot of silt (such as a muddy and channelized canal) won't hold many smallmouth bass, if any at all. They also gravitate to any sort of structure, especially woody debris, steep drop-offs, and submerged small islands (humps) where they can be found trying to locate their prey among the rubble or waiting to ambush prey as it swims by. In open, sandy areas, smallmouth bass will be more actively moving (probably transiting from one rocky shoreline to the next) and hunting small fish as they swim along. In rivers and streams, they are more closely associated with moving water than largemouth bass and will seek out water that is flowing around half

Ryan Birringer found this smallmouth bass ambushing small fish next to a concrete wall. Every few moments, the water would erupt as the bass pounced on fish being swept toward the wall by the river's current. Ryan landed a streamer close to the bass and, while keeping a tight line, set the hook as soon as he felt a jolt on the other end.

a foot per second or less, which is about the speed of a very slow walk. Any sort of deeper water located near riffles could hold smallmouth bass.

The metabolism of smallmouth bass gets active when water temperatures rise above 50°F (10°C) and their optimal water temperature for feeding and growth is 78°F–84°F (26°C–29°C). Juvenile smallmouth primarily feed on aquatic insects, zooplankton (tiny drifting aquatic animals), and small fish; adult smallmouth feed predominately on other fish, frogs, and crayfish. Crayfish are an immensely important food item for smallmouth and can make up a considerable portion of their diet. Smallmouth bass spawn in the spring when water temperatures are between 54°F–74°F (12°C–23°C), which typically occurs from mid-April to mid-June but can be earlier or later in the season depending on latitude. There are also several other species of bass that have a more limited range of where you can find them, such as Guadalupe, redeye, spotted, and shoal bass.

Bluegill, green sunfish, redear sunfish, pumpkinseed, and several other similar species are among the most reliably consistent fish to catch on a fly rod since they seem to eat just about anything they can fit into their mouths. They are found in ponds, lakes, canals, culverts, channelized streams, large rivers, and maybe even your bathtub if they could wiggle up through the drain. They often move into shallow, warmer water along with the bass, typically spawning after the bass have finished reproducing. Some species, like bluegill, spawn multiple times throughout the summer. You'll find them around numerous types of cover, including aquatic plants, sunken parts of a bridge, and docks—essentially, anything acting as a protective "reef." Most of these fish will be found in water above 85°F (29°C).

Another species of the Centrarchid family worth mentioning is crappie. When it comes to pursuing this fish with a fly rod, it is most often done on lakes and ponds during spring and early summer. During this time, crappie move into shallow water and station around weedy areas of a lake or pond, making them easily accessible to urban anglers. However, as water temperatures warm, they retreat to deeper depths and may only venture near the shallows during dawn and dusk.

CATFISH

There are about forty-five species of freshwater catfish in North America, but channel catfish is by far the most abundant of them. Like many centrarchid species, channel catfish are heavily stocked in urban waters, particularly ponds. This is due to their rapid growth rates, cost-effective hatchery production, survivability, and susceptibility to various angling techniques. Another common catfish in urban areas is the bullhead catfish, which is considered more tolerant of harsh environments and poor water quality than channel catfish.

Both these catfish can survive in a variety of water temperatures, from freezing to above 90°F (32°C), but are most active when the water is 75°F–85°F (24°C–29°C.) The average weight for these fish is around 2–4 pounds (1–2 kg) but they can grow much larger. Being omnivorous, they feed on aquatic insects, small fish, crayfish, frogs, aquatic plants, and more. They have keen senses of smell and taste, and, like common carp, they also hear very well underwater due to an anatomical structure called the Weberian apparatus that acts as an amplifier of sound waves. The splat of a heavy streamer or bottom-dwelling fly landing on the water's surface can trigger them to strike. (Fun fact: Piranha also have the Weberian apparatus, which help them detect vibrations in the water from struggling prey. As far as I'm aware, there are no established piranha populations in North America, and besides, they are shy and try to avoid humans.)

Going after catfish in rivers is a fun pursuit. They will be stationed right against the river bottom, so when water levels drop during summer and fall, channel catfish become more accessible to fly fishers. However, during summer and fall they will be more spread out in the river. Search for them around ambush points like deeper water around bridges, sunken trees, and in "holes"—depressions or pockets in the stream or riverbed where the water is noticeably deeper than the surrounding area. They also prefer some amount of current flowing nearby or right along the edge of the hole.

Other Freshwater Species

Of course, other freshwater species live in urban waters beside the ones I've listed. To give you an idea of what other amazing fish you might hook into, here are some additional species worth knowing about.

BOWFIN AND GAR

Bowfin and gar, two very unique species, are commonly called "living fossils" because their species first appeared over 240 million years ago during the Triassic Period. They have the uncommon ability to breathe both water and air, so you may see them tipping their mouths out of the water to gulp air, especially when the water is warm and stagnant. Both species inhabit freshwater rivers, streams, canals, and swamps. They even manage to get into ponds when small creeks or ditches, connected to the ponds, swell up during rainstorms and open up migration corridors. Shallow waters with aquatic plants are common places to encounter these fish as they slowly swim or sit, waiting to ambush their prey. Both species are piscivores, preying on fish as well as crayfish.

Gar have heavily armored bodies with long, toothy bills that are very boney. Because of their boney mouths, some anglers use flies made of unbraided nylon rope to entangle in the fish's teeth. Untangling this mess can be troublesome and could harm the fish, especially if the rope fly breaks off. Alternatively, and more humanely, anglers and guides have found success

Beyond freshwaters in the southern and eastern United States, gar can be found in some marine environments of the Mississippi River drainage, such as brackish estuaries and other coastal areas. Members of the gar family include the longnose, spotted, and alligator gar. The alligator gar, growing up to 6 feet (2 m) in length, is an exceptional species for fishing. Photograph courtesy of Tyler Winter

hooking into gar with streamers that use lighter (finer diameter) hooks that can penetrate their boney mouths. Point being, it's far better to rely on hook points to catch a gar than to see it swim off with its mouth fixed shut due to an entangled and broken-off rope fly.

Bowfins are found along the eastern and southern United States and parts of southeastern Canada and typically grow to 20 inches (50 cm) in length. They don't have boney mouths like gar, so hook penetration is much easier.

SUCKER

Sucker, a broad term for a group of species within the Catostomidae family, is a fish that you may have already encountered. The Catostomidae family is made up of over seventy species, including white sucker, Sonora sucker, redhorse, smallmouth buffalo, and blue sucker.

Most suckers are detritivores, meaning they consume organic matter and algae from off the bottom of rivers, streams, lakes, and ponds, as well as crustaceans and aquatic insect larvae. Catching one often requires getting your fly to rest on the bottom and patiently waiting for the sucker to find its way to it. Timing is critical because setting the hook too early or

A largescale sucker caught on the Spokane River in Washington. A sucker's mouth, similar to a carp's mouth, is downward-facing and shaped like a suction cup, designed for efficiently feeding on algae, detritus, and small invertebrates along the bottom.

too late can lead to a snagged fish. But when you skillfully hook a sucker in the mouth instead of randomly snagging its body, it's an accomplishment worth celebrating.

Certain species of sucker can grow over 24 inches (61 cm) in length and it can be maddening trying to hook into a massive sucker as it goes about calmly feeding right in front of you. Some suckers seem to have poor eyesight so you can get close to them, giving you a chance to catch one. Sight fishing with a highly visible nymph or bottom-dwelling fly is one of the most effective ways to convince these fish to eat, and as a fly fisher you have to watch them eat the fly before setting the hook since there is little other indication of a take. Fly fishing for these species is tough, I'll admit, and they'll challenge your skills as an urban angler.

FRESHWATER DRUM

The freshwater drum, or sheepshead, is a member of the Sciaenidae family, which also includes redfish, a saltwater species. Freshwater drum are the only member of the Sciaenidae family that resides its entire life in freshwater. These hard-fighting, opportunistic feeders have a diet that includes small fish (particularly gizzard shad), aquatic insects, crayfish, and mussels, making them ideal targets for a fly rod.

Typically ranging from 5–15 pounds (2–7 kg), they inhabit rivers and lakes, preferring clearer water. When water temperatures get above 60°F (16°C), they start spawning in shallow, gravelly areas. As the water temperature continues to rise, they often linger in these shallow zones, offering numerous sight-fishing opportunities throughout summer. As you search for freshwater drum, with fly ready in hand, keep an eye out for their gray or copper-colored bodies and watch for them tailing in shallow water. A well-executed cast can have them pouncing on your fly, but a poor presentation or excessive false casting can easily spook them off.

TROUT

Rainbow and brown trout are two species of trout that can be found more commonly in urban areas. Rainbow trout will spawn in rivers or streams in the spring, while brown trout spawn later in the fall. Both are coldwater species, most active when water temperatures are 55°F–65°F (13°C–18°C); prolonged temperatures above 70°F (21°C) are fatal for them. In urban areas, they can be found in reservoirs and ponds, as well as rivers, streams, and canals so long as water temperatures don't remain above 70°F (21°C) for extended periods. While this typically restricts them to rivers in cities located at more northern latitudes, some urban areas in warmer climates have dams that release cold water from their bases,

A redband trout, a subspecies of rainbow trout, caught in downtown Spokane, Washington.

which keeps temperatures in the river cooler throughout hot summer months (more about dams will be discussed in the next chapter).

Ponds throughout the country are routinely stocked by fishery managers with fully grown rainbow trout during winter months. While most of these ponds warm up and become uninhabitable for trout in the summer, it nonetheless provides anglers with an opportunity to hook into trout during the winter and spring seasons. Most of these stocked rainbows are not picky eaters and will readily take most flies presented to them.

In colder waters that support trout year-round, you'll find them more difficult to catch. Trout that are primarily raised and nurtured in a healthy ecosystem (compared to trout that are fully grown in a hatchery), will often fixate on one particular food source. Small rainbow and brown trout—less than 12 inches (30 cm)—primarily feed on aquatic and terrestrial insects that are available to them underwater or on the surface. As they grow larger, they begin to also feed on small fish, such as sculpins or other small trout, and crayfish. A trout's fixation on a particular food source will depend on the weather, season, insect activity for the day, and other factors.

TEMPERATE BASS

Temperate bass include several species from the Moronidae family: white bass, yellow bass, white perch, striped bass, and hybrid striped bass. Out of these species, only the white perch and striped bass inhabit both freshwater and saltwater environments. The hybrid striped bass is a hatchery-raised cross-species between white bass and stripers, which many anglers refer to as "wipers." Temperate bass are mainly found in large reservoirs and any rivers or streams connected to them. Most striped bass roam the ocean coasts but either migrate up rivers to spawn, are stocked in lakes, or have become landlocked due to dams and other obstructions.

Temperate bass are most active when the water is between 55°F–75°F (13°C–24°C) and are often found in shallow areas of lakes—1–15 feet (.3–4 m)—at these temperatures. In the spring, they begin moving into rivers to spawn and will also follow schools of small fish (shad, herring, shiners) in nomadic behavior. Hybrid striped bass will also undergo spawning migrations, but since they are sterile hybrids, they are unable to reproduce, which is why populations of hybrid bass can only be maintained through stocking programs; think of wipers as mules—a horse and a donkey can reproduce to make a mule, but a mule and mule are incapable of reproducing to make another mule. Some rivers that are connected to these reservoirs can have several species of temperate bass moving through them, providing anglers with waves of opportunities. Therefore, it is a good idea to check with your state's fish and wildlife department for lakes or reservoirs that hold populations of these fish.

Temperate bass are very aggressive feeders. They can form large predatory schools, corral small fish in the shallows or near the surface, and cause an explosive feeding frenzy. Although they can be found feeding throughout the day, low-light conditions—dusk to dawn and cloudy days—are great times for them to hunt. Lastly, ponds are sometimes stocked with hybrid striped bass to help control fish populations and provide exciting angling experiences, and because they are more resilient to low dissolved-oxygen levels and harsher water temperatures.

Saltwater Species

Saltwater species living along ocean shorelines and in other saltwater bodies in cities provide additional challenges and opportunities for the urban angler. The saltwater species listed below are ones that are more accessible to anglers walking along the shoreline or wading in shallow-water areas. Beaches, harbors, bridges, estuaries, piers, jetties, marinas, tidal creeks, and right off the shoreline are many pieces of habitat where these species can be found if they live in or migrate along your coastline.

I also fished around for research studies that supported a list of generalist saltwater species commonly found in urban environments, but I pulled up very little, at least compared to the wealth of information available for urban freshwater species. One exception is the Atlantic killifish (*Fundulus heteroclitus*), and science backs up its urban survival skills, but at 3 inches (7 cm) long, it's not exactly a thrilling opponent on a fly rod, so it's not included in the list that follows.

FLOUNDERS

There are many species of flounders found throughout the Atlantic, Gulf, and Pacific coasts, including fluke (summer flounder), Gulf flounder, starry flounder, and certain species of halibut (yes, species like California halibut can be caught with a fly rod from the beach). Flounder are flat fish with both eyes on one side of the body, and a species can be either righteye or lefteye. For example, fluke are lefteye flounder, so the right side of their body lies on the seabed. Although they lie flat and have excellent camouflage, they are ambush predators that rapidly swim to catch their prey, and even sometimes go to the surface to nab a meal. Their diet is fairly broad and includes small fish along with squid, shrimp, and crabs.

Due to their numbers, widespread distribution along the coasts, and tendency to hunt shallow water, they are an enjoyable target for any urban saltwater angler. They can be in water 6 feet (2 m) deep or less and within a variety of habitats, such as beaches, piers, mouths of creeks, and sandy shallow flats, especially when deeper water is nearby. Waiting in holes and trenches caused by waves, they'll swiftly strike at small fish that swim slowly overhead. Summer months can be the more active season to catch flounder and targeting them can turn an unproductive day around when other fish species have migrated away or left the shallows.

SPOTTED SEATROUT

Spotted seatrout, or speckled trout, are an abundant fish living in urban

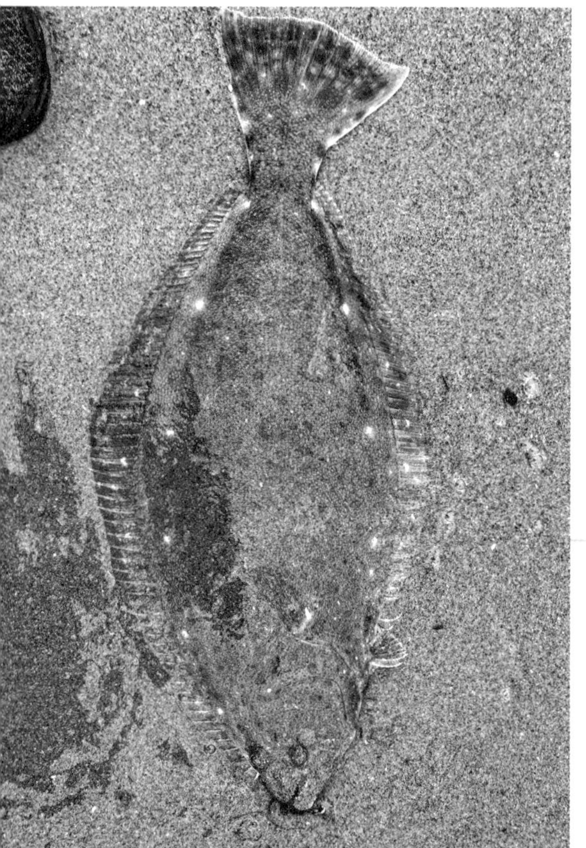

Flounder, like this Pacific halibut, are masters of camouflage; they blend seamlessly into sandy or rocky ocean floors with their mottled, color-shifting skin to ambush prey and avoid predators. Photograph courtesy of Carl Crawford

Spotted seatrout have a distinctive pair of sharp canine teeth that's perfect for ambushing small fish, but be sure to handle them carefully when removing your fly!

waters from the mid-Atlantic, down around Florida, and along the Gulf Coast. They are a temperate fish, preferring water 60°F–80°F (16°C–27°C), and will migrate into creeks or offshore during colder winter months. Smaller spotted seatrout will feed on crustaceans and shrimp, while larger ones, averaging 2–3 pounds (approximately 1 kg), switch to eating smaller fish like mullet. Schools of these fish can be found in shallow water, especially areas that have seagrass or plenty of broken structures for them to hide around. Docks, piers, jetties, and around bridges are other common places to locate them. Waiting in the current, they use the tide to bring small fish to them, so locating any moving water can be key.

SURFPERCH

There are several species of surfperch within the Embiotocidae family that live up and down the Pacific coast from Mexico to Canada. They are available to anglers year-round and are seemingly abundant. However, not much is known about their population numbers. Surfperches are roughly the size of large bluegill and are bottom feeders, eating small crustaceans like shrimp and crabs, along with aquatic worms and other invertebrates. As their name states, they can be found in the surf very close to the beach, schooling up to look for their food, especially on an incoming tide. Any deep holes or depressions out in the surf could hold a school of them. They also congregate around jetties, sunken wrecks, pilings, and kelp. One interesting fact about this species is that the female carries the fry (juvenile fish) inside her and gives live birth to her young rather than laying eggs.

STRIPED BASS AND BLUEFISH

We looked at striped bass in the freshwater section earlier, and now we'll check out their behavior when they are in saltwater. Striped bass are born in freshwater and then migrate to saltwater to feed, mature, and, eventually, head back into freshwater environments to reproduce; a single striped bass can reproduce multiple times throughout its life. Striped bass, or "stripers," can be found nomadically migrating along the Atlantic, Pacific, and Gulf coasts. On the East Coast, they'll be around mid-Atlantic states and as far south as Florida in the winter months and then start migrating up to New England to spawn in rivers during the spring as water temperatures warm above 50°F (10°C). Then they'll continue migrating northward, going up into parts of Maine and Nova Scotia, as waters warm in the summer (although some areas may have small numbers of resident stripers during the summer). In the fall, they reverse their migration, returning to the mid-Atlantic states by winter. Less is known about their ocean migration patterns on the Pacific coast, but stripers can be found from Los Angeles and up the coast into rivers in Oregon and as far north as the Columbia River in Washington.

Striped bass gravitate to the shoreline, which puts them into casting range for many urban anglers. Jetties, shallow flats, and beaches are prime hunting grounds where stripers will feed on fish, squid, eels, and shrimp. Even though they prefer a wide range of food options, they can be selective in what they are currently feeding on when you locate

Striped bass often gravitate to rocky beaches and shorelines with riprap. These environments provide habitat for small fish, crustaceans, and other prey, making them feeding grounds for striped bass. The structure of rocks and riprap also creates ambush points and shelter from strong currents, further attracting striped bass.
Photograph courtesy of Ben Carmichael

them. They can be skittish in shallow waters and on sunny days but will aggressively feed from dusk to dawn. Striped bass can grow to large sizes, but for much of inshore, urban fishing you're more likely to run into smaller "schoolie" stripers.

Bluefish are intense predators with sharp teeth and sleek, streamlined bodies built for speed. Like striped bass, they live and migrate along the Atlantic coast from Florida to Maine; however, unlike stripers, they do not live on the Pacific coast. During winter, they inhabit the southern Atlantic states, and in early summer through early fall, they move north to live along the New England coast. In the Northeast, they'll begin to push into shallow water as inshore water temperatures climb above 60°F (16°C) and will only go offshore to spawn. When they are near the shoreline, they will gravitate to similar habitat as striped bass to mainly feed on fish. Unlike stripers, they are less skittish and picky, feeding with reckless abandon on schools of small fish.

Understanding and Appreciating Urban Fish Diversity

There are many other species of fish we will encounter in urban waters, of course, and taking an active interest in them makes fishing more fruitful and fun. All fish species tell us things about the health and status of our waters and aquatic habitats. Some species of fish are also *native species* that can serve as historical links, helping us learn what our local waters were like before cities were built—knowledge that has long been part of Native American traditions. These native species provide additional insights into how our urban fish communities are doing today and inspire urban anglers and local communities to envision a brighter future.

While it is easy to find information and facts about certain species, such as rainbow trout or largemouth bass, it can be a struggle to find material on any number of other fish you will come across. Urban areas have sadly lost a lot of amazing species that used to swim in our waters, some for thousands or millions of years. While pollution and human infrastructure play dominate roles in this, the management of our fish communities and populations also needs to be addressed.

Historically, white European and Anglo men have dominated fisheries research and management, and their views have largely influenced perceptions of which fish species are considered most significant and important. This has led to a focus on certain species, such as trout and largemouth bass, while often overlooking a diversity of other species.

Despite the good intentions behind many management and conservation efforts, there is frequently a lack of diverse perspectives and meaningful public engagement in the decision-making processes that manage fish populations and species in urban areas. This ongoing issue continues to impact entire aquatic ecosystems, as well as cultural and community traditions, food resources, fishing opportunities, and local economies.

Additionally, the labels assigned to fish complicate and intensify these challenges. Labels such as *native transplant*, *invasive*, *naturalized*, *exotic*, *game*, *sport*, *food*, *rough*, and *trash* are confusing, frequently misleading, and typically reflect the biases of fisheries managers, researchers, and anglers rather than a comprehensive understanding of each species' social-ecological role. In urban environments—where habitats have been dramatically redesigned by infrastructure, development, and pollution—these labels can lose their relevance entirely. Even if a fish is native to the broader region, it is living in a fundamentally altered, foreign ecosystem. For people, especially kids exploring urban creeks and drainage ditches close to home, the excitement of encountering a fish—any fish—is what truly matters. That moment of discovery can spark a sense of wonder and

A close-up of carp scales reveals overlapping plates of armor and ruggedness, reflective of the carp's remarkable adaptability and resilience in urban waters.

invite them to come back, explore more deeply, and build a lasting and caring connection with the waters and fish around them.

Common carp are not historically native to North America, and they are often blamed for degraded habitats and declining biodiversity. Yet in many urban areas, their abundance has provided many people with meaningful opportunities to connect with local waters. Rather than dismissing a species solely as a problem, we can view their presence as a starting point—a way into deeper conversations about stewardship, access, and the future of our shared ecosystems.

Learning More About the Fish in Your Urban Waters

Beyond the species I've covered briefly, there are a lot more fish species you'll encounter in urban areas. What follows are a few great resources that I encourage you to check out in order to learn about a particular species you are interested in. These resources also provide excellent avenues to help advocate for particular fish species in your area.

NATIVE FISH FOR TOMORROW (NF4T)

This organization advances the conservation of native fish, especially native rough fish. Historically, "rough fish" has been a derogatory term to categorize certain species of fish as having low or zero value. I've had many talks with Tyler Winter, one of the NF4T directors, who has done some incredible work for this group, including reclaiming the term "rough fish" and helping to get the Native Fish Bill passed in Minnesota. The Native Fish Bill is a first of its kind in the United States, giving native fish comprehensive protections and restitution. If you want to advocate for native fish and are interested in getting your state to adopt more holistic fishing regulations and policies, start here. www.nativefishfortomorrow.org

CONSERVATION FISHERIES

This nonprofit focuses on the preservation of aquatic biodiversity in streams and rivers, including the preservation of smaller fish that are amazing and cool to learn more about. www.conservationfisheries.org

GAR LAB

Run by aquatic ecologist Solomon R. David, PhD, "The Gar Guy," this website provides, for free, research papers on gar and bowfin. The site primarily focuses on gar and bowfin, but there are other fish resources as well. solomondavid.net

OTHER RESOURCES FOR LEARNING ABOUT FISH SPECIES

There are many other excellent resources and organizations dedicated to protecting and revitalizing fish populations and their habitats, from Trout Unlimited and Stripers Forever to the American Fisheries Society and the Coastal Conservation Association. A quick internet search will turn up additional groups and valuable insights to help you get involved in efforts to advocate for the aquatic life living in your local urban waters.

Which Species Will You Find in Your Waters?

To learn more about the fish in your city, and where you might find them, we need to study the waters they live in. Throughout the next three chapters, we will explore urban waters more deeply, looking at the aquatic habitats created by cities and how fish respond to them. The intent is to deepen your understanding of urban waterscapes and further sharpen your ability to "read urban waters." We'll do this by looking at human-built infrastructure in urban rivers, streams, lakes, and ocean shorelines and how to locate fish around prevalent urban structures.

Additionally, over these next three chapters, I seldom get into the specifics of what fish species you might find because that will depend on many factors, including water quality, habitat availability, the region you live in, and local conservation efforts. Be prepared to encounter any number of fish species, such as predatory fish that eat other fish (like smallmouth bass, gar, and stripers), schools of fish that eat lots of insects floating on the top of the water (like bluegill and green sunfish), and fish that root around and feed off the bottom (like common carp, freshwater drum, and corbina).

The best way to prepare for encountering a variety of fish species is to develop your skills as an adaptable angler. As you gradually try each new technique—whether it's using dry flies, wet flies, streamers, bottom-dweller flies, or nymphs under an indicator—think of it as adding a new tool to your fishing tool kit. Don't feel pressure to master them all right away. Building your skill set bit by bit will expand your ability to catch new species in unexpected situations. Again, there isn't enough room in this book to cover each fly-fishing technique, so take advantage of the resources listed at the end of the book.

Each skill you gain opens up more possibilities, bringing a sense of excitement and exploration to your fishing adventures. Working on your techniques will gradually prepare you to cast confidently in any scenario, turning every outing into a chance to find and catch something new. But some skills, like trying to keep a running fish on the line while standing atop a footbridge, just can't be practiced ahead of time!

Nate McCord demonstrates the sought-after skill of fly fishing from a bridge—a technique best learned by experimenting and being prepared for plenty of trial and error.

All modern cities manage waterways in similar ways: as over-engineered, channelized systems that result in strikingly similar aquatic habitats.

CHAPTER 8

Urban Waterways

Cities have a variety of rivers, streams, creeks, canals, and ditches, which I'll collectively refer to as *waterways*. These range from narrow, grassy ditches slicing through neighborhoods to vast rivers such as the Mississippi that cut entire cities in half. Some are straightened and concrete-lined canals, while others have bends and curves with tree-lined banks.

What all urban waterways share in common is that they have been viewed primarily as utilities and many of their characteristics are defined by human-built infrastructure. They're engineered to manage floods, supply drinking water, generate power, support industrial activity, process waste, and withdraw water for irrigation.

As you explore your own city, there is a lot of infrastructure throughout urban waterways, both hidden and in plain sight. All of these human structures and modifications affect aquatic habitats, influence which fish species can survive, alter fish behaviors, and, ultimately, determine how we fish these environments.

To start off this chapter, we first need to look more closely at how waterways functioned before humans altered them through engineering projects.

Untamed Waterways

Rivers, streams, and creeks are inherently very sinuous. Without any human water-control infrastructure, they will snake across a landscape. As they flow along, their powerful currents cut into banks, eroding the land and releasing sediment that is carried downstream to be deposited elsewhere. This process, called erosion and deposition, causes waterways to shift and change course over time. Erosion and deposition continuously play out over years and centuries. While these processes can be slow, leading us to believe that waterways hardly ever change, they are relentless.

Waterways also periodically flood the surrounding landscape, and the portion of land that a waterway floods over is called a *floodplain*. Trees, bushes, and other vegetation grow close along waterways and act as a buffer against catastrophic flooding and erosion. This lush habitat is called a *riparian zone*.

Waterways that are free to meander and flood not only generate new habitats but cycle and distribute nutrients, benefiting both aquatic and terrestrial ecosystems. And a winding waterway creates a diverse array of habitats, including shallow riffles and deep pools, which are essential for fish and other aquatic life. Riparian zones purify water before it enters waterways, helping to improve water quality, shading the water to keep it cool, and providing habitat for many species of fish.

Your city might have waterways featuring beneficial characteristics such as riparian zones and a meandering course. Often, these waterways are smaller, making it easy to cast across from bank to bank. One example is Rock Creek in Washington, D. C.'s Rock Creek Park. These places are excellent to explore and can lead to better fishing opportunities. However, no matter how untouched a waterway in your city might seem, it still reflects the influence of human activity and infrastructure. Not only are these areas popular with other anglers, but they are often also used for various recreational activities. A lot of guidebooks have been written to help you fly fish

A heavily channelized waterway in Omaha, Nebraska. Photograph by Morgan Dorsey

This image highlights the dynamic and erosive power of the Mississippi River as it meanders through a rural landscape, creating a diverse array of habitats. Several crescent-shaped lakes (called oxbow lakes) adjacent to the main river channel are visible, remnants of the river's previous paths and potential future courses. The surrounding landscape is the floodplain, where areas become inundated by floodwaters. Photo by Best Backgrounds/Shutterstock

along more "natural" waterways, and I have listed some of those resources at the back of this book.

To get the most out of fishing in your city, you'll want to include fishing in the very "urban" waterways—the ones that are set in human-built infrastructure or are heavily influenced by it. The focus for the remainder of this chapter will be taking an in-depth look at how humans dramatically reshape our waterways and how you might go about fishing in such altered ecosystems.

Waterways Reshaped by Channelization

Waterways that meander, change shape, and occasionally flood are problematic for cities. Constructing buildings within a floodplain places people and their livelihoods in the crosshairs of these relentless forces. To combat this, engineers are often called upon to tame the ever-changing behavior of waterways.

One extreme process that engineers use to restrict the movement of a waterway is *channelization*. The process of channelization involves straightening, widening, or deepening a river. Typically, the main reasons to channelize waterways are to simplify drainage for flood control, prevent

While they might appear bleak, urban anglers can't ignore channelized waterways, given how many have been designed into our cities. Fishing in these waters requires a certain level of adaptability, resiliency, and resourcefulness.

flooding into the surrounding landscape, and improve navigation for ships and barges.

Channelizing a waterway is like taking a winding, scenic road and turning it into a straight, efficient highway. Just as the highway removes the curves and twists of the original road to create a direct route, channelization removes the bends and meanders of a waterway, straightening it out to control its flow and limit flooding. This process makes the waterway more predictable and manageable but at the cost of the diverse habitats that the original, winding waterway provided.

Channelization works to restrict the waterway from carrying out its free-flowing, beneficial behaviors that many fish species and aquatic communities rely on. Channelization also isolates waterways from their floodplains and the habitats that depend on periodic flooding. Thus, channelization is perhaps the most comprehensively destructive activity for aquatic and riparian ecosystems, and channelization projects have eliminated vast amounts of favorable habitat for many species of fish.

Channelization comes in many forms. At one extreme, waterways can be confined and run in a straight line for a mile or more, such as the Chicago, Los Angeles, and San Antonio Rivers. Other waterways, while not channelized to such an extreme degree, have nonetheless been significantly altered. Examples include the West Fork Trinity River in Fort Worth, Texas; the South Platte River in Denver, Colorado; the Pearl River in Jackson, Mississippi; the Boise River in Boise, Idaho; and the Olentangy River in Columbus, Ohio. Often, you might see sections of waterways severely channelized into a straight line, usually to make room for a highway.

While this engineering process has removed a significant amount of aquatic habitat for fish, remarkably, some fish species survive in these waterways depending on the extent of channelization. For urban anglers, these waterways are also some of the most accessible places in our cities, and although most appear barren at first glance, there are some surprising fishing opportunities. The key is learning how to find fish in such places.

LOOK BEYOND THE MONOTONY

Some channelized waterways can be incredibly featureless places to fish, little more than a watery canal running in a straight line. Instead of blindly casting all the water, which will likely leave your arm sore and without a fish in the net, take the time to observe your surroundings. With patience, spots that hold fish will reveal themselves.

Look for Turbulent Water and Riffles: Riffles (small, choppy waves on the surface) indicate shallow, faster water that typically flows over gravel and rocks. These areas provide excellent habitat for aquatic insects and other small organisms because their fast-moving, shallow waters boost oxygen levels, distribute nutrients, and the gravel and rocks provide varied surfaces for shelter and feeding. Fish gravitate to these areas because of the higher quantity of food (aquatic insects and other small organisms). Casting a streamer or a two-fly rig (like a dry-dropper rig) into and downstream of riffles is an effective way to search these spots for fish. Any sort of islands or large structures in the waterway can also help form these fish-holding features.

Find Where Smaller Waterways Converge: Look for spots where smaller waterways dump into the main channelized waterway. These smaller waterways could be creeks, ditches, or even tunnels coming out of the side of the bank. Food items, such as small fish or insects, are swept down these smaller waterways, and fish might be waiting to ambush their next meal. Streamers and wet flies can be effective in these spots.

Check the Bridges: Bridges provide shade and cover for fish, and bridge piers (the vertical support structures) help to break up the current into seams of water that concentrate food items. A good method to use here is casting and retrieving a streamer. The current around bridge piers also forms deeper troughs of water around and downstream of the piers. These deeper troughs are excellent places to float an indicator with a weighted nymph or worm pattern underneath.

Check Close to the Banks: If there are any trees and bushes growing over the water, explore these spots. Insects and other food items drop from the trees into the water where fish are waiting. A floating fly like a foam beetle pattern or small bass popper is a good way to check these spots, as well as a two-fly rig (like a small Woolly Bugger suspended under a bass popper). Many fish, such as carp, suckers, and smallmouth bass, will also feed right up against the banks of waterways, especially in the mornings or evenings and when water levels start to rise.

Look at the Bottom: Channelized waterways can be filled in with a lot of sediment. Look at the bottom of the waterway for any rocky and gravelly areas that could be a hunting ground for fish like smallmouth bass. These are also areas where carp and other bottom-feeding fish root around for food items, such as aquatic worms and small insects. Additionally, check for any drop-offs where the water abruptly transitions from shallow to deep. You might notice these drop-off zones where the water color changes from light to dark. Fish will gravitate to drop-offs, looking for food along the ledge, and at times work into the shallow water to feed.

LOOK FOR OBJECTS IN THE WATER

When a waterway is channelized, obstacles such as tree trunks, branches, and entire sunken trees can slow down the current and cause flooding. Periodic "clearing and snagging" operations, such as those carried out by municipal public works and environmental management agencies, remove these obstacles, which are often referred to as "large woody debris." Numerous aquatic insect species depend on large woody debris for habitat and nutrients. When this woody debris is removed, aquatic insect populations significantly decrease, along with the fish that feed on those insects. Many urban areas don't have trees growing close to sections of a waterway to begin with, eliminating any chance of woody debris making it into the water. If you do happen to find any large woody debris in the water, take advantage of the situation because it acts as a reef that attracts many fish.

Try casting streamers and dry flies close to any objects or structures you find and then retrieve the fly back toward you. Alternatively, cast a streamer beyond the object and then retrieve the fly back toward it, which will imitate a small fish or crayfish fleeing to the reef for protection. Additionally, check the area around the object for any fish feeding in the current or along the bottom of the waterway. Try getting a bottom-dwelling fly or an unweighted nymph close to the mouths of these fish (use the "drag and drop" covered in chapter 4).

ELEVATE YOUR GAME

If you are struggling to locate and catch fish, then get to a high vantage point from where you can look over a stretch of the waterway. Pick a sunnier day

Objects in the water provide habitat for fish, such as boulders and larger rocks, shopping carts, bikes, and remnants of old bridges. For instance, while on the Los Angeles River, Analiza del Rosario and I searched around piles of broken concrete slabs for carp and other fish. Those slabs helped to slow the flow of water in the channel, creating riffles on the surface. Underneath those riffles was a slightly more complex habitat where small fish and other aquatic organisms lived and found refuge, especially during periods of high and fast flows.

Bridges and elevated walkways and bike paths all provide high vantage points for looking down into the water.

Besides spotting fish, you might also see shallow zones such as islands, sandbars, shoals, and, on the inner bends of waterways, point bars. Channelized waterways can be deep and have very steep banks, making it tough to get down to the water and wade safely. Shallow zones offer easier access to the water and more room to cast. Use satellite view on any mapping application to find these spots as well. In the bottom-right of this photo, you'll also notice riffles that are formed due to the nearby island.

with little to no wind, and when the water isn't highly discolored due to runoff. Having polarized sunglasses will also help you to see through the water to spot fish. If you own binoculars, consider bringing those as well.

Begin scanning the water, taking your time as you search for fish. This is also where being in a group of anglers is a huge advantage. In Denver, Nic Hall, Nate McCord, Rick Mikesell, and I covered a lot of ground going from one high point to the next, scanning the water for carp and white suckers. At times, we would spread out and call or text one another when we found fish. Only when someone located a fish would we either get down into the water or make a cast from the bridge. If one angler went down into the water, we would help by keeping an eye on the fish and direct the angler's cast to that fish. It was a true team effort, but it was far more productive than blindly casting over empty water.

Now that we have some basic tips for fishing in channelized waterways, let's look more closely at the specific methods infrastructure engineers use to channelize a waterway, such as lining riverbanks with rocks or concrete, constructing dams and levees, and placing structures in a river to direct the flow of water. We'll cover strategies and techniques for fishing in these areas. Even though not all the engineering structures discussed in this chapter may be present in your local waterways, these insights will enhance your understanding of the engineered environment and give you some ideas for fishing in your local waters.

Armored Waterways: Battling Erosion

One method that engineers use to channelize waterways, and more generally to prevent erosion and restrict meandering, is called *armoring*. This method involves piling the banks with riprap or completely lining and covering the waterfront with slabs of concrete. There are many other methods to armor waterways, including using gabions (cages filled with rocks) and concrete structures called tetrapods (which look like jacks, the game pieces).

Armoring helps protect land from strong currents and erosion. However, armoring causes flooding and erosion further downriver as the waterway seeks out other spots to erode instead. To prevent erosion further downriver, engineers might continue to armor the waterway, extending the process until entire lengths of a waterway are locked under riprap or concrete.

While riprap protects the banks of waterways against erosion, it limits the growth of vegetation along the waterfront. Grasses, shrubs, and trees struggle to grow in piles of rock and stone. When there is less vegetation growing along the banks, there is less shading and water temperatures can rise significantly. Additionally, with fewer trees near the water, the

Concrete blocks and piles of riprap line the banks of the Missouri River near downtown Omaha, Nebraska. Photograph by Morgan Dorsey

quantity of large woody debris and leafy material in the waterway is reduced, decreasing overall aquatic insect populations and habitat for fish.

In extreme cases, entire waterways might have their banks and substrate lined with concrete, creating the most homogenous habitat imaginable. Few species of fish can survive in completely concrete canals, and if the water level is only a few inches deep and running swiftly, about the only fish you'll find are little mosquitofish. However, if there's at least a couple feet of water and the current isn't running too swiftly, you could find common carp and grass carp in concrete canals. If you add in some bridges, culverts, maybe some trees, and shallow islands to the concrete canals (which adds a little more diverse habitat), you could start to find other species, such as largemouth bass, green sunfish, catfish, and tilapia.

In limited amounts, a pile of riprap can act as a magnet for small fish and crayfish seeking places to hide. You might even find smallmouth bass hunting up against the riprap. An effective fly-fishing technique in this situation is using a heavy jig streamer, holding your arm and rod out ("high-sticking"), and twitching the fly along the riprap. You can also cast out the streamer into deeper water and retrieve it back toward the riprap.

In colder months, armored banks, warmed by sunlight, increase the surrounding water temperature more quickly than vegetated banks. That can draw in fish since they provide a warm-water refuge. In these cooler months, the fish will be less active, but you can still catch a couple by using an indicator rig to slowly drift one or two nymphs along the riprap. As the indicator slowly floats downstream, walk beside it—without recasting—so your flies can efficiently cover an entire length of the waterway.

When you find a bend in an armored waterway, watch how the current pushes into the riprap (or concrete wall). As water deflects off the riprap, it forms eddies that trap food items such as insects, small fish, and crayfish. These eddies are excellent spots for species such as bass, walleye, and trout to feed and ambush prey that is helplessly swept in the current.

At these eddies, cast out a streamer or large wet fly and allow it to be carried by the current toward the eddy. Once your fly is in the eddy, fish might aggressively strike at any moment. Be ready to set the hook by keeping the rod tip close to the water, pinching the fly line against the cork handle, and using your hand that isn't holding the rod to pull ("strip") line in to remove any slack on the water. When a fish strikes, give one quick strip while keeping the rod tip pointed at the water (a "strip set"). Once the fish is firmly on the hook, raise your arm to bend the rod into the letter "C". When the rod is in this C-shape it acts as a shock absorber, helping prevent the fly from breaking off. At this point, you can either continue to strip line in or use the reel to bring the fish toward you.

In Minneapolis, Ryan Birringer fishes a turbulent eddy pushing foam against a rocky bank. Keeping tension on his streamer by stripping line slowly allowed him to detect subtle strikes beneath the swirling foam. After feeling a fish strike, Ryan performed a quick strip set to firmly hook the fish, then raised his rod arm to bend the rod into a distinct "C-shape." This rod position acts as a shock absorber, cushioning the fish's movements and preventing the fly from breaking off, which is essential when fighting a fish in turbulent water or in a strong current.

Levees: Confining Waterways

One surprising form of infrastructure found in many of our cities is *levees*. Levees are raised sections of land along the banks of a waterway, constructed from materials such as soil, gravel, riprap, and slabs of concrete. They resemble elongated, narrow hills or very steep banksides. Sometimes, they are covered in grass and foliage to try to blend them into the landscape. The primary purpose of a levee is to mitigate floodwaters from inundating a portion of the floodplain.

There are levees in cities across the country that work to shield us from flooding, but there are no absolute protections, and levees do fail. Moreover, scientists and engineers have determined that levees actually increase flooding in other areas. Levees raise the water level, accelerate the flow of water, and create bottlenecks, which then push floodwaters into communities and towns that cannot afford (or are not given funding for) similar flood-control infrastructure.

Millions of us live, work, recreate, and, yes, fish around levees. To see if your city has any, visit the US Army Corps of Engineers (USACE) National Levee Database, which includes a map of all known levees. www.levees.sec.usace.army.mil

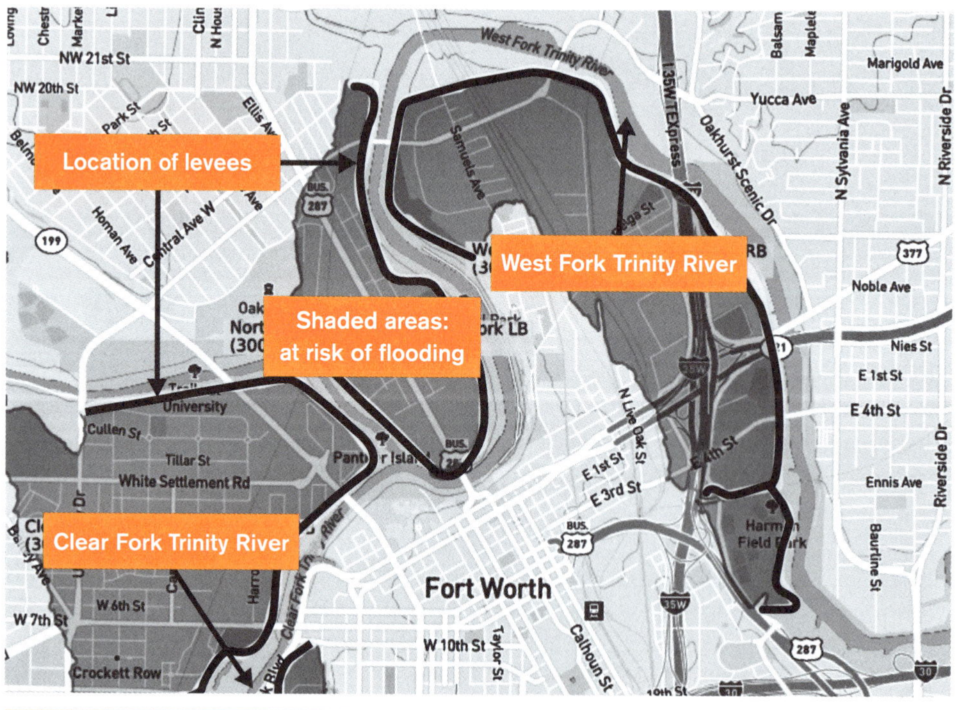

Location of levees in downtown Fort Worth, Texas. Source: USACE National Levee Database

For urban anglers, levees provide an elevated position from which to spot fish down in the water. Levees can also be massive pieces of infrastructure where water levels rise and fall throughout the year, if the water gets that close. Although levees are generally featureless places, as water levels drop, structures and debris once hidden underwater become visible. Take note of these structures, and on future fishing outings, when water levels just cover those structures and debris, focus your fishing efforts on those spots (if the debris isn't washed away in strong currents). Other spots include any tunnels or pipes that are discharging water from the side of the levee, and any marinas or docks.

Dams: Regulating Waterflows

A dam is a barrier constructed across a waterway to control the flow of water for any number of functions, such as water storage, hydroelectric-power generation, flood-risk management, transportation enhancement for ships and barges, recreational boating, and water diversion for municipal, industrial, and agricultural uses. The design and construction of dams vary widely, from small low-head dams to massive hydropower

An aerial photograph of what the levees around Forth Worth, Texas, look like, which easily can be mistaken as benign grassy hills. Photo by Vibe Images/Shutterstock

dams, utilizing materials such as soil, rock, concrete, stones, bricks, or any combination thereof.

When dams are built on waterways, they restrict the flow of water, and upstream of the dam larger bodies of water, *impoundments,* form. These impoundments are sometimes renamed as reservoirs, lakes, or ponds, and many of the lakes in our cities are waterways impounded by dams. In the next chapter, we'll delve deeper into fishing strategies for shorelines around those bodies of still water. Here, our primary focus is on the waterways downstream of dams, sometimes referred to as *tailwaters*.

To find dams in your city, visit the National Inventory of Dams website (nid.sec.usace.army.mil). This resource provides maps and details about dams nationwide. It is also helpful to do a little internet research into the dams you come across. Understanding the specific details of the dams in your area, even those located miles upstream from your city, can be incredibly helpful for fishing, as dams have far-reaching effects on waterways and fish populations.

Dams in urban areas are interesting places to fish around. There are many unique situations that you might encounter, which can't be fully explored in this book. To get you started, below is some basic information about dams and fishing strategies that you can use.

DAMS: WATER QUALITY

When discussing dams here, I am referring to large dams on waterways, which dramatically impact downstream ecology. Examples of larger dams include Longhorn Dam in Austin, Texas; Buford Dam outside Atlanta, Georgia; Geist Dam in Indianapolis, Indiana; and Griggs Dam in Columbus, Ohio.

No dam is too large to fish around. In Minneapolis, I spent time with Rick Phetsavong and a group of anglers fishing around the massive lock-and-dam system on the Mississippi River. Rick even guides clients to fish near these enormous infrastructures, proving that the only limitations to where you can fish are the ones you set for yourself.

If you have a large dam on your urban waterway, the first question on your mind should be: *Where do I see water coming out from the dam?* You can either look for this information online or go look at the dam in person. If you are going to check out the dam for yourself, the best time to do this is during summer months. Once you've found where the water is being released from, you can use table 8.1 on page 159 to help determine the water's characteristics and the fish species you might expect in the waterway below a dam.

During summer, many impoundments become thermally stratified—a condition wherein water separates into distinct temperature layers, with

Table 8.1. Influence of Dam Release Levels on Downstream Conditions and Fish Species

Release Level	Characteristics of Release Water	Fish Species You Might Encounter Downstream of the Dam During Summer Months
Surface release: (epilimnetic) water spilling over the top of the dam or through gates near the top of the dam	Warm Well oxygenated Nutrient depleted Possibly discolored due to sediment	Smallmouth and largemouth bass, carp, various sunfish, catfish, gar, freshwater drum, various suckers, walleye, sauger, pike, temperate bass, creek chub, pickerel
Deep release: (hypolimnetic) water coming out the bottom of the dam or from a building called a powerhouse	Cold Oxygen depleted Nutrient rich Clearer	Trout, mountain whitefish, various suckers, walleye, sauger, perch, pike, temperate bass

warmer water near the surface (the epilimnion layer) and colder water near the bottom (the hypolimnion layer). If you've ever jumped into a deep lake during summer and felt the sudden shock of cold water as you dove deeper, you've experienced this layering firsthand. Dams that draw in and release water from the epilimnion layer of an impoundment are called "surface release dams," and the released water is typically warmer and well oxygenated. "Deep release dams," by contrast, pull from the hypolimnion, where water tends to be colder and oxygen depleted.

Table 8.1 provides general guidance on the fish species likely to be found downstream of a dam based on its release level. However, other factors, such as the depth and shape of the impoundment, can influence water temperature and oxygen levels. For example, some impoundments are too shallow to stratify during the summer and instead remain warm from top to bottom. In these cases, even if water is released from the bottom of a dam or through a hydroelectric powerhouse, the outflow will still be warm water. As a result, the habitat downstream of the dam may favor warmwater species like smallmouth bass rather than coldwater species such as trout.

Dams might also have intakes that pull in water from different depths of an impoundment (called multi-level release), mixing warm and cold water together. All of this can get confusing, and a simple solution to getting accurate information is to carry a thermometer and check water temperatures immediately downstream of the dam.

Another thing you might notice in the table is that deep release (hypolimnetic) dams release clearer water. All dams act as sediment traps that block sand, silt, clay, and other particles from continuing downstream. It's a huge problem because it shortens the functional life of dams by filling in impoundments with sediment. In fact, about 1 percent of the total volume of water stored in impoundments worldwide (approximately 6,800 km^3)

is lost annually due to sedimentation; that's roughly seven billion dump trucks worth of sediment going into impoundments each year.

Since dams are effective sediment traps, we as anglers can use that to our advantage. If waterways are discolored due to sediment, you can try venturing closer to dams, particularly deep-release dams, to find clearer water and potentially better fishing because the fish will see your fly better.

DAMS: CHECKING THE FLOW OF WATER

Dams disrupt the flow of water, but the extent of flow alteration depends on the dam's design and function. Large dams can either mimic historic seasonal flows (run-of-the-river dams) or significantly alter water flow on daily and seasonal bases (storage-release dams). Storage-release dams might allow normal flow but hold back water during storm events to prevent downstream flooding. They might also store and withdraw water for purposes like irrigation or municipal water supply, or release water in pulses to generate electricity based on demand (hydropeaking).

Flow alterations from a dam can be complex, and the discharge levels greatly affect fishing conditions for anglers. Fortunately, you can check flow conditions from your computer or phone thanks to monitoring streamgages operated by the United States Geological Survey (USGS). We'll cover how to use these very helpful USGS monitoring systems in chapter 10.

DAMS: FLY FISHING TIPS

Many urban anglers like to fish near dams. Fish, insects, and other organisms often get washed over or churned through turbines and spit out of dams, making them easy prey for fish waiting nearby. The base (or toe) of a dam is a chaotic area where water crashes down into what's called a stilling basin. Hydroelectric dams also have outlets from powerhouses that empty into stilling basins. These basins, typically made of concrete or riprap, are designed to absorb and dissipate the energy of the water coming out of the dam. When water flows are lower, you can get a good look at these structures.

The stilling basin is a high-energy spot where it's difficult for fish to hunt and ambush prey. However, around the stilling basin, you'll find

This dam's spillway gates are closed, providing a clear view of the stilling basin at the base of the dam. This area consists of little more than a large, flat concrete slab with chute and baffle blocks. When water pours through the spillway gates, it crashes into these blocks, creating a chaotic and turbulent zone where fish are unlikely to swim. Instead, most fish will position themselves just beyond the turbulent water, waiting to ambush food that gets spit out of the dam.

eddies and other areas where the chaotic water meets slower currents. This is where you want to cast streamers, retrieve poppers across the surface, or drift nymphs under an indicator.

Further downstream of the stilling basin, you might find small islands, boulders, rocks, and sandbars. These features create pools and riffles for fish. Using a dry-dropper or streamer, search the riffles, deeper water, and spots where fast and slow water meet to form seams. The species you find in this habitat will change throughout the seasons as fish migrate up close to a dam and then back downstream.

Lastly, if the water flowing out of the dam is flooding the surrounding area, don't get discouraged. When water levels rise, many fish push closer to the banks and feed among the flooding vegetation. Often, parks and other green spaces are located near the base of a dam, and these places will periodically become submerged. It's fun wading around a sunken park or frisbee golf course, casting bottom-dwelling flies for fish around a park bench or in tall grass. You might also see fish such as suckers and carp feeding in such shallow spots that their backs are out of the water.

SAFETY TIP

Avoid Low-Head Dams

Urban waterways often have numerous smaller dams, many of which are barely taller than the average person. These structures can range from historical remnants of old mills to modern installations that store and withdraw water for agricultural, industrial, or municipal use. Many small dams encountered in urban settings are known as *low-head dams*. These simple structures, typically a few feet to around 15 feet (4 m) high, are often built from concrete. They operate as run-of-the-river dams and, despite their small size, significantly alter water flow, the same as any other dam, by creating impoundments upstream that impact the aquatic environment.

Low-head dams present significant hazards, especially when climbing on, or wading close to, these structures. As water plunges over these dams, it creates dangerous vortices beneath the surface. These recirculating currents can trap anglers, kayakers, canoers, swimmers, and children playing near the dam, often with fatal results. The deceptively benign appearance of these small dams masks the potential danger, which has led to hundreds of deaths since the 1960s.

Petitioning your city and advocating for the removal or modification of low-head dams will help make waterways safer for everyone to enjoy.

DAMS: IMPACTS ON HABITAT AND FISH

Dams provide many benefits to our cities, and without certain dams, entire cities and urban fisheries wouldn't exist in their current forms. For instance, the South Platte River in Denver historically used to run dry during certain times of the year, particularly in the summer. But now Chatfield Dam provides a year-round supply of water for Denver's urban fishery.

At the same time, dams have far-reaching impacts on habitats and fish. Whether large or small, dams alter water flow, temperature, and sediment transport, thereby affecting aquatic habitats and species. Dams aid in the channelization of waterways and alter flow regimes that drastically transforms habitats. For example, the lower Boise River used to be a meandering, braided, gravel-bed river. After Lucky Peak Dam was built, the river became channelized and regulated, which destroyed the historic biodiversity and productivity of the waterway.

Dams wipe out native fish species. After the construction of Hoover Reservoir in Columbus, Ohio, 18 percent of all species were lost in Big Walnut Creek. After the Chattahoochee River was impounded by the Buford Dam in Georgia, and with subsequent hypolimnetic releases (cold water released from the bottom of the impoundment), most native warmwater species were eliminated downstream for approximately 48 miles (77 km). In Oklahoma, around 19 percent of fish species depletions were caused by dams blocking fish migrations.

Dams can completely halt water flows, effectively sacrificing one waterbody to sustain another. This often exacerbates disparities in who has access to, and benefits from, local water resources. Lastly, many dams throughout the country are coming close to the end of their lifespans or have already passed them, posing hazardous risks to local communities while further degrading aquatic habitats (see Additional Facts About Dams in the United States, page 163).

Additional Facts About Dams in the United States

Total Dams: There are over 91,000 known dams in the United States.

Hydroelectric Power: Only 3 percent of dams generate hydroelectric power.

Ownership: More than half of all dams are privately owned.

Lifespan: The average lifespan of a dam is around sixty years. By 2030, seven out of ten dams in the US will be over fifty years old.

Deficient Dams: There are over 2,300 deficient high-hazard-potential dams.

Dam Failures: Since 1980, an average of twenty-four dams fails each year, and the frequency of dam failures is increasing.

Directors: Routing the Flow of Water

Besides armored banks, levees, and dams, you might encounter a variety of other devices used to alter waterways, such as stream barbs, river dikes, bendway weirs, wing dams, rock vanes, and spur dikes. These terms are not synonymous, but to keep things simple, I am going to collectively refer to these structures as *directors*.

Directors are found in many waterways, from small streams to the Mississippi River. They vary in shape, size, and configuration but are typically recognizable as fingerlike structures jutting out from the bank into the waterway, usually angled upriver or downriver. Directors are constructed from materials such as stones, large rocks, concrete, and timber piles, and they are often built in a series along the bank. They can be fully or partly submerged under the water, and you will more easily see them during times of low flow.

Engineers use these structures for a variety of purposes, including to divert or hydraulically redirect water flow to protect specific bank

Me on a small river director, specifically a rock vane, that was built in the Olentangy River in Columbus, Ohio. At higher flows, this director is usually underwater.

locations from erosion, manage sediment distribution in the river, deepen the main channel to facilitate ship and barge navigation, and dissipate energy to maintain a stable riverbed. There is some research that suggests directors can provide beneficial habitats for fish, but determining their long-term effects is challenging due to their frequent combination with other engineering interventions.

That said, directors reintroduce habitat complexity to waterways that have been simplified by channelization. They create varying depths and flows along their structures, offering diverse environments within a confined space such as riffles and pools. This heterogeneity of depth and flow is critical for fish to develop and spawn.

Directors provide hunting grounds for fish to ambush prey and calmer water for fish to cruise around foraging for food. Downstream of the structures, areas with slower flow and shallow depths form, becoming places for fish to reproduce. The rocks and stones used to construct directors create reef-like structures that offer hiding spots for aquatic insects, small fish, and crayfish. The reefs, pools, and shallow zones all help to support various life stages of fish, effectively acting as aquatic nurseries. Lastly, engineers sometimes modify directors by adding notches, known as notched dikes, which allow more water and sediment to flow through the structure. This improves sediment transport and increases habitat diversity by creating more complex flow patterns, offering fish better access to cover, feeding areas, and spawning grounds.

Directors can be productive spots for urban fishing. Here are a few things to keep in mind when you come across any of these pieces of infrastructure.

Eddies at the Bank: Where the director meets the bank of the waterway, eddies can form both on the upriver and downriver side of the structure. These eddies trap lots of food items, making them prime spots to cast a streamer or drift weighted nymphs under an indicator.

Slack-Water Pools: Immediately downstream of the director, slack water forms a pool where fish seek refuge from the main current. Try casting out streamers and unweighted nymphs, retrieving them slowly. Further downstream, shoals and sandbars can attract carp, smallmouth buffalo, and freshwater drum, which root around in the substrate for aquatic insects and crayfish. If you spot fish in these shallow areas, use bottom-dwelling flies and aim to land the fly just off the nose of the fish.

Late-Summer Considerations: In late summer, the slack water downstream of the director can become isolated from the main channel, forming a warm, stagnant pool with depleted dissolved oxygen. Harmful algal

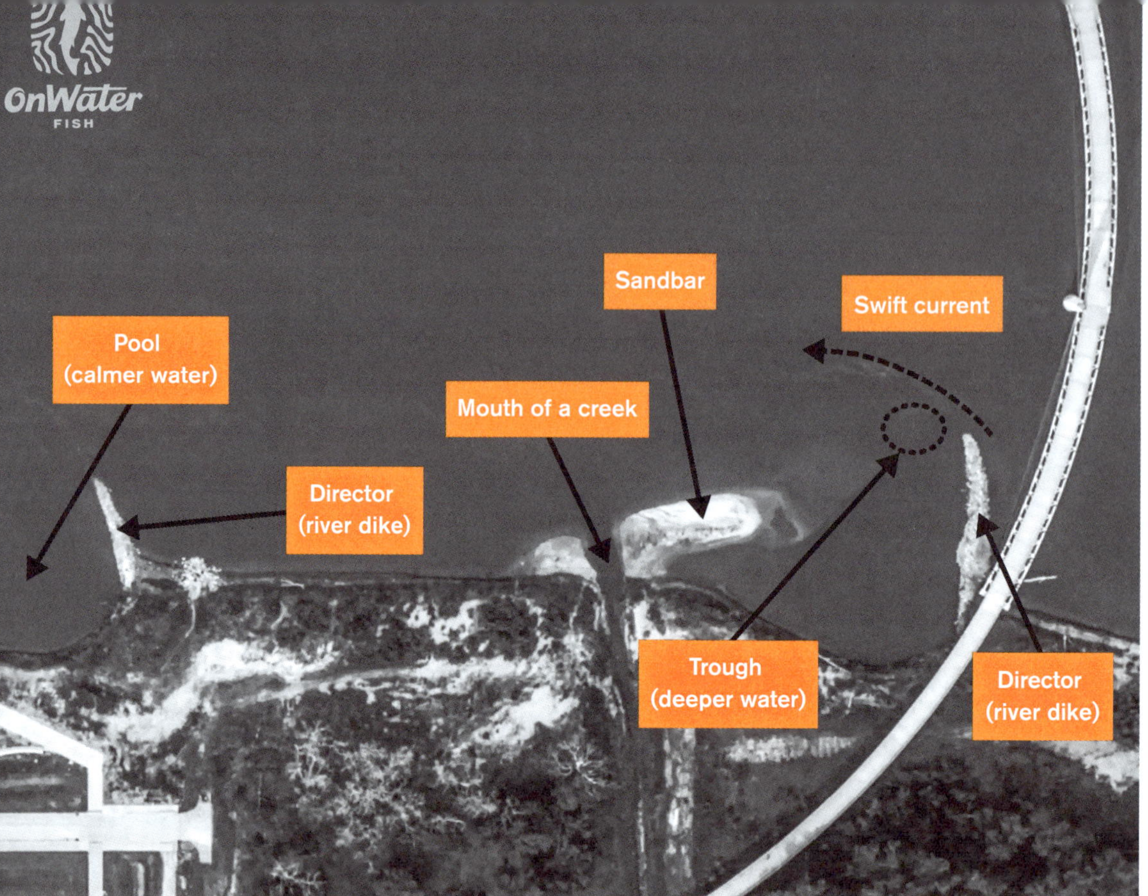

A top-down look at two directors (river dikes) located in the Missouri River next to downtown Omaha, Nebraska. Depending on the water level, these may be partially submerged below the surface of the water at certain times of the year.
Satellite image provided by OnWater Fish

blooms (HABs) might also form in these backwater areas, preventing fish from venturing into them.

Ambush Spot: At the end of the director, where it meets the swift main channel of the waterway, deep troughs form. Larger fish often wait near these scour holes to ambush prey swept through the current. Casting out and retrieving a streamer through the trough can lead to surprising catches; a sinking line helps here to get the fly even deeper.

Getting Out onto a Director: Walking out onto this piece of infrastructure is a personal decision and there are risks because they are often placed in areas with strong currents. However, if conditions permit—low and slow water, for example—then walking out onto a director helps you fish all the spots around it. Many urban waters are also deep and challenging to wade in due to channelization, so directors allow you to access parts of a waterway that otherwise would only be accessible by boat. Wear proper footwear and step carefully, as the rocks and rubble can shift underfoot.

In Indianapolis, after the 120-year-old Emrichsville Dam failed in 2018, a utility company chose to install a rock ramp instead of building a new concrete dam. This solution offers better fish passage while ensuring water supply for municipal and industrial uses. Photograph by Daniel Woody

Alternative Water Control Infrastructure

In urban waterways, you will encounter other types of water control infrastructure beyond the traditional ones discussed in this chapter. They come in various designs and shapes, depending on the site where they're built. Some resemble concrete ramps with rocks protruding from them, while others consist of boulders and large rocks precisely placed in a waterway by an excavator. They might be called rock ramps, rock weirs, check structures, grade control structures, energy dissipators, Newbury rock riffles, or stepped grouted sloping boulder drop structures. The names are confusing and not important to anglers.

What is important is this: There is a growing shift away from traditional water-control infrastructure and toward designs that aim to accommodate diverse water uses in urban areas. For example, in downtown Dayton, Ohio, dangerous low-head dams were removed from the Miami River and replaced with alternative drop structures. These new structures now provide opportunities for white-water paddling while improving water quality. Along Denver's South Platte River, there are many ramp-like structures that mitigate erosion while providing enhanced riffle-pool habitats around the site of the structure.

As cities have begun to recognize the additional values of urban waterways, alternative water-control infrastructure has been appearing more frequently. You, too, may find such structures. If you do, here are some tips for fly fishing around them.

Upstream of the Structure: Try casting small streamers or bottom-dwelling flies close to the fish you spot upstream of the structure, where water might be deeper and slower. You can also try drifting dry flies, such as patterns imitating beetles or grasshoppers, in this area.

On the Structure: If the structure is long enough, like the rock ramp in Indianapolis, with at least a couple feet of water flowing across it, there can be riffles and pools that hold fish, depending on the depth of water. Using poppers, dry flies, and streamers is a good way to check the turbulent water in this area.

Downstream of the Structure: Lines of bubbles that form downstream of the structure where fast and slow water meet are seams, or "feeding lanes" for fish. Drift nymphs under an indicator or use a two-fly rig, like a dry-dropper, in these places. Casting streamers through the foam and turbulence as water spills off the structure and into these feeding lanes is also effective. Further downstream of the structure, you might find calm, shallow water where fish will be foraging for food along the substrate, and you can sight cast to individual fish using lightly weighted nymphs or bottom-dwelling flies.

Compared to traditional water-control infrastructure, newer alternatives often provide localized benefits, offering modest improvements for fish habitat and water quality where they're installed. But those gains rarely match what was lost through decades of channelization, damming, and other sweeping alterations. And just like the traditional infrastructure they replace, these alternatives can still deepen inequities when they determine who gets access to the water and whose needs shape the design. When community voices are sidelined and historical harms are overlooked, even the most innovative structures can reinforce the same exclusionary patterns. Without a broader commitment to inclusive planning, long-term transparency, and ecological accountability, we risk building shinier versions of the same old mistakes.

CHAPTER 9

Urban Shorelines

Throughout your city, you may encounter various bodies of water such as ponds, lakes, or sections of saltwater environments. Since this book is for the wading or shore-bound angler, this chapter will focus on where these water bodies meet the land. In other words, how to fish along the *shoreline*.

Urban lakes and ponds are convenient places to fly fish. The paths along their shorelines provide easy access to the water, often making wearing waders unnecessary.

In downtown Denver, one side of the South Platte appears as a raging river, while the other side resembles something more like a pond.

Urban shorelines can have numerous features and habitats for fish, such as beaches, rocky areas, boat docks, boardwalks, piers, and various coastal defense structures. In this chapter, we'll explore where you might find fish and catch them with a fly rod. Many of the fly-fishing techniques we covered in the previous chapter are also applicable along shorelines. In fact, the lines between what is a river, pond, or lake are often blurred in urban areas, where human-built infrastructure can create unusual water features. In your city, you may encounter bodies of water that don't fit neatly into traditional categories.

There are no fly-fishing tactics or techniques exclusive only to streams, rivers, lakes, ponds, or ocean shorelines. Whatever fishing skills you learn or come up with, mix and match them based on the water and conditions on any given day. Experiment, be creative, be adaptable—remember, there's no one way that urban fly fishing "should" be done.

An Important Resource for the Saltwater Angler

Depending on where you live, you might be fishing along a saltwater shoreline where tides can rise and fall by several feet in a single day, causing currents and water levels to fluctuate significantly. When fishing in the intertidal zone—the area where the ocean meets the land—tides will

The top photo is during high tide along the Boston Harbor shoreline, when the water was up close to the walkway. The bottom photo is during low tide, which reveals numerous structures that were hidden from view during high tide. When you see structures in low tide, make a mental note or take a photo because they could be places that attract fish when the tide rises again.

further influence where and when you find fish. Watching and observing the tide is another layer to reading the water.

While you are on the water, observe the water level. Is it coming in or going out? Is the water rising or falling? What structures, above or below the water, do you notice, such as blocks of concrete, pilings underneath a dock, or maybe a drop-off into deeper water? When you make these observations, continue to watch the tides as they come in or go out, and note the currents caused by those tidal cycles.

There are several online resources, such as www.tides4fishing.com and the app Tides Near Me, that you can use to track the tides and swell (*swell* refers to a series of long, rolling waves that form in the open ocean due to distant winds and storms). Pulling up tide and swell charts for your city will give you helpful information, such as when high or low tide will occur, the height of the waves, and the wave period (the time interval between successive wave crests).

Many saltwater anglers also want to know which tide is best for fishing: high or low tide, rising or falling? Ask any saltwater angler, from West Coast to East Coast, about their preferred tides, and you will receive a variety of answers. For instance, Carl Crawford, a Los Angeles fly fisher, likes to fish at low tide, specifically when the tide starts to rise again. This allows him to walk further out onto beaches and cast flies into the surf for species like surfperch and halibut as they follow the tide inland. On the other hand, Boston fly fisher Rafael Del Razo prefers to fish high tide at night, as this pushes fish closer to boardwalks and piers, allowing him to make short casts to them beneath streetlights.

As you are learning to fish in urban saltwater, it is most important to get out and fish, regardless of the tide. Then, while you are on the water, by reading and observing the water level and any currents, you will discover the specific fishing spots that work best when the tide is high, low, or somewhere in between. Referencing tide and swell charts, before or during your time on the water, will further sharpen your own insights about optimal fishing conditions.

Getting in the Water

Consider looking for places where you can get into the water to further explore the urban shoreline. In the water and away from the shore, you will have more room to cast without having to worry about obstacles such as trees, streetlights, people, and fences. Here are some tips for getting into the water.

Check Water Access Laws and Water Quality: Refer back to chapters 2 and 6 on this; additionally, when you get to the water, check for any posted signs that say getting into the water is prohibited.

Check the Tides: If you are saltwater fishing, you don't want to make your way onto some sort of structure only to get stuck because of a rising tide.

Look for Shallow Areas: Stand atop a piece of high ground or a bridge and look for shallow areas such as sandbars, shoals, and sunken islands; also, check satellite imagery for any of these shallow areas.

Find Other Areas to Access the Water: Check around the shoreline, either in person or online, for areas where it's easier to get into the water, such as beaches and estuaries.

Along many urban shorelines, the water is too deep for wading. In these scenarios, there are still a couple ways you can access the water to fish and net your catch.

Look for Ramps or Use a Drop Net: In some urban areas there might be concrete or dirt ramps that connect to the water. If allowed, you can use these ramps to access the water to land a fish. If there aren't any ramps, some anglers use a drop net (or a net on an extendable pole) when fishing on top of piers and elevated boardwalks. A drop net is a large, circular net with a rope for lowering and lifting fish from elevated spots. To use it, lower the net into the water, position the fish over it, then lift steadily to land the catch without stressing your line (it's much easier to use with two people).

Go to the Marina: Some marinas have options to rent watercraft, which can be affordable with a group of

If you are wading along ocean shorelines, be mindful of the tides and ensure you can safely return using the same route you took when the tide was lower. Avoid getting caught in a situation where rising water forces you onto dry land, as this could lead to unintended trespassing on private property.

friends. City parks might also have options to rent rowboats and swan paddleboats. Whether or not they allow fishing from the boats is something you'll have to ask.

There are many adventures to be had in urban ponds and smaller lakes, and, yes, you can even find ponds and lakes where it is possible to get in the water. In Minneapolis, Ryan Birringer took me to a public golf course where we teed off looking for bass, sunfish, and carp in a small waterway that cut through the fairways. We weren't having any luck in the stream, so we waded farther down to where it spilled into a small lake. Around the mouth of the stream, the water was shallow and sandy enough for us to stand in the lake and cast streamers into where the stream's current met the calmer lake water. That was the spot. Ryan, after his third cast, started hooking into and landing several northern pike. We went from a fishless day to scoring above par for the course!

Critically Important Shorelines

Like waterways, shorelines are dynamic places where erosion, deposition, and flooding occur to create rich and productive habitats for fish. Some of these shoreline habitats are called estuaries (an area where freshwater and saltwater meet) and marshes (an area of land where water covers the ground for considerable periods of time). These places immensely benefit humans and cities for a variety of reasons, including protecting us from floods, storm surges, and sea-level rise. When cities build over these shorelines with hardened infrastructure, we lose these beneficial, life-sustaining habitats. Sadly, most major cities have paved over these ecosystems. For example, there is only one salt marsh remaining in Boston, and in Houston the Armand Bayou Nature Center (ABNC) strives to protect one of the largest urban estuary preserves in the United States, which is why fishing is prohibited in the ABNC.

If your city has any of these shoreline habitats, it is important to check local fishing regulations to ensure you are permitted to fish there. Preserving these places is critically important to the future of our local fisheries. If fishing is permitted, then you might find some incredible opportunities there. Much has been written about how to fish in these habitats, so I have included some recommended reading at the end of this book.

CITY BEACHES

Many cities contain beaches along oceans, lakes, and ponds, which provide many angling opportunities. One challenge is that beaches are

The Nanaimo River estuary in British Columbia is a rich and vibrant ecosystem that sustains a wide variety of animal species and plant life. Estuaries, where freshwater rivers meet the saltwater of the ocean, are among the most productive environments on the planet, serving as critical habitats for countless species and providing essential nursery grounds for fish and other marine life. Photograph by Tomas Kulaja/Shutterstock

popular places for everyone, and it's tough to fly fish in a crowd. But plenty of anglers fly fish along urban beaches.

If your city has any beaches, here are a handful of tips for fly fishing along them.

Low-Light Conditions: Go fishing early, late in the evening, or even at night; this will help you avoid most of the crowds and give you a chance to potentially hook into the largest fish of your life. When light levels are low, many large predatory fish venture closer to shallow water and within easy casting range. When you do hook into something, the battle is on!

Bring a Partner: Have a partner to check behind you while casting so you don't hook other people, especially as they stop to take photos right in the zone of your backcast.

Non-Beach Weather: If the weather is cooler, cloudy, or rainy, you can expect fewer crowds. Again, these low-light conditions could entice larger fish to patrol closer to shore.

Hedge Your Bets: If you only have a couple of hours to fish in the morning before the crowds appear, it helps to have a group of anglers to spread out along the beach, casting and searching for fish. Once someone locates a school, everyone can join up and maybe each catch a fish together.

There is an entire world of ocean life teeming along beaches, just below the waves. Carl Crawford, who has coached many new fly fishers on the art of casting and fishing in the surf, explains how there are endless experiences for you to discover:

> *I initially got into fly fishing for trout, but given the expense and hours spent driving to trout waters, it made sense to locate as many nearby urban fishable waters as possible. That's when I stumbled upon fly fishing in the surf and found my new favorite local fishing spot—the beaches of the Pacific Ocean.*
>
> *A major attraction is the variety of species in different sizes, and you never know what you're going to encounter next. Due to the raucous nature of the surf environment, the fish tend to be notably stronger than similarly sized freshwater fish. The ocean is always accessible and never subject to the drought conditions that we experience in Southern California. It doesn't require a full day's commitment, and you can always find a great healthy eatery nearby afterward to top off the day's experience, even if the fish were uncooperative!*

In Los Angeles, Analiza del Rosario, Caroline Craven, and I met before sunrise to fly fish along Santa Monica Beach. At any other time of the day, it is packed, but early in the morning it felt like we had the place to ourselves. Casting lines into the crashing surf and watching the sun light up the ocean in pinks, reds, and golds was bliss. We didn't catch any surfperch, but once the crowds grew, it was easy enough for us to pack up and head to the Los Angeles River to meet with more friends for a little carp fishing.

When fishing along the beach, an abundance of caution is required since it is common to have beach walkers enter the range of your backcast. They will often stop to watch you cast, causing you to pause to ensure their safety. It can be frustrating, but it's our responsibility as anglers to be vigilant. Another area of caution is how you approach the water to avoid trouble with a rogue wave or aggressively rising tide.

Conservation efforts have had significant positive effects on our local surf habitats around Los Angeles. I remember during the 1970s and '80s, there were multiple oil spills that polluted our waters for months at a time. Thanks to conservation efforts and regulations, this has been largely mitigated, benefiting our shoreline, its inhabitants, and those who love to recreate in the water.

I've met a number of fly-fishing partners on the beaches, forming ongoing relationships. Many people in our community are willing to help you out, whether it's learning basic fly-fishing tactics, how to cast, or fly tying.

Urban Ponds and Small Lakes

Some of the most accessible bodies of water in our cities are urban ponds and small lakes. What's the difference in size between an urban pond and a small urban lake? It really depends on how cities and people label them. For our purposes here, urban ponds and small lakes are bodies of water that you could easily walk or travel around in less than an hour or two, allowing you to explore and fish all of the structures and features around the shoreline.

These bodies of water offer fishing opportunities throughout the year for species such as bluegill, green sunfish, pumpkinseed, common carp, grass carp, largemouth bass, smallmouth bass, and catfish. You can also find other species of fish that people illegally dump into the pond or lake, such as koi, goldfish, and various exotic aquarium pets. Whatever fish species you come across in urban ponds and lakes, you'll want to be ready to use various fly-fishing techniques and tactics to catch them.

Perfect Your Roll Cast: The shorelines along urban lakes and ponds might seem like tough places to fly cast due to crowds. But I watched fly fishers, city to city, fish these bodies of water by perfecting their roll cast. The more you work on this cast, the more you'll be able to effectively fly fish along urban ponds, lakes, and other areas where lots of people are milling about and where space to cast is limited.

Indicator and a Nymph: Placing an indicator onto your leader a few feet from the end of your fly line is an easy rig to set up. Then attach a

Urban ponds are unique bodies of water that offer a range of fly-fishing experiences, from beginner-friendly opportunities to some of the most technical challenges you'll encounter in a city.

nymph, such as a Hare's Ear or even a small Woolly Bugger, and make a cast. Once the fly is in the water, slowly retrieve it back to shore. Stop the indicator periodically and keep an eye on it; if it twitches, it could indicate a fish taking your fly.

Dry-Dropper: A floating fly, such as a foam beetle or "bread" fly, with a sinking egg pattern is another excellent rig to use. Tie the floating fly onto the end of your leader and then attach about a 12-inch (30 cm) piece of monofilament to the bend of the hook. At the end of the monofilament, tie on a sinking fly, like an egg pattern. Cast it out and be ready for fish to take either the floating fly or the dropper (you'll know that a fish took the dropper when the dry fly plunges under).

Check Around Fountains: Fountains help to improve water quality in urban ponds and lakes by increasing dissolved oxygen levels in the water. These fountains can attract fish, particularly later in the summer. During these hotter months, aim to get your flies closer to where the fountains are aerating the water.

Inlets and Outlets: Water entering or leaving a pond or small lake through canals, creeks, or even pipes are places for larger fish to ambush prey.

Urban ponds and small lakes are frequently lined with concrete walkways, and the concrete continues under the water. You might actually see concrete steps or drop-offs right along the shoreline. Try to fish close to these drop-offs by casting your fly parallel to shore and retrieving it along the edge of the deeper water.

They will stay hidden nearby and pounce on small fish, crayfish, leeches, and any sort of swimming insect that is caught in the current.

Urban ponds and small lakes are fun places to spend time outside looking for fish, and they are great spots to take someone who is new to fishing. It's low stress and, during late spring through early fall, the fish are close to the shoreline, placing them well within range of a fly rod. In Minneapolis, Jennifer Hsia and I didn't have to cast far to catch handfuls of bluegill and crappie. In fact, we had a blast reaching out with our fly rods and dapping small nymphs between aquatic plants and watching the fish charge at our flies.

Each pond and small lake also has its own character and fishing opportunities. After Jennifer and I packed up at that first pond, we went to another one that was utterly loaded with massive carp bathing in the sun. The carp were being picky—as they always are—but I finally got one to take a fly, and Jennifer fully committed by going into the pond to net the lunker for me. You can't ask for a better fishing partner than someone willing to fill up their boots with pond water!

Throughout the rest of this chapter, we'll look at an assortment of human-built infrastructure that you might find along urban ponds, lakes, larger reservoirs, and saltwater shorelines. Many of these engineering structures are coastal-defense strategies, which mitigate the risks of damage caused by coastal flooding, sea level rise, and storm surges.

Armored Shorelines

Our cities have armored much of the shoreline using riprap, building large seawalls, laying down tetrapods, and employing a variety of other methods. When cities built over habitats such as estuaries and marshes, we essentially removed the buffers that protected us from coastal flooding. Whenever we armor our shorelines, waves seek out other areas of the shoreline to erode, and this is one reason why entire shorelines have become armored as people try to protect buildings and homes from flooding.

Adding to the problem, our shorelines need sediment to help prevent them from completely eroding away, and much of this sediment is trapped in impoundments behind dams. When sediment can't make it to our shorelines, beaches disappear. Cities might then opt to dredge sand to re-nourish beaches or simply continue armoring the shoreline, both of which are expensive and fail to solve the underlying problems.

Much of the publicly accessible shoreline in the heart of cities, whether along ponds, lakes, or saltwater environments, consists of walkways atop walls. The water level could be anywhere from a foot to several feet below you, making netting a fish tough but not impossible. This is where ingenuity and creativity come in, along with planning how you will land the fish before making a cast.

As you venture around these walkways, it helps to have both a floating and sinking line (for information on sinking lines, refer to chapter 1). Having a floating line will allow you to target shallow areas and places where debris has fallen into the water without getting your fly constantly snagged. Having a sinking line will give you a way to cast out into the deeper surrounding water where other fish might be cruising. Streamers like a Clouser Minnow, Lefty's Deceiver, or Woolly Bugger are great flies to efficiently search for fish by casting out and retrieving the streamer over larger areas of water.

Fly fishing along these walkways doesn't have to be complicated. In Denver, Rick Mikesell had us fly fishing at night for bass along a concrete shoreline simply by holding our fly rods low and at an angle. As we walked around the lake, we guided small streamers close to the wall, essentially "walking the dog."

Beneath walkways, there could be many vertical structures like pilings. Especially in saltwater environments at night, the tide will push fish and squid into these pilings, and larger fish will cruise around the perimeter, nabbing any prey stuck in the current. In these situations, you definitely want to use heavy, abrasion-resistant monofilament, such as 15–20-pound (7–9 kg) fluorocarbon. When you hook a fish, it could try to run you back into the pilings to break you off. Point the fly rod down toward the water, keep a good bend in it, and work to pull the fish away from the pilings.

After work, Rafael Del Razo casts and retrieves streamers for fish drawn to the dock by the glow of nearby streetlights in Boston, Massachusetts.

Shorelines are often reinforced with walls and vertical barriers, which can make fishing more challenging. Still, these built-up edges sometimes work in our favor. Restaurants and cafes along the waterfront occasionally draw fish close by chumming the water with food scraps, creating a surprisingly productive place to cast a fly.

Marinas, Docks, and Piers

Structures such as marinas, docks, and piers will often have pilings supporting and suspending them above the water. These supports create shelter and protection for various aquatic species, including small fish, eels, crustaceans, macroinvertebrates, and frogs, depending on whether you're fishing in saltwater or freshwater. Pilings act like artificial reef structures, serving as spawning grounds and nurseries for fish.

Boats moored at marinas and docks are also prime locations for larger predatory fish, which hide underneath to ambush prey. While boats frequently come and go, keep an eye out for those that remain docked for extended periods. These stationary boats create a more consistent habitat, making them ideal targets for your casts. Floating and intermediate lines paired with streamers work well when fishing around marinas, docks, and piers. In freshwater, try poppers, sliders, or jig streamers for bass and sunfish during the summer. When casting, aim to place your fly close to a piling, boat, or some other structure, as this greatly increases your chances of enticing strikes from fish using these protective areas to hunt.

Note that many marinas are private and off-limits to the general public. However, some marinas are protected by breakwaters, which are often accessible to the public and can get you within casting range of where the fish are.

THE PITCH CAST

In tight spaces where traditional overhead or roll casts aren't possible—such as between boats, underneath smaller bridges, or into culverts—you can use a simple and effective technique called a "pitch cast." This method is particularly useful for accurately placing a fly in confined areas and at short distances—25 feet (8 m) or less—where an overhead cast might hit an obstacle. If you have experience with using a conventional spinning or casting rod, then you might already be familiar with this cast. By relying on the heavy weight of the fly to drive the cast, it's also more forgiving for beginners and can be done with minimal practice. Here's how to do it.

1. **Use a Heavy Jig Streamer:** Attach a heavy jig streamer to the end of your leader; George Daniel's Spark Plug is a great jig streamer to use with this cast. The heavy weight of this fly is important because it provides the momentum needed for the cast.
2. **Prepare Your Fly Line:** Pull or "strip" some fly line off your reel and hold the loose line lightly in the fingers of your hand that is not holding the rod. This slack line will help you add distance to your cast.
3. **Swing the Fly:** Hold out the rod in front and slightly off to one side of your body. Gently start swinging the jig streamer back and forth

under the rod tip, like a pendulum. This back-and-forth motion helps build momentum for the cast.

4. **Pitch the Fly:** Once the fly has enough momentum, stop the rod when the fly is swinging forward and near the peak of its swing. At the same time, release the slack line from your hand that is not holding the rod to allow the fly to shoot forward toward your target. The motion is similar to a gentle "flick." The fly will land on the water with a subtle plop, just enough to entice nearby fish to dart out and strike.

SAFETY TIP

Casting Close to Boats and Docks

In rare instances, people have gotten upset with me for casting flies too close to their boat or dock. It's a bit awkward to watch someone lose their temper. To mitigate any potential altercations, pinch down the barbs on your flies and consider using weedless flies, where monofilament covers the hook point, making it less likely to snag anything.

Breakwaters

Breakwaters, both on the ocean and larger freshwater lakes, come in various forms that can either be shore-connected or fully detached from the land. However, for the shore-bound urban angler, one of the most accessible types of breakwaters are often found around marinas and ports.

Breakwaters that are used around marinas and ports diminish the strength of waves and wave-induced currents to create calmer water for ships, boats, ferries, and port operations. Typically constructed from rock, concrete, or interlocking armoring units, these breakwaters can be substantial in size to effectively diminish wave impact.

The waves and currents beyond the breakwater (the windward side) can be intense, creating turbulence that traps small fish, crustaceans, and floating insects near the structure. As a result, fish feeding in these turbulent waters often linger close to the breakwater, sometimes right at your feet, making long casts unnecessary. Clouser Minnows and Lefty's Deceiver fly patterns work well as would any similar-looking streamer. For saltwater fishing, Carl Crawford has enjoyed days standing on breakwaters while the tide is coming in, which can provide fruitful opportunities. As the tide rises, it brings the water level higher up the rocky sides of the breakwater, presenting closer shots to fish. This method has helped Carl reel in calico bass and various species of perch from his vantage point.

This aerial view shows a shore-connected breakwater protecting a marina from ocean waves. On the left side of the photo, the open ocean sends waves crashing against the breakwater, while wave-driven currents push food items, such as small fish, close to the structure. On the right side, the inside of the breakwater is sheltered from the waves, creating calm waters with shallow areas where sandbars can form. Shore-connected breakwaters like this one are often accessible to anglers, providing a place to walk out and fish. Photograph by Luke Gibson

On the harbor side of the breakwater (the lee side), you'll find much calmer waves and currents. A prime starting spot is at the end of the breakwater, where the open ocean or lake enters the protected zone via an inlet. Here, larger fish often lie in wait, ready to ambush prey swept in by the outside waves and current, and you can use poppers or drift flies under an indicator. Lastly, check any shallow water and drop-offs, as well as pilings around the docks that are within casting range.

DREDGING OPERATIONS

At times, fishing in marinas might not be great due to recent dredging operations during which cranes are brought in to pull up sediment and move it out of the marina. Depending on the size of the marina, these dredging operations can severely cloud the water, diminishing your chances of catching fish. However, if the marina is large enough, these dredging activities might stir up small fish and other prey, potentially causing a feeding frenzy nearby.

Dredging also occurs in many other places, such as between jetties as well as in freshwater rivers, to keep channels open for ships and barges. Dredging operations can be limited and infrequent or they can happen almost year-round, covering wide areas. Extensive operations can heavily

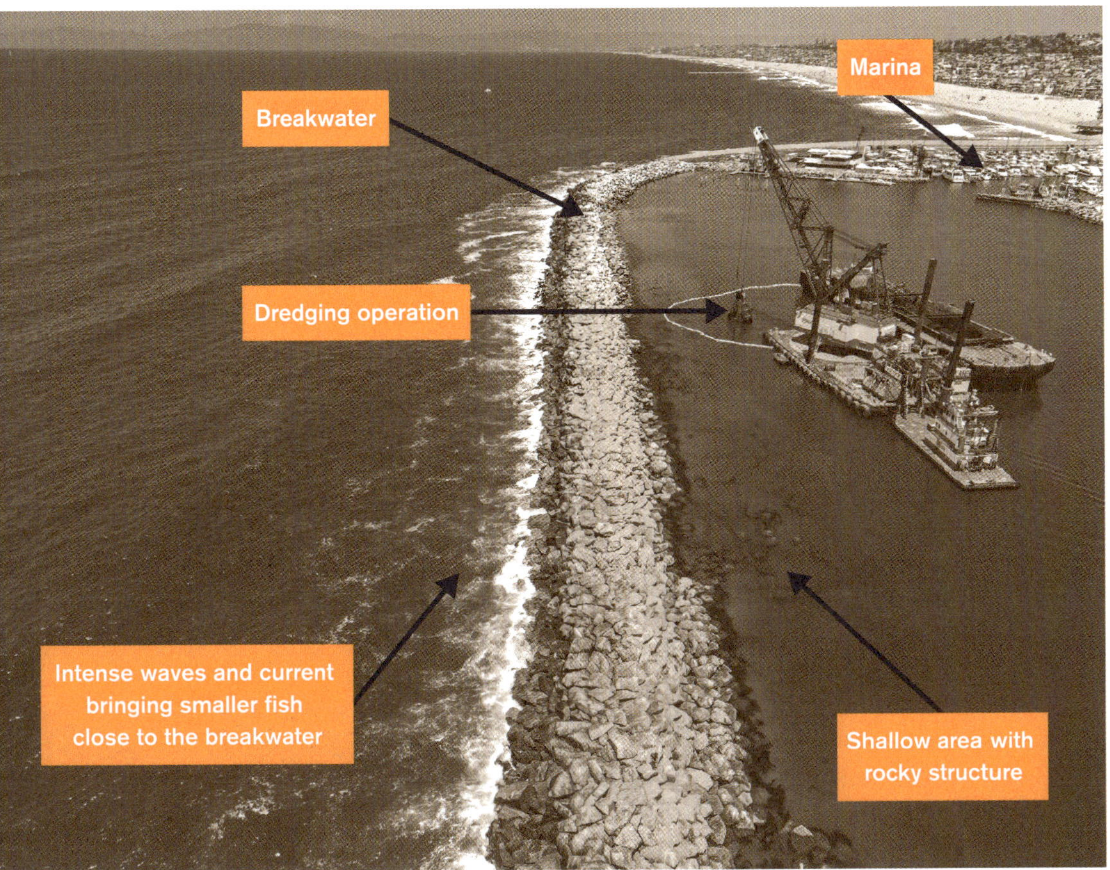

The breakwater in this photograph is the same one shown in the previous image. Here, we can see an active dredging operation removing sediment that has accumulated on the lee side of the breakwater. This photograph also provides a clearer view of the contrast in wave action between the windward and lee sides. Additionally, we can spot piles of rock that have become dislodged from the breakwater, forming a small boulder field that serves as habitat for fish. Photograph by Luke Gibson

damage or destroy aquatic habitats, and might even require scuba divers to go in ahead of operations to wake up sleeping sea turtles that are at risk of being crushed.

FLOATING BREAKWATERS

Breakwaters may also be floating structures rather than built up from the bottom of a body of water. These floating breakwaters can be constructed from various materials, including wood, plastic, tires, or composites, and may feature a boardwalk-like platform (much like a dock) that is great for casting. Floating breakwaters are typically deployed in calmer areas of larger bays or sounds where the waves are less extreme compared to open coastlines. As a result, the breakwater will be positioned much closer to the water's surface, making it easier to net a fish.

When fishing from a floating breakwater, it's not uncommon to find fish lurking right beneath your feet. If there are few people out and it is quiet, move slowly and walk softly to avoid alerting fish while you make short casts with a streamer right along the structure. This is also a great tactic to use while throwing a popper for sunfish or bass in a lake.

DETACHED BREAKWATERS

Another type of breakwater you may come across is a detached breakwater, which might also be called an artificial reef or an offshore or nearshore breakwater. Unlike shore-connected breakwaters, detached breakwaters are constructed away from the shoreline, often running parallel to it and serving as barriers to waves and wave-induced currents. The actual structure itself is typically situated well beyond the casting range of shore-based fly fishers.

The primary purpose of a detached breakwater is to create a zone of calmer water along the beach on its leeward side. By reducing wave energy, these breakwaters facilitate sediment deposition, leading to the formation of beaches, shallow flats, and more stable seabeds. These features provide essential habitats for fish and various food sources. In warmer coastal regions, the calmer waters created by detached breakwaters can foster the growth of sea grass and other marine vegetation, further enhancing the habitat.

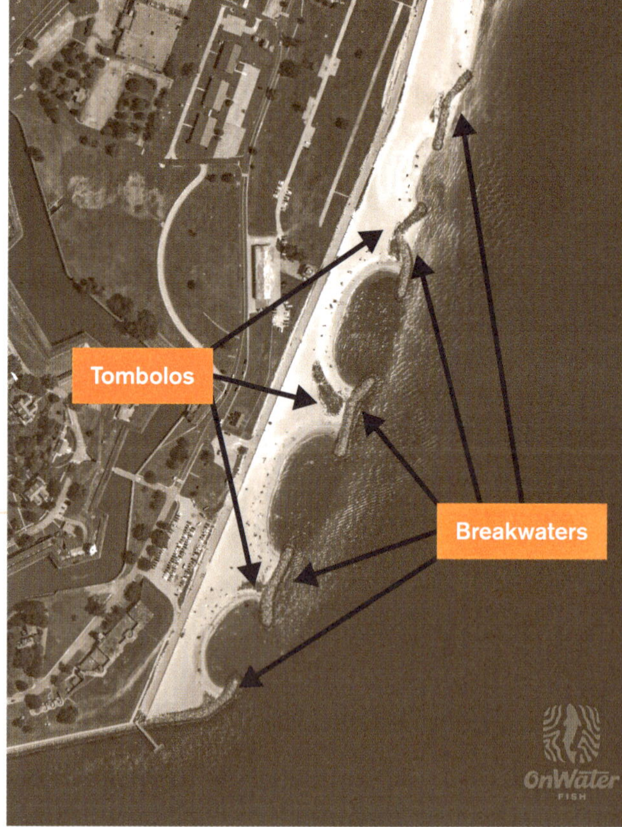

Occasionally, sediment accumulation might lead to the formation of a tombolo, which is a shallow landform that reaches out from the shoreline and connects with the breakwater. In such cases, you might be able to wade out on the tombolo, getting closer to the breakwater and more fishing opportunities near the structure. Satellite image provided by OnWater Fish

Casting streamers proves fruitful for actively scouting the water, attracting a variety of freshwater and saltwater species such as stripers, flounder, or smallmouth bass, especially in murky waters. When sight casting to individual fish, using a "bottom-dwelling" fly pattern can be highly effective. This approach is particularly useful for targeting fish that are foraging for food in shallow areas.

Groins

A groin is a shore-connected structure that extends about a 100 feet (30 m) perpendicularly out into the water; they look similar to the directors we discussed in the last chapter. They come in various shapes, such as T or Y heads, zigzags, or straight lines. While they can be made from various materials, you'll typically encounter groins made from rock, timber, or concrete blocks. The purpose of a groin is to dissipate wave energy and slow down the alongshore drift of sediment, which is driven by the longshore current running parallel to the beach. By interrupting this current, groins help trap sand on the updrift side, reducing erosion and widening the beach. However, as sand accumulates on the updrift side of the structure, the beach on the downdrift side begins to retreat. To combat erosion farther down the shoreline, more groins are built, often resulting in a beach lined with these structures.

It's best to observe the currents and waves before making your first cast to see if there are any foam lines or seams of

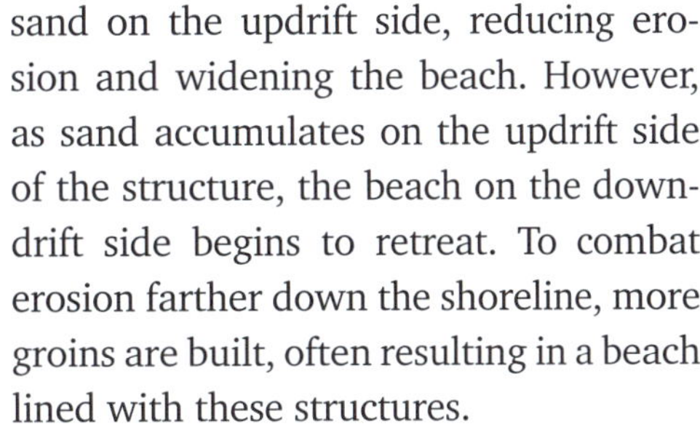

In Boston, Ben Carmichael and I waded in the calm water created by offshore breakwaters (seen in the background). The tide was rising and pushing through the breakwaters, creating lanes of steady current that schoolie striped bass were using to hunt for food. To catch the bass, Ben used an intermediate line to keep a small streamer under the water. He would then cast out as far as possible, tuck the fly rod under his arm, and, using both hands, steadily retrieve the streamer back to him (called a roly-poly retrieve). The bass would chase and pursue the fly, occasionally nipping at it, and eventually chomping down.

You might come across a beach that has groins built up and down the shoreline, providing a day's worth of fishing spots to explore. Photograph by Luke Gibson

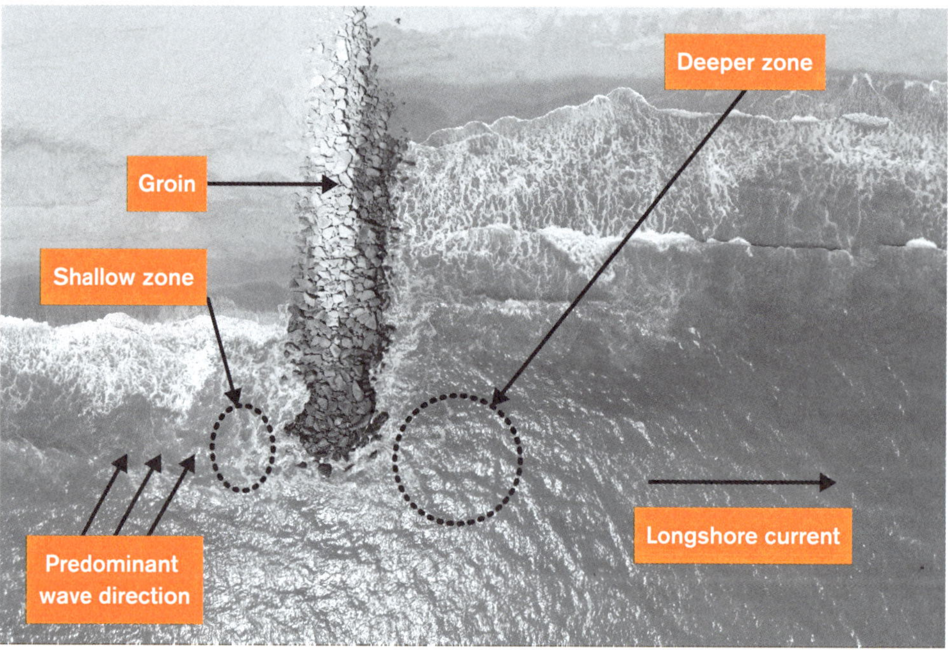

When waves are kicking up on an ocean or lake, one side of the groin may have a sheltered area while the other side takes most of the brute force of the waves. The sheltered area of the groin can be a calm refuge for fish, and if the groin is constructed out of rock, it acts as a reef for crustaceans and smaller fish. Predatory fish can be found hunting around groins, either waiting near the end of the groin for fish trying to swim around it or moving along the edges to intercept fish that try to flee back to the rocks. On the updrift side, the predominant wave direction pins smaller fish and crustaceans close to the structure, which gives predatory fish multiple chances to nab an easier meal. Photograph by Luke Gibson

water that are signs of food being concentrated. While standing on the beach, cast streamers near where the structure connects with the land both on the updrift and downdrift sides, since food such as crabs and small fish can get pushed near the shoreline. Then, if possible and permitted, walk onto the structure while making casts out and away from it and quickly retrieve the streamer back to you. The end of the groin can also be a good spot to make a series of casts in all directions (called fan casting).

SAFETY TIP

Walking onto Groins

There are safety concerns with groins. If walking onto a groin is permitted, the rocks can be very slippery, so having a sturdy pair of boots with studs or slip-on cleats (like Yaktrax) will provide better footing. Take your time and move slowly in order to avoid twisting an ankle. Also, if you are fishing atop the groin, pay particular attention to the tides and current as conditions can quickly change, potentially creating hazardous situations where waves can topple you over or push you into the structure. These structures are built in high-energy areas, so if the waves are too strong, it's best to stay on the shore and fish around the structure.

Jetties

Jetties look very similar to groins, but they serve a distinctly different purpose. Jetties are built usually at the mouths of harbors, bays, and deltas in order to confine the flow of water, which deepens a channel for ship traffic. Like groins, they are generally built with rock and concrete; but unlike groins, they extend significantly farther out into the water, are much wider, and are usually built in pairs. A single jetty will also take much longer to fully cover than a single groin.

Many of the same fishing tactics used around a groin can be employed on a jetty. However, the water within the navigation channel will be deep and fish may be deeper down in the water column waiting to ambush their prey. In this situation, a full sinking line will help to get your streamer down to depth as you retrieve the fly back toward the jetty; the shooting taper line discussed with the "Heavy Hitter" setup in chapter 1 is a great sinking line to use along a jetty.

Carl Crawford pointed out to me that a good approach to fishing a jetty or a series of groins is to move atop the structures with the incoming or outgoing tides. For example, you can start at the end of the structure and, as the tide starts to come in, you can slowly move back toward land, following the rising water; or do the reverse with a falling tide. The tides

It can be difficult to move and fish along a jetty on a crowded day, but you might find a time when you have the place to yourself. Note that the same safety concerns with groins apply to jetties, and they can be especially dangerous in higher tides and storms. Photograph by Luke Gibson

will create currents that form seams where faster water meets slower water. It is often turbulent right along these seams, and small fish, crustaceans, and other food sources will be tossed around, becoming disoriented, and predatory fish will be waiting close by.

Fish will travel around the structures hunting for food, but if you are not getting any bites, it might be best to pick up and continue moving down the beach since the fish could be in different zones of the surf. Groins and jetties are good spots to start or end a day, but don't burn yourself out if the fish aren't there.

Lastly, groins and jetties can be effective places to drift flies (either nymphs or streamers) under an indicator rig, especially if you are fishing on a lake for freshwater species. You can use the waves, current, and wind to your advantage by making a short cast and allowing the current to take your flies away from the structure, which gives you a very prolonged drift. At the end of the drift, slowly retrieve your fly back to you while making sure to pause every few moments to entice any following fish to bite.

Lindsay Mlynarek uses a two-handed switch rod paired with a sinking line and a streamer to target drop-off areas along a jetty. She's also using a stripping basket to help keep the fly line from falling and getting snagged into the crevices between the large blocks on the jetty.

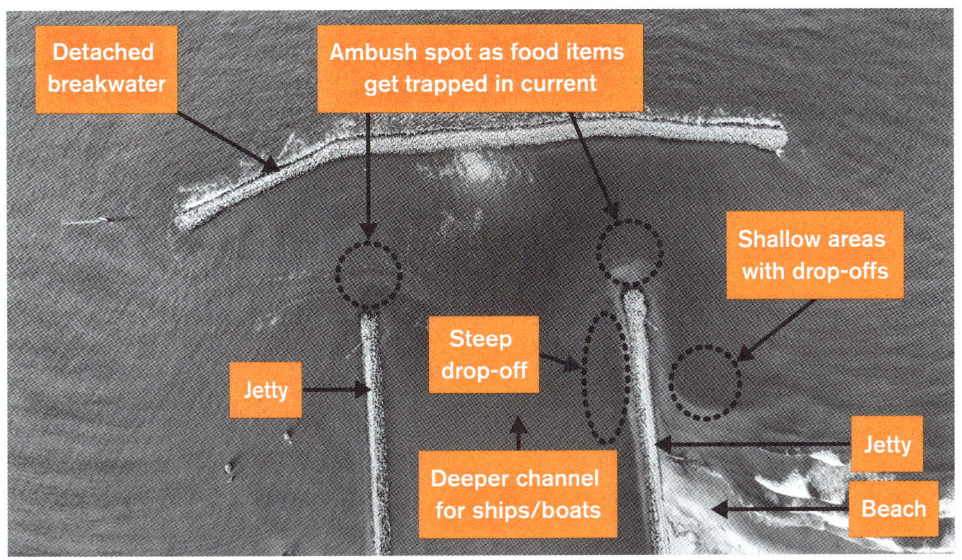

Here is an aerial view looking straight down onto the two jetties from the previous photograph. These jetties, in tandem with the detached breakwater, are used to create a deeper channel of water for ships and boats to navigate in and out of a nearby marina. Photograph by Luke Gibson

These two photos illustrate how rapidly conditions can change in urban waters. The photo on the left shows a section of river where we fished one day; within twenty-four hours, a rainstorm swelled the river with urban runoff. While similar changes can happen in nonurban settings, the frequency and intensity of these water-level fluctuations are a defining feature of urban waterways.

CHAPTER 10

Changing Conditions of Urban Waters

Urban waters are always in flux, even if the concrete shorelines and riverbanks make them seem permanent and unchanging. Water levels, flow alterations, and water quality can shift not just with the seasons, but from week to week, day to day, or even hour to hour—and the fish respond to these shifts as they occur. As urban anglers, staying aware of these changing conditions and adapting our approach is essential. That means observing the present conditions rather than relying solely on past experiences or expectations. In urban environments, where change is constant and sometimes unpredictable, flexibility and curiosity are often more important than worrying about the "right" fly to use.

Seasonal Changes

The best time of year to go fishing depends on many factors, especially regional climate and what species of fish you are looking for. Fish behavior undergoes significant changes in response to shifts in the seasons. For example, as summer transitions into fall, some fish species migrate in search of shallow water and suitable spawning grounds, while others experience a slowdown in metabolism and gravitate toward slower, deeper waters to conserve energy. Generally speaking, if you live in the northern half of the United States, or in Canada, fish activity is highest from spring through fall, when most species are feeding frequently. In contrast, in the southern half of the United States—especially in the Gulf states, southern California, and warmer cities like Phoenix—fish tend to stay active throughout the year due to consistently milder winters.

Beyond those general guidelines, human-induced climate change is disrupting the seasonal cues that fish depend on, and this challenge is further intensified in urban environments, where pollution and water control infrastructure can disorient fish behavior. These factors make it more challenging to predict seasonal fish habits in urban areas.

A useful way to understand the seasonal patterns of fish in your city is to spend time on the water, fishing and observing. Keeping an eye on

In downtown Spokane, Washington, Ethan Crawford gets his first glimpse of the redband trout he is hooked into.

water temperatures while fishing also provides valuable insights, helping you identify which species are active at different times of the year and where they tend to concentrate within the urban waterscape. (Refer back to chapter 7 for information on species activity patterns and how they correspond to different water temperatures.) Sharing observations and insights with other local anglers makes this process easier, offering a deeper understanding of how fish respond to a city's unique conditions.

There are very dedicated anglers out on their local waters year-round, decoding how the behaviors of fish change throughout the seasons and when they are most active. My good friend Ethan Crawford is one of the fishiest people I know. He has fished the Spokane River through all sorts of weather, day in and day out. Ethan has learned the behaviors of the native redband trout in the river, and even when the fishing season is closed, he still ventures down to the river to watch the trout, note the insects they are eating, and observe where along the river he finds the fish. On a few occasions, Ethan has even motivated me to walk down to the water in the dead of winter to drift nymphs under indicators (holding hand warmers to fend off the numbing cold) and catch maybe one really good urban trout.

Beyond seasonal changes, conditions in urban waters often fluctuate on a weekly, daily, or even hourly basis. As urban anglers, we want to be prepared for this. Today, your favorite urban waterway might be shallow and clear, ideal for sight casting flies to fish. Tomorrow, it could be swift, deep, and discolored, requiring you to drift nymphs under an indicator or use jig streamers to search for fish holding tight to the banks. Conditions and habitats can also vary significantly along sections of waterways and shorelines. In one area, you might find plenty of fish to target, while just a short distance away, another spot along the same waterway or shoreline could be entirely devoid of fish. For the remainder of this chapter, we'll explore what drives these changes in urban waters and how you can learn to read them and adjust your approach to fish more effectively.

"Hoses" and "Straws"

One of the more influential factors shaping water conditions in cities is the way people add to or withdraw from waterways, lakes, ponds, and coastal shorelines. Water moved through pipes, pumps, tunnels, and smaller waterways might be returned to the same body of water or sent miles away to a completely different one. These additions and removals can be thought of as "hoses" and "straws" that directly affect conditions for fish and aquatic habitats.

"HOSES"

When you look out across an urban waterway, pond, lake, or ocean shoreline, you'll notice small ditches, canals, and pipes that spill out water on some days and run dry on others. These are "hoses" that transport water from somewhere else to be discharged into a body of water. If you are curious about where the water is coming from, you can use satellite imagery on a mapping app to trace the "hose" back to its source. You might find it leads to a municipal wastewater treatment plant, industrial plant, pond, or small dam, or it might simply disappear under the concrete landscape. If you are particularly curious about the origins of the water and its contents beyond the scope of this book, you can refer to the EPA's Enforcement and Compliance History Online (ECHO) website (echo.epa.gov). States and cities might also offer their own environmental compliance databases similar to the federal EPA's ECHO tool, so it's worth a quick search to see what might be available in your city and state. For example, the Washington State Department of Ecology's Environmental Information Management (EIM) system contains monitoring data collected by state scientists and partners, covering air, water, soil, sediment, and more. Anglers can search, view, and download data relevant to any point-sources discharging effluent into local waters. (Refer back to the end of chapter 6 for information on point-source discharges as well as tips for using the ECHO tool.)

The more detective work you do, the more you will discover clues as to why fishing is either productive or nonexistent around a certain "hose." For example, in Denver, fishing around the confluence of Clear Creek and the South Platte River can be slow. This is due to the highly acidic waters of Clear Creek, which are caused by mine waste piles way up in the mountains. Anglers in the area have even confirmed this by testing the waters with simple and inexpensive pH test strips. In urban waters, if a particular fishing spot is always unproductive, there's a reason for that.

There are plenty of examples of "hoses" in urban waters to investigate, but let's take a closer look at the most ubiquitous one: municipal wastewater treatment plants.

MUNICIPAL WASTEWATER TREATMENT PLANTS

No other piece of infrastructure epitomizes urban fishing more than the municipal wastewater treatment plant (WWTP). Something about it calls out to urban anglers. Maybe it's the effluent cascading down an outfall, the faint scent of chlorine in the air, or the hum of air compressors pumping oxygen into treatment tanks. Whatever it is, it will get any urban angler jazzed to cast out and see what's beneath the surface!

To catch this carp, Nate McCord patiently watched as it fed beneath a thick layer of foam near a wastewater treatment plant outfall. The foam would occasionally obscure his view, causing him to lose sight of the fish. When a break in the foam appeared, he made his cast and kept a tight line to feel the moment the carp took the fly.

Talk to any veteran urban angler, and they'll share their excitement about fishing near a municipal WWTP and the unique aquatic habitat it creates. When you see fish feeding beneath the foamy surface, you know it's going to be a great day! Needless to say, you could write a whole book about fishing around municipal WWTPs, and all of the ways people catch fish around them. Of course, given the popularity of these spots, be prepared to share the frothy water with others.

Located along freshwater and saltwater bodies, these plants influence a wide range of environments. First, the water discharged from a municipal WWTP can at times be cleaner than the receiving body of water, though I still wouldn't go licking any monofilament to tighten my knots. Municipal WWTPs operate year-round, providing consistent fishing spots even in late summer when flows are low or dried up in other areas. You might also smell chlorine, used in the final steps to remove harmful organisms from the water before discharge. While chlorinated water is harmful to aquatic life, today's municipal WWTPs often include dechlorination methods before releasing the treated water.

The temperature of the water discharged from a municipal WWTP can differ from the receiving body of water. In winter, the effluent can warm smaller waterways dramatically, potentially disrupting fish spawning and metabolism. Additionally, WWTP effluent might have lower dissolved oxygen levels, causing fish to avoid these areas during warmer months. However, this "oxygen sag" often recovers further downstream, where fishing improves again.

Since municipal wastewater treatment plants are ubiquitous and provide better fishing opportunities in urban areas, below are a few insights and tricks to fishing around them.

Visit Your Municipal WWTP: I know this might seem ridiculous, but I know many urban anglers, myself included, who have benefited from visiting their municipal WWTP, especially in terms of learning about your specific WWTP and its water quality. You might even meet some very experienced anglers working there. Tyler Winter, an angler and board member for Native Fish for Tomorrow, is also a water quality scientist for a municipal WWTP in the Twin Cities area. Professionals like Tyler can give you the exact details you're looking for.

Locate Municipal WWTPs Along Waterways and Lakes: The best fishing spots are near municipal WWTPs located next to urban waterways and lakes or impoundments. Ocean shoreline municipal WWTP outfalls often extend well offshore through pipes and diffusers, beyond the range of the shore-bound angler.

Use a Floating Fly Line: Depending on your city and region, various fish species may congregate around municipal WWTP outfalls. You might find bottom feeders, fish swimming steadily in the current, and fish pushing their faces up through the foam feeding on the surface. A floating fly line allows you to cast streamers, bottom-dwelling flies, nymphs, poppers, sliders, and more to target all of these fish.

Try a Sinking Fly Line: The area around a municipal WWTP outfall will often have ledges, drop-offs, swirling currents, and thick, foamy water. An intermediate full-sinking line or sink-tip line helps you to punch a streamer through turbulent water to deeper areas where larger fish wait.

One other interesting tip is that chironomids (non-biting midges that look similar to mosquitos) are commonly found in municipal WWTPs due to their tolerance of low dissolved oxygen, which allows them to survive in the nutrient-rich, oxygen-poor upper sludge layers of wastewater ponds. In fact, in some WWTPs, chironomids are a valuable component of wastewater pond ecology, helping to break down organic matter and cycle nutrients. Municipal WWTPs can produce large swarms of mating chironomids that fly over and land on nearby bodies of water, creating a feeding frenzy among the fish. To be prepared for such a situation, have a couple smaller dry flies in your box, like a Parachute Adams (mentioned in chapter 1), to tie on and cast out to any fish rising to the surface.

"STRAWS"

In addition to the many "hoses" adding water to ponds, waterways, lakes, and ocean shorelines, there are "straws" removing water. When we turn on the faucet or the showerhead, that water is coming from somewhere. The same is true for when water is used for watering lawns, fighting fires, filling pools, manufacturing, creating hot water to sterilize surgical equipment, and providing climate control for massive indoor football stadiums and AI data centers.

Water can be siphoned from one body of water and transported into and throughout cities through canals, ditches, and pipes. In the Phoenix area, for example, a network of 131 miles (211 km) of canals drains the Salt River and routes the water through the urban landscape, providing the city's water supply. A local utilities company stocks several thousand grass carp (white amur) into the canals each year to control aquatic plants and algae, and grates are in place to prevent the grass carp from escaping. There are an estimated forty-four thousand carp in the canals, which provides ample fishing opportunities throughout the neighborhoods.

In coastal cities like San Diego, water also flows into the urban system directly from the ocean. The Claude "Bud" Lewis Carlsbad Desalination Plant, one of the largest in the United States, converts seawater into drinking water that supplies 10 percent of San Diego County's water supply. Once used, that desalinated water becomes part of the larger urban water cycle, running through homes, businesses, and treatment systems before being discharged, reused, or recirculated. And like many desalination facilities, these plants discharge hypersaline brine (saltier than seawater) into nearby coastal waters. If not properly diluted, dense, salt-laden outflows can sink, resist mixing, and create "dead spots" where marine life struggles.

One more example of "straws" are pumps that draw up clean water from aquifers and groundwater. Groundwater is integral to the health of urban waters by recharging them with cool, clean water, which is especially important for waterways during hotter, drier months to support aquatic habitats and fish. However, when humans excessively pump up groundwater, it has far-reaching negative impacts, including reducing freshwater flows to estuaries, inhibiting fishery production along the coast, and lowering water tables, which leads to saltwater intrusion and the contamination of drinking water. Without proper water conservation, cities can over-extract aquifers and groundwater beyond their recharge rates, leading to permanently depleting these vital sources of clean water.

One place where you can see groundwater in action is on the Los Angeles River. For much of its length, the river has a concrete bottom, but the section that Analiza del Rosario took me to has a soft bottom, which allows groundwater to trickle up and provide year-round freshwater to the river. This influx of groundwater helps to cultivate trees and vegetation, forming a much better habitat for carp, bass, and catfish.

All of these "hoses" and "straws" cause frequent fluctuations in urban waters. However, there are other factors, such as impervious surfaces and water control infrastructure, that cause conditions in urban waters to drastically change. These shifting conditions, sometimes occurring within hours, require urban anglers to adapt their fishing strategies accordingly, but anticipating these changes is difficult without additional resources and knowledge. Fortunately, there is a free and invaluable resource available to all of us that not only enhances our success but also helps prioritize personal safety when fishing in urban waterways.

Streamgages

Streamgages are monitors that collect critical data about water conditions, and they are installed in waterways nationwide by the United States Geological Survey (USGS). Anglers in cities across the country rely on streamgages to navigate and fish their urban waterways effectively. These gages offer valuable insights, helping to explain why conditions in urban waterways fluctuate. By monitoring these changes, we can anticipate their effects on fishing opportunities and personal safety.

HOW TO USE USGS STREAMGAGES

1. **Access the Dashboard:** Streamgages are a free online resource that you can access at www.dashboard.waterdata.usgs.gov/app/nwd/en. This URL will take you to the National Water Dashboard, which is a map of the United States covered in colorful dots.
2. **Select Streamflow Data:** Click on "Layers" in the top-right corner, select "USGS Stations," and choose "Streamflow," followed by the "Status" drop-down menu. This narrows the focus to data for specific types of waterways: "High flow," "Low flow," "Not flowing," and "Streamflow." You can also turn off other layers if they are showing up on the map, such as the weather radar. Turning off the radar reduces clutter on the screen, helping you to search the map more easily; you can turn it back on as you become familiar with the interface.

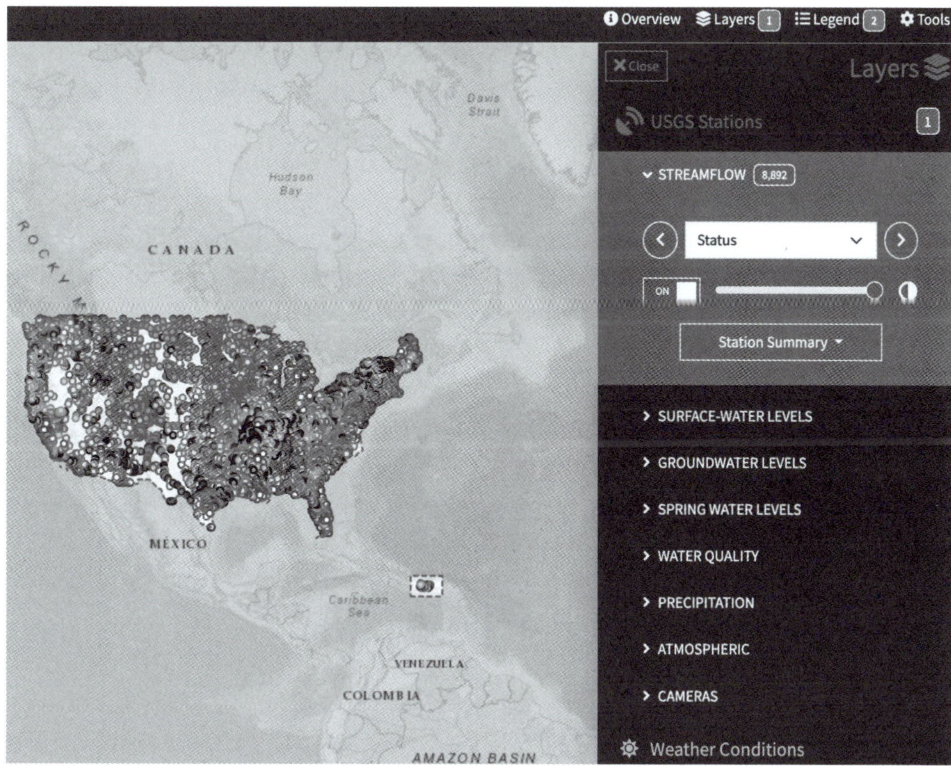

Source: USGS.gov

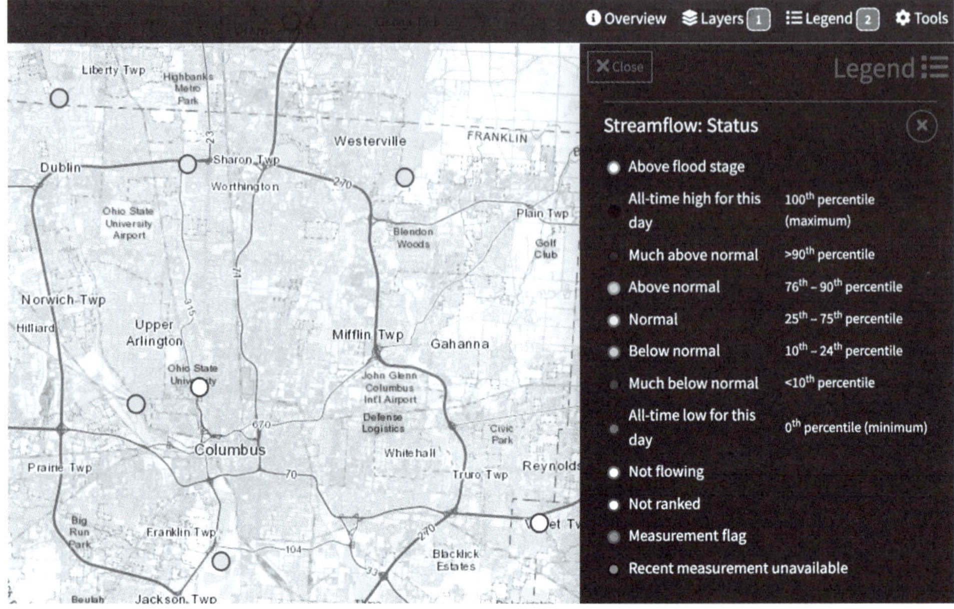

Source: USGS.gov

3. **Zoom to Your City:** Type in your city and state in the top-left corner search bar. Opening up the "Legend" will provide a color-coded key showing what each colored dot means in terms of flow and flood status.
4. **Find a Streamgage:** Click on one of the dots in your city. This will open a new page with a graph. Next, click "Site page" in the top-right corner, which will open up another page that will deliver the detailed data. If you're using your phone, when you click on a streamgage dot, select "Site page" in the pop-up menu.
5. **Select the Data to Display:** Scroll down below the graph to the section labeled "Daily data" and click "Show these data types." Click "Graph it" next to "Discharge, cubic feet per second." Once it says "Graphed" scroll back up to the graph.

The free version of the onWater Fish app also provides the USGS streamgages when you tap on a waterway on the map in the application. This is very handy for when you are out on the water.

UNDERSTANDING THE DATA

Now that you have a graph of a streamgage pulled up, let's consider what it's telling you. First, you are looking at a graph that is displaying the streamflow, or *discharge*, for a section of a waterway in your city.

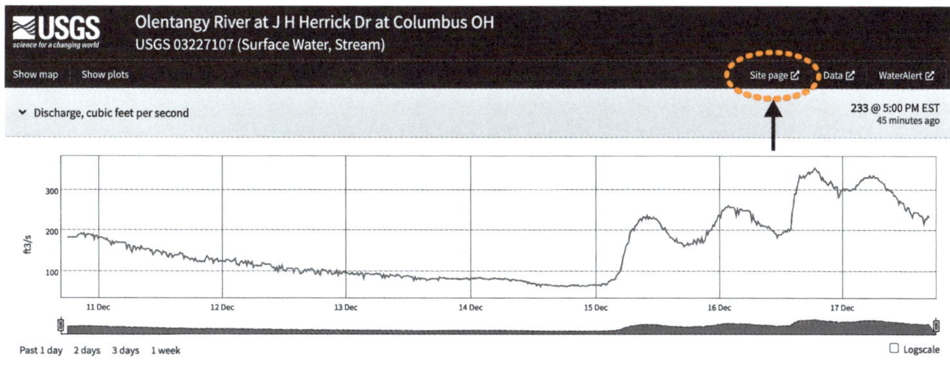

Source: USGS.gov

	Data type	Data date range
Graph it	Gage height, feet [Stage, Radar]	2015-01-07 - 2025-02-23
Graph it	Gage height, feet DS bubbler, [Stage, pressure transducer]	2020-11-24 - 2025-02-23
Graphed	Discharge, cubic feet per second	2015-01-14 - 2025-02-23

Source: USGS.gov

Discharge is the volume of water moving past a specific point in a waterway per unit of time.

Discharge = Area × Velocity

Discharge is commonly expressed in cubic feet per second (cfs). For example, you might hear an angler say, “The river is flowing at 380 cfs today.” What they are referring to is the volume of water passing a specific point in that river each second—essentially, the river’s discharge. While discharge does not provide you with specific information for the speed or depth of a waterway, it tells you how much water is flowing through it, giving you an overall picture of water conditions for that section of the waterway. So, what does that mean? And how do these discharge graphs specifically help urban anglers?

APPLYING THE DATA TO A REAL-WORLD SCENARIO

Knowing the discharge of a waterway is only useful with additional knowledge of that waterway. Let’s look at a specific streamgage to explain what I mean by this. The graph on page 204 displays the discharge for the Olentangy River in Columbus, Ohio, for the week of July 12 to July 19, 2024. Looking at the graph, on July 19, the flow was around 68 cfs. That measurement means next to nothing without additional knowledge of that river. So, what additional knowledge do you need? Well, it's as simple as going over and looking at the water.

When I lived in Columbus, I fished the Olentangy a lot. However, before I left my apartment, I would check the streamgage on my computer or phone. Then I would walk over to the river and note the conditions of the water. Within a handful of trips to the river, I started to build a picture of what that section of the Olentangy looked like at different discharge amounts.

When the Olentangy River was at 200 cfs or lower, I learned that the water would be low and clearer, great for wading and sight fishing for carp and suckers. However, if the Olentangy was discharging between 200 to 500 cfs, then I knew the river was much higher, faster, and, usually, a bit off-color. At these higher discharge amounts, instead of wading farther out into the water and sight fishing, I would stay close to the riverbank and jig streamers around bridges and other structures where fish could be seeking

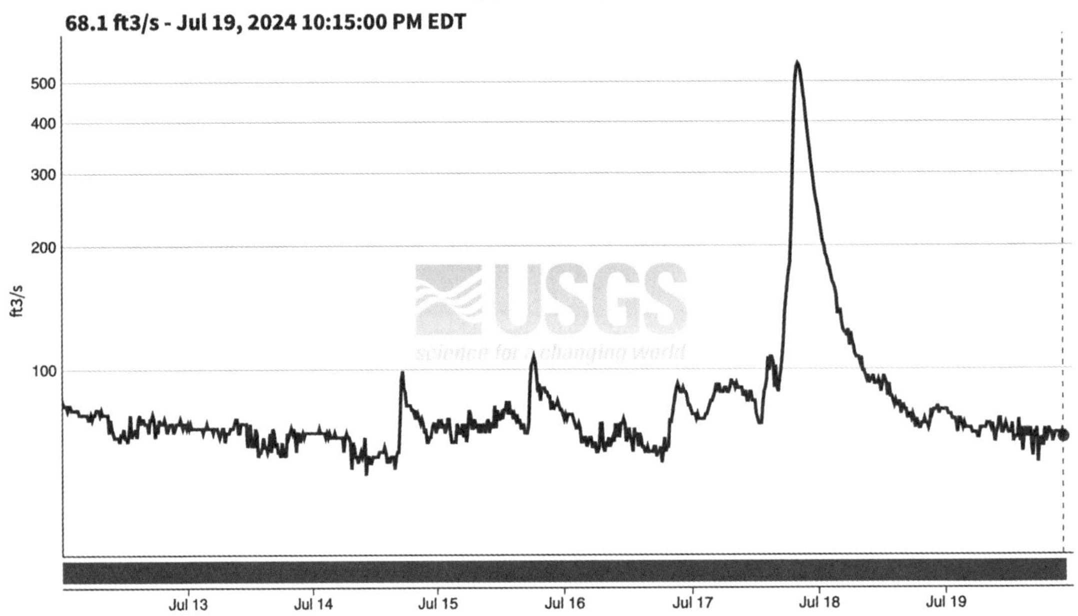

The graph above displays discharge data for the Olentangy River from July 12 to July 19, 2024. With these graphs (after you click "Site page" on the desktop version), you can change the time frame to display the previous week, month, or year. Below the graph you can also click "Change time span" to put in a custom date range, which is useful if you want to see what the discharge was for that waterway at some date in the past. Source: USGS.gov

protection from the increased flow in the river. If the river was discharging anything above 500 cfs, then I knew that section of the Olentangy was blown out and I would go back to the USGS map and check streamgages at different locations in the city or head to a favorite pond.

So, looking at the graph for the Olentangy River, we can see that conditions on that section of the river for that week would mostly be great for wading in the river and sight fishing for carp and suckers. However, on July 18, the river spiked up to 500 cfs. If I had checked the streamgage before heading out that evening, the spike on the graph would have alerted me that too much water was flowing through the river to go wading or use tactics like sight fishing. Armed with this knowledge, I would adjust my strategy before even leaving my apartment, packing heavier fly patterns like jig streamers to target fish that were likely pushed closer to structures offering calmer water during the increased flow.

When I first moved to Columbus, Ohio, I had no prior knowledge of how to fish the Olentangy River under different discharge amounts. By using local USGS streamgages to monitor the waterway and observing conditions firsthand, I was able to significantly shorten my learning curve. Simply pulling up the streamgage data at home allowed me to identify the best times for fly-fishing techniques like sight fishing for carp in shallow water.

USING STREAMGAGES IN YOUR CITY

When using a streamgage to check the discharge of a waterway, it's important to visit the waterway in person to observe the actual conditions. Ideally, it would be best to get as close as possible to the physical location of the streamgage monitor, which is what's displayed on the National Water Dashboard map. For example, the streamgage shown in the Olentangy River graph collects data near the John H. Herrick Drive bridge in Columbus, Ohio. So, I would go to that bridge—or near it, like the King Avenue bridge, which was close to where I lived—to compare what the graph was telling me to what I actually saw.

For your city, maybe you pull up a discharge graph for a particular local waterway and it is reading at 500 cfs. You then look at that waterway and see that it's pretty low and clear at 500 cfs. Or, on the other hand, you pull up another streamgage for a different waterway, and the discharge currently reads just 40 cfs. But when you go and look at this other waterway, 40 cfs means there's too much water flowing in it for wading.

The more often you compare the discharge graph to what you actually see for that section of waterway, the more you'll build a mental picture of what it looks like at different discharge amounts. This is also easy to practice as you travel around your city. When you're near a waterway, pull up the map and see if there's a nearby streamgage and then read the discharge graph. (Some streamgage webpages also have webcams that show a real-time look at the waterway.)

Once you build up that mental picture, you can then pull up these graphs at home and have an immediate idea of what the conditions are on that waterway. If you and some friends are interested in fishing a certain section of it, check the discharge for that section to give you a heads-up on what fishing gear and tackle you might need. Using these discharge graphs will help you to predict fishing opportunities and adjust your strategies based on current conditions—while saving you a lot of time.

A particularly long waterway in your city might have multiple streamgage monitors distributed throughout the city when there are numerous dams or converging waterways. In Denver, Nic Hall, Nate McCord, and Rick Mikesell would pull up these graphs on their phones and check conditions at different spots along the South Platte River. If the discharge was too high or low at one spot didn't necessarily mean the entire urban river was the same. Checking other streamgages on the South Platte River would help decide on what spot to fish next. Remember, urban areas are an overlapping mosaic of various factors that impact waterway conditions. Downstream from any streamgage, you may encounter dams, municipal WWTPs, converging waterways, canals siphoning off water, or other features that influence the volume of water flowing through the waterway. Spikes in the streamgage graph result from rainstorms and other factors, such as a dam releasing additional water. To better understand these fluctuations, use a mapping application to examine what might be upstream of the streamgage that's contributing to changes in discharge.

If there isn't a streamgage monitor on the urban waterway you are interested in fishing, you can still check any nearby waterways that do have gages. This is the case for most small urban waterways. Streamgages are expensive, and so they won't be installed on all the streams, creeks, and ditches across the city. However, checking the map for nearby similar waterways that do have gages might offer helpful insights.

ADDITIONAL FEATURES

On the National Water Dashboard, there are many other features to explore. For instance, in your city there might also be "super gages" that continuously monitor water quality, such as the temperature of the water, and dissolved oxygen and pH levels. To find these gages on the National Water Dashboard, click the "Layers" tab, then click "USGS Stations," and then add the "Water Quality" layer to the map. You can apply this additional data to build even better fishing strategies for your urban waters. For example, let's say there is a super gage on a waterway in your city that is telling you the water temperature is 70°F (21°C). Let's also say there are bass and carp in that waterway. At 70°F, you can anticipate that they will be in a feeding mood since that water temperature gets their metabolism going, which automatically increases your chances of catching them. Then, on a different day, you go back and check that gage and it now reads 60°F (16°C). At that colder temperature, those bass and carp will be more sluggish, meaning you will have to work a bit harder and adapt your fishing techniques to get them to take a fly or lure.

If your city has few or no USGS super gages, check to see if any local community-based organizations have installed their own monitoring equipment. In Spokane, Washington, for instance, the Spokane Riverkeeper has placed sensors along local waterways to track water temperature, and the data is freely available to the public.

The more familiar you become with the streamgages in your city, the more you'll notice how frequently conditions on urban waterways can fluctuate dramatically, sometimes within a few hours. A nearby waterway might shift from shallow and calm one day to a raging torrent the next, only to quickly return to shallow conditions before surging again. These rapid and extreme changes create challenging conditions for fish trying to survive in urban environments and pose serious hazards for those fishing or engaging in other recreational activities on urban waterways. But here's the really important question: Why do these extreme fluctuations occur so frequently in urban waterways? To understand why, we need to revisit some key topics we've already discussed and explore how streamgages help reveal their impacts.

Water Level Fluctuations in Nonurban Waterways

In chapter 6, we explored how impervious surfaces, such as roads, parking lots, and rooftops, contribute to pollution in urban waters. However, the impacts of impervious surfaces, along with water control infrastructure, extend beyond pollution. They significantly alter the flow patterns and characteristics of waterways and at times create dangerous situations for anyone recreating in them. To better understand these impacts, let's again take a brief look at waterways in nonurban landscapes.

Nonurban landscapes often feature waterways surrounded by ample soil and vegetation that can absorb and filter water from rainfall and snowmelt. This landscape acts like a giant sponge, soaking up water and gradually releasing it into nearby waterways and groundwater over days and weeks. This area of land that drains into the waterway is called the *drainage basin* or *watershed*. A crucial component in this process is the *riparian zone*, an area of soil and vegetation immediately along the edges of streams and rivers.

While seasonal flooding occurs in nonurban waterways, such as in late spring when snowpack melts or during large rainstorms, the surrounding spongy landscape helps mitigate catastrophic flooding. Nonurban waterways also benefit from higher baseflows, meaning water levels remain higher during dry periods because the surrounding landscape slowly releases stored water.

REAL-WORLD EXAMPLE: UPPER COLDWATER RIVER, MISSISSIPPI

A real-world example of the characteristics of nonurban waterways is the upper Coldwater River just southeast of Memphis. Its drainage basin consists primarily of a nonurban landscape with largely intact riparian zones. Additionally, the upper Coldwater River has not been significantly altered by channel modifications such as dams, levees, or other methods that would restrict its dynamic flow. If you want to see the section of river I am talking about, search for "Byhalia, Mississippi" on any mapping application, and look 4 miles (6 km) north.

Looking at the graph on page 209, a USGS streamgage located where Highway 78 crosses the waterway shows relatively stable flow with some

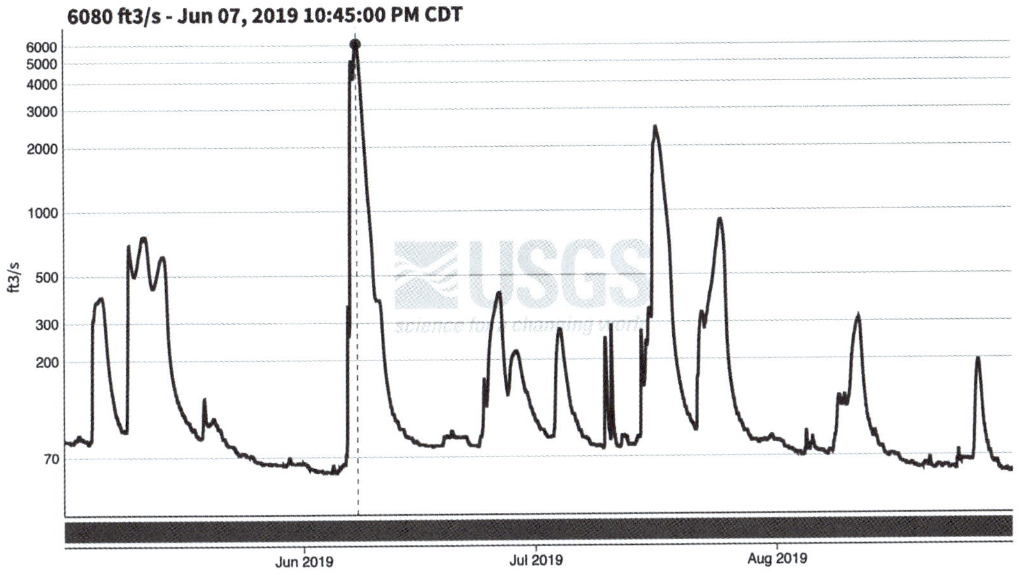

This graph shows streamgage data for the Coldwater River, a winding river with largely intact floodplains and a minimally developed watershed. Each spike in the graph represents a surge of water entering the river from the surrounding landscape due to rain events. After each surge, the river gradually returns to its baseflow of approximately 70 cfs. Source: USGS.gov

high-water events caused by large rainstorms (the spikes on the graph). For instance, a particularly intense rainstorm on June 7, 2019, caused the waterway to peak around 6,100 cfs. However, aside from such events, the surrounding landscape absorbs most other rainfall and gradually releases that runoff into the waterway, providing a baseflow of around 70 cfs.

Water Level Fluctuations in "Flashy" Urban Waterways

In contrast, urban landscapes are covered in impervious surfaces like roads, sidewalks and roofs that act like a waterproof tarp. Rather than absorbing water, this tarp repels it and sends it rushing toward urban waterways. Urban waterways tend to fill quickly, as this volume of water is essentially released all at once instead of over days and weeks. Even small rainstorms can overload an urban waterway multiple times in a single week. In an effort to deal with all this runoff, urban waterways are often engineered as giant pieces of infrastructure to transport floodwaters quickly. Many urban waters are designed to condense runoff into channels and push it through that channel as fast and efficiently as possible. All this runoff is then shoved downstream, potentially causing flooding in another part of the city or neighborhood.

This common characteristic of urban waterways is called *flashiness*. In other words, they rapidly fill with water and then quickly empty, repeating this whiplash of a cycle over and over. Furthermore, because water is gained and lost so quickly in urban waterways, especially smaller ones, they experience more extreme peak flows and much lower baseflows.

REAL-WORLD EXAMPLE: NONCONNAH CREEK, TENNESSEE

We can see a good example of this characteristic "flashiness" of urban waterways in Nonconnah Creek, which flows through Memphis. This waterway is less than 10 miles (16 km) away from the upper Coldwater River and has a similarly sized drainage basin. However, the drainage basin for Nonconnah Creek is almost entirely covered in impervious

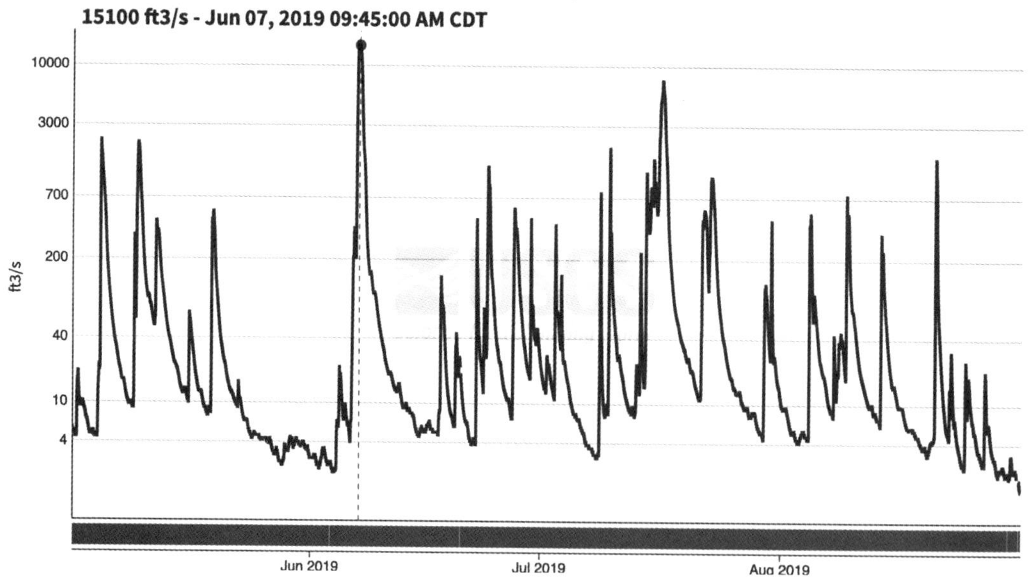

Even relatively small rain events cause water flow in Nonconnah Creek to spike dramatically due to the watershed being covered with impervious surfaces. Because this waterway is designed to rapidly expel runoff, the flow drops just as quickly. Source: USGS.gov

surfaces; the waterway has been extensively channelized, and the remaining riparian zones, where they exist, are exceedingly narrow. (To see this urban waterway on a mapping application, search for "Autumn Ridge, Memphis, Tennessee," and go north for about a mile.)

The graph on page 210 displays a streamgage chart for Nonconnah Creek (during the same timeframe as the upper Coldwater River graph), which shows rapid rises and falls in discharge amounts. Even small rain events cause the waterflow to spike to high levels. We can also see that the intense rain event on June 7 surged the waterflow in Nonconnah to 15,000 cfs, which is almost three times as much as the spike in the nearby upper Coldwater River. Lastly, since all this water is lost rapidly, Nonconnah's baseflow is extremely low, only around 5 cfs, compared to Coldwater River's 70 cfs. That means the water in the Nonconnah is incredibly low during drier periods, reducing available aquatic habitat for fish.

FLASHY URBAN WATERWAYS: IMPACTS ON FISH AND AQUATIC HABITATS

While fish species are adaptable to the occasional flood or high-water event, the sheer frequency of these events in urban areas overwhelms and stresses even the most resilient species. The flashy characteristics of urban waterways significantly impact in-stream habitats for fish and other organisms, leading to the loss of fish populations, aquatic biodiversity, and ecological function. Channelization and repetitive urban runoff degrade water quality, destroy habitats, and cause chaotic fluctuations in water temperature and oxygen levels. These chronic stressors create long-term, persistent challenges for aquatic ecosystems, compromising ecological health over time.

Impervious surfaces and channelization also reduce the water available to be slowly released into waterways during drier seasons. Consequently, urban waterways experience significantly reduced water flow during hotter, drier periods, resulting in lower baseflows. While low baseflows are part of the hydrological cycle of waterways, the persistent low levels common in urban settings stress fish, leading to increased mortality and reduced populations. In extreme cases, waterways that historically flowed year-round may now have sections that dry up entirely, particularly in late summer—and we all know what that means for the fish.

FLASHY URBAN WATERWAYS: RISKS FOR PEOPLE

Angler safety is another concern. For example, you wouldn't want to be near Nonconnah Creek when its water levels are surging, within hours, from 5 cfs to over 15,000 cfs. To avoid such chaotic and dangerous conditions, it is essential for anglers to monitor weather forecasts for any approaching storms and understand how to use USGS streamgages for the waterway we plan to fish.

Rapid fluctuations are a common hazard of many urban waterways across the country. While urban waterways can usually be safely waded and fished most of the time, intense rainstorms cause flooding that may trap the unsuspecting angler in the water. In addition, swift, rising waters can mobilize dangerous debris, such as tree branches, shopping carts, tires, and even heavier objects like cars and refrigerators. After a major storm, take a moment to notice how your favorite fishing spots have transformed; familiar objects may have moved or disappeared and been replaced with new ones.

In Minneapolis, Ryan Birringer and I fished along a small urban creek on a day when the waterflow was perfect for wading. We explored with ease up and down the creek, catching smallmouth bass and carp along the way. At one point, he casted to carp from a bridge that stood a good 11 feet (3 m) above the water. A couple weeks later, after I was back home, Ryan sent a photo of that same bridge completely submerged due to heavy rainstorms. The water level had spiked with runoff, flooding the creek and

surrounding area. Yes, Ryan did fish in the creek once the water level stopped rising. Although the water remained incredibly high, he approached the waterway cautiously, adapting his tactics by using heavy jig streamers near structures to target walleye and smallmouth bass. He even managed to catch a few fish as they swam along a flooded walking path!

Flood hazards also extend well beyond the realm of fishing, posing serious risks and financial burdens for communities and businesses near waterways. Even areas farther away can suffer as stormwater systems become overwhelmed, leading to backups where the water has nowhere to go. Compounding the problem, properties labeled as "beyond the floodplain" by the Federal Emergency Management Agency (FEMA) often lose eligibility for the National Flood Insurance Program, creating a situation that hits low-income communities hardest, leaving them vulnerable to high recovery costs.

Officials sometimes dismiss these as "freak rain events," as was the case after the Memphis flooding on June 7, 2019. Yet, extreme rainfall is on the rise nationwide, driven by human-induced climate warming that increases the atmosphere's capacity to hold water vapor and fuels more

Two weeks later, Ryan sent me this photo, showing that same bridge completely underwater. The two parallel lines are the top parts of the bridge that Ryan is leaning against in the first photo. Photograph courtesy of Ryan Birringer

Ryan Birringer on a bridge in Minneapolis, roughly 11 feet (3 m) above the water, casting to carp.

intense storms. These conditions are also harder to predict as forecasting models often rely on historical data gathered from a relatively stable climate period. This growing unpredictability not only challenges community preparedness and response but also complicates the design and maintenance of urban water infrastructure, revealing the limits of systems built for predictability and exposing how fragile our built environments can be when pushed out of equilibrium.

Traditional Infrastructure Under Pressure

Traditional urban water infrastructure—stormwater systems, flood control, coastal defenses, and water supply networks—is struggling to cope with evolving conditions such as more frequent, intense weather events and shifting watershed characteristics. It's like a ship built for calm seas suddenly being caught in a storm. In response, some cities are deciding to stay the course and invest in more large-scale "gray projects," such as underground storage tanks, stormwater tunnels, bypass channels, and reservoirs.

One example is Indianapolis's DigIndy project, a $2 billion, 28-mile (45 km) tunnel network built 200 feet (61 m) underground. Designed to capture up to five billion gallons of combined stormwater and sewage, it will channel runoff water to a treatment plant before discharging into a local waterway, the White River. While the project represents a significant effort to reduce pollution in Indianapolis's rivers, it encountered problems even before full completion. Planned two decades ago, DigIndy relied on climate models that failed to fully account for the impacts of climate change and the increasing frequency of extreme rain events, limiting its ability to meet today's needs for water quality improvement.

Despite efforts like the DigIndy project, urban waters remain dynamic and unpredictable. The combination of more frequent extreme weather, widespread impervious surfaces, and continued reliance on hard infrastructure has created a harmful feedback loop—one that puts mounting pressure on communities, livelihoods, and ecosystems. These growing challenges are prompting many cities to rethink their approach to managing and redesigning urban water in ways that better reflect today's realities.

The city of Spokane, Washington, implemented a system combining "green" and "gray" infrastructure to capture and treat urban runoff before releasing it into the Spokane River. However, before the system was fully operational, part of the structure collapsed, overwhelmed by an unusual amount of rainfall. While occasional setbacks are inevitable, improving the health of urban waters remains an essential and worthwhile endeavor. This event also underscores the need for an adaptive strategy that builds flexibility into the design and planning process.

Reenvisioning Urban Waters

Many cities are now embracing an adaptive approach to water management by integrating traditional "gray infrastructure" with "green solutions" to create hybrid systems. These strategies blend the efficiency of conventional projects with sustainable elements like permeable pavements, rain gardens, retention ponds, and vegetated roofs that mimic historic watershed functions by capturing, filtering, and gradually releasing runoff.

Many urban ponds, for instance, often serve as retention or detention basins designed to manage runoff.

Other efforts to revitalize urban waters include seawalls engineered with built-in tide pools for marine life, urban stream redesigns that incorporate meanders (riverbends) and riparian buffers, and the adoption of responsible water use practices. Such approaches not only address water management challenges but also enhance water quality and aquatic habitats, while generating job opportunities in design, construction, maintenance, and community outreach. These are great first steps, but what is also needed are bold, large-scale projects that will reimagine and redesign urban waterscapes—and some projects, potentially in your city, are already proposing transformative changes. Yet redesigning urban waterscapes doesn't happen in isolation; it's deeply rooted in the way we build and nurture our cities and communities on a whole.

Large-scale projects intended to redesign urban waters are stalling out due to procedural gridlock, lawsuits, and resistance to change. Many of these waters border long-established, under-resourced communities historically excluded from decision-making. For these efforts to truly succeed, they must prioritize inclusive, transparent, and meaningful engagement with these communities right from the beginning. When revitalization efforts are grounded in the needs and voices of long-marginalized communities—and when decisive action is allowed to proceed without becoming lost in endless delays and procedural gridlock—then transformative change becomes genuinely possible.

Fly fishing itself carries a legacy of elitism and exclusion, and bringing this history into urban spaces is not something I take lightly. I've wrestled with this tension throughout the journey of writing this book. I've witnessed firsthand how fly fishing can unify communities and spark deep connections to local ecosystems—it's powerful and important. Yet I've also experienced the opposite: resistance to newcomers, possessiveness disguised as tradition, and a false sense of intellectual or spiritual superiority.

I originally came to urban waters because I lost my trout streams. But as I waded deeper into these currents—murky, complex, and alive—the reasons why I go fishing evolved. I want bold, transformative changes for urban waters, but not in a way that recreates the same exclusionary culture in new forms. If revitalization simply means guarding waters instead of sharing them, then it's no revitalization at all. There is another way—a way whereby urban waters are ecologically revived and become shared spaces that invite curiosity, inclusivity, and a renewed sense of belonging. That's the change I want to see, and those are the waters I hope to fish in.

CONCLUSION

Making Your Cast

Urban fishing opens up worlds of adventure, but to unlock the full range of exciting possibilities, you'll want to do more than just grab a rod and head to the nearest body of water. As we've seen throughout these pages, city waters contain many unique fish species in both freshwater and saltwater, and there are various techniques you can use to catch them. The urban ecosystem is a maze of concrete, soil, flora, fauna, water control infrastructure, industrial factories, weather events, and floodplains where conditions shift and change on a seasonal, and daily, basis.

We waded through a range of topics, stories, and practical considerations to gain a foothold in the complexity of urban waters. However, as much as we covered, there is no perfect script for urban fishing, and this book is merely a starting point. That might seem daunting, especially if you were hoping for exact instructions on where to stand and when to cast, but the open-endedness is precisely the point: Fishing is less about step-by-step instructions and far more about letting your curiosity lead the way. With each new experience on the water, both your technical know-how and your understanding of urban waters will grow and come into greater focus.

Urban waters are places of discovery and play—vibrant, ever-changing spaces that are far more than pieces of engineering, utilities, or aesthetic choices. Fishing these waters both challenges and surprises you, pulling you into unexpected settings and exciting encounters. Fishing transforms you from a passive spectator into an active participant, awakening your instincts: *Flash!* A fish plucks food from the silt. The hum of powerlines fades as you move in. You feel the fence at your back as you cast. The fly lands, sinks, and settles beside a sunken skateboard. The fish turns, moves toward the fly. You hold your breath. The fish takes. Your arm jolts up, the rod bends down, and life strums out on the other end!

Urban fishing is a reminder that our cities, so often layered with concrete and transmission lines, harbor pockets of vibrant life. For many, it starts with the simple desire to fish close to home. The moment the rod bends over is a visceral encounter showing "nature" does not end where city limits begin.

It's gripping, in-the-moment fun.

With your fishing rod in hand, you engage in a longstanding human experience. On public waters, this shared experience fosters genuine connections that have the potential to grow into communities where people uplift and support one another. In these waters, skilled fishers share advice, strangers from across town swap stories about what the fish are biting on, and anglers continually teach, learn from, and inspire one another. There's no membership fee, no application form, and no central authority deciding who's "in" or "out." Like a vibrant box of lures, flies, and bait, these moments of connection can come together to create and sustain a vital sense of belonging.

Venturing deeper into your local waters strengthens your bond with them. It's about knowing where the water comes from each time you turn

Urban fishing underscores a simple truth: The living, aquatic world persists and regenerates, even at the outfall of a wastewater treatment plant. If we nurture that world, we stand to gain far more than a few photo-worthy catches. We gain healthier fish populations, shorelines that invite neighbors and families to gather, and more resilient cities.

on the tap. It's about noticing runoff as it carries traces of human detritus, realizing it doesn't simply vanish down a storm drain. And after the thrill of a catch, it's about recognizing fish as living beings, as part of a complex ecosystem—not just here for our entertainment.

How we treat our local waters reflects our societal values. When waterscapes are exploited, degraded, or overly restricted, they signal a preference for short-term gains over long-term ecological, economic, and social well-being. Conversely, prioritizing dynamic, living-system solutions demonstrates a commitment to sustaining ecosystems. When industries, land managers, and individuals thoughtfully consider the full journey of a drop of water, both public health and local economies can thrive. And when waters are accessible and managed equitably, the benefits are safeguarded for all.

The fate of our waters is not set in concrete. It can be influenced by everyday people who care enough to show up. Fishing opens up transformative opportunities for those who never saw themselves as stewards or agents of positive change in their own neighborhoods. It provides a tangible way to engage with nearby waters, recognize their value, and feel empowered to protect and make them a thriving part of the community again. Whether it's volunteering at a local clean-up, sharing a fishing story with family and friends, or teaching someone new how to fish, simple yet meaningful acts shape new connections with the communities around us and the world at large.

With all of that in mind, and as we reach the end of our guided trip together, remember that urban fishing offers endless possibilities. *This is your adventure to experience.* If you've made it to the end of this book, you're ready for the challenges and self-discovery of urban fishing. You will eventually pull from the water your own personal reason for fishing in the city—one that might reveal itself when a passerby notices your fishing gear and stops to ask: "How's the fishing?"

Whether we fish frequently or only when time allows, whether our fishing rod is the latest model or a hand-me-down, each cast we make is a small expression of a different vision for our waters.

ACKNOWLEDGMENTS

This book is the culmination of many discussions, phone and video calls, and time spent with anglers, biologists, engineers, stream ecologists, sociologists, water quality scientists, and leaders within conservation and nonprofit groups and the fly-fishing industry. Thank you to everyone who volunteered their time to talk and spend time with me for this unusual project of writing a book about urban fly fishing. I would very much like to thank a few anglers in particular: Dr. Robert (Bob) Bartlett, Ryan Birringer, Emma Brown, Ben Carmichael, Carl Crawford, Dr. Brandon Dale, Nic Hall, Dr. Jennifer Hsia, Lino Jubilado, Nate McCord, Mike Medina, Rick Mikesell, Rick Phetsavong, Analiza del Rosario, and Tyler Winter for the additional time and effort you dedicated to helping me.

I would also like to thank Robert (Rob) Driscoll for giving me my first job as an urban fly-fishing guide, and to my fellow guides, Ethan Crawford, Ethan Fields, and Chad Triplett, for helping me to become a better angler and teacher throughout the seasons. To Tom Rosenbauer, for being a mentor through all your books, videos, and podcasts and for supporting this project from the very beginning. And to my editor, Anna Bliss, for seeing the heart of this unconventional book and skillfully guiding me to shape it into its very best form.

To my family and friends, thank you for indulging countless fishing stories—whether about wastewater treatment plants, sedimentation, channelization, or large-scale suckers. To my parents, you instilled in me a love for both the outdoors and the act of teaching, gifts that continue to shape my life. To my wife, Lindsay—my cased caddis, gathering tiny pebbles while the current shifts around us. When all scatters, you bring me back together. With you, we build our life together. I love you, immensely. And I owe you more homemade pasta dinners than I can count.

FURTHER RESOURCES

Below is a collection of online resources, books, and podcasts covering a broad range of fly-fishing topics to expand your confidence, skill sets, and self-reliance on the water. While these resources primarily focus on fly fishing in nonurban settings for particular species, many of the techniques and strategies presented can be adapted to urban waterscapes and a variety of fish. As you explore these materials, consider how they apply to your local urban waters, and follow your curiosity to tailor these methods to the fish species you enjoy pursuing with a fly rod.

Online Resources

This collection of online resources provides a broad range of educational materials for anglers of all skill levels.

ORVIS FLY FISHING LEARNING CENTER

This is an extensive online learning center with articles, videos, illustrations, and a glossary of fishing terms. It is a great resource for learning everything from the basics of fly fishing to more advanced techniques. The learning center includes such topics as:

- how to cast a fly rod and tie knots
- how to attach fly-fishing leaders to your line
- how to target specific fish species
- how to fish with streamers, attach an indicator on your leader, and set up a two-fly rig
- how to fish in diverse environments, such as small streams and coastal beaches

www.howtoflyfish.orvis.com

MAD RIVER OUTFITTERS

Mad River Outfitters, a fly shop in Columbus, Ohio, has an excellent YouTube channel, covering a multitude of topics. Two valuable video playlists by Mad River Outfitters on YouTube that I recommend are:

- "Fly Casting": a video playlist covering everything from the basics of how to cast a fly rod to more advanced casts like the "double haul"
- "Getting Started in Fly Fishing": a series of videos answering all of your fly-fishing 101 questions

TAKE ME FISHING

The Recreational Boating and Fishing Foundation (RBFF) is a national, nonprofit organization that will help you to learn how to fish (not just fly fish) through an entire website of free educational resources.

www.takemefishing.org

If you're a Spanish-language speaker, visit Vamos A Pescar.

www.takemefishing.org/es

FLY FISH INSTRUCT

Fly Fish Instruct has a library of online workshops and courses, including a free online introductory course to fly fishing. The introductory course is geared toward anyone who is completely new to fly fishing or has minimal experience.

www.flyfishinstruct.com

FLY FISHERS INTERNATIONAL

Fly Fishers International contains a wealth of online education material with videos, articles, manual, and workshops. Many resources are free, but to access everything you will need a membership.

www.flyfishersinternational.org

THE TRIPLE HAUL

This is my personal site with free articles on fly-fishing tactics, techniques, and gear. I highly recommend reading the article, "How to Build Your Own Leaders for Fly Fishing," which is an in-depth article about fly-fishing leaders, including how to build your own and how to set your leader up for indicator, two-fly, and streamer fishing. I also have an article specifically on setting up a dry-dropper rig (a two-fly rig comprised of a floating fly with a sinking fly suspended beneath), "Fly Fishing How To: 3 Ways to Create a Dry-Dropper Rig."

www.thetriplehaul.com

Books

The books listed in this section are designed to improve your fly-fishing techniques and offer a deeper understanding of the waters you fish. These titles cover everything from casting fundamentals to advanced tactics. Several of them explore methods of citizen science (the involvement of the public in scientific research) and ecology (the study of how organisms interact with each other and their environment) that you can use to actively contribute to the health of your local waters.

For a general guide to fly fishing that walks you through everything from casting a fly rod and tying knots to presenting flies to fish and using techniques for various bodies of water, I recommend *The Orvis Fly-fishing Guide*, Revised 2017, by Tom Rosenbauer.

These three books are focused on specific fish species with in-depth tactics and techniques:

- *The Orvis Guide to Fly Fishing for Carp: Tips and Tricks for the Determined Angler* by Kirk Deeter
- *Smallmouth: Modern Fly-fishing Methods, Tactics, and Techniques* by Dave Karczynski and Tim Landwehr
- *Matching Warmwater Baitfish: Patterns and Techniques for Smallmouth and Largemouth Bass, Muskie, and Other Predators* by Kevin Feenstra.

The following books focus on fly fishing in saltwater environments, such as along beaches and estuaries:

- *Lefty Kreh's Fly Fishing in Salt Water, Third Edition*, by Lefty Kreh
- *The Saltwater Edge: Tips and Tactics for Saltwater Fly Fishing* by Nick Curcione
- *Fly Fishing the Surf: A Comprehensive Guide to Surf and Wade Fishing from Maine to Florida* by Angelo Peluso
- *Fly-Fish the Surf* by Lee R. Baermann
- *The Orvis Guide to Fly Fishing for Coastal Gamefish* by Aaron J. Adams

These books are centered on fly fishing for trout (though the methods and tactics can easily be adapted to other species in similar bodies of water in your city):

- *The Orvis Guide to Small Stream Fly Fishing* by Tom Rosenbauer
- *The Orvis Guide to Stillwater Trout Fishing* by Phil Rowley
- *Strip-Set: Fly-fishing Techniques, Tactics, & Patterns for Streamers* by George Daniel
- *Fly Fishing Evolution: Advanced Strategies for Dry Fly, Nymph, and Streamer Fishing* by George Daniel

If you are interested in becoming involved in advocating for your local waters, contributing to citizen science, and learning more about the unique ecology of your city, these recommendations are for you (see also books and studies listed in the bibliography):

- *Field Guide to Freshwater Invertebrates of North America* by James H. Thorp and Christopher Rogers
- *The Field Guide to Citizen Science: How You Can Contribute to Scientific Research and Make a Difference* by Darlene Cavalier, Catherine Hoffman, and Caren Cooper
- *Handbook of Citizen Science in Ecology and Conservation* edited by Christopher A. Lepczyk, Owen D. Boyle, and Timothy L. V. Vargo
- *Braiding Sweetgrass: Indigenous Wisdom, Scientific Knowledge, and the Teachings of Plants* by Robin Wall Kimmerer
- *The Routledge Handbook of Urban Ecology, Second Edition*, edited by Ian Douglas, P M L Anderson, David Goode, Michael C. Houck, David Maddox, Harini Nagendra, and Tan Puay Yok
- *Engineering in Plain Sight* by Grady Hillhouse

Podcasts

These entertaining and educational podcasts offer everything from techniques and gear reviews to advocacy, storytelling, and episodes on urban fly fishing:

- The Orvis Fly Fishing Podcast
- So Fly Fishing
- Anchored with April Vokey
- The Wet Fly Swing Fly Fishing Podcast

BIBLIOGRAPHY

Adams, Catherine M., Dana L. Winkelman, and Ryan M. Fitzpatrick. "Impact of Wastewater Treatment Plant Effluent on the Winter Thermal Regime of Two Urban Colorado South Platte Tributaries." *Frontiers in Environmental Science* 11 (2023): https://doi.org/10.3389/fenvs.2023.1120412.

Alter, Elizabeth S., et al. "Evolutionary Responses of Marine Organisms to Urbanized Seascapes." *Evolutionary Applications* 14, no. 1 (2020): https://doi.org/10.1111/eva.13048.

Anguelovski, Isabelle, et al. "Green Gentrification in European and North American Cities." *Nature Communications* 13, no. 1 (2022): https://doi.org/10.1038/s41467-022-31572-1.

Bascom, Willard, and Kim McCoy. *Waves and Beaches: The Powerful Dynamics of Sea and Coast,* rev. 3rd ed. Patagonia, 2021.

Beach, Dana. *Coastal Sprawl: The Effects of Urban Design on Aquatic Ecosystems in the United States.* Pew Oceans Commission, 2002. www.pewtrusts.org/-/media/legacy/uploadedfiles/wwwpewtrustsorg/reports/protecting_ocean_life/envpewoceanssprawlpdf.pdf.

Behrndt, Rachel. "Panther Island Receives Additional $20 Million; Leaves $98 Million to Fully Fund Project." *Fort Worth Report,* March 3, 2023. fortworthreport.org/2023/03/03/panther-island-receives-additional-20-million-leaves-98-million-to-fully-fund-project/.

Billingham, Eliza. "Persistent Rain Damages Spokane's Award-Winning Stormwater System Before It's Fully Operational." *Inlander,* December 5, 2024. https://www.inlander.com/news/persistent-rain-damages-spokanes-award-winning-stormwater-system-before-its-fully-operational-29027666.

Brown, Larry R., et al., editors. *Effects of Urbanization on Stream Ecosystems.* American Fisheries Society, Symposium 47, 2005.

Bryan, C. Frederick, and D. Allen Rutherford, editors. *Impacts on Warmwater Streams: Guidelines for Evaluation,* 2nd ed. Southern Division, American Fisheries Society, 1995.

Bullard, Robert D. *Dumping in Dixie: Race, Class, and Environmental Quality,* 3rd ed. Westview Press, 2000.

Chapman, Peter M. "Determining When Contamination Is Pollution: Weight of Evidence Determinations for Sediments and Effluents." *Environment International* 33, no. 4 (2007): 492–501. https://doi.org/10.1016/j.envint.2006.09.001.

DeGood, Kevin. "A Call to Action on Combating Nonpoint Source and Stormwater Pollution." Center for American Progress, October 27, 2020. https://www.americanprogress.org/article/call-action-combating-nonpoint-source-stormwater-pollution/.

Dhar, Gopal, et al. "Influence of the Organophosphorus Insecticide Phosphamidon on Lentic Water." *Journal of Environmental Biology* 25, no. 3 (2004): 359–63. pubmed.ncbi.nlm.nih.gov/15847349/.

Douglas, Ian, et al., editors. *The Routledge Handbook of Urban Ecology,* 2nd ed. Routledge, 2021.

Dupke, Susann, et al. "Impact of Climate Change on Waterborne Infections and Intoxications." *Journal of Health Monitoring* 8, no. Suppl 3 (2023): 62–77. https://doi.org/10.25646/11402.

Eades, Richard T., et al., editors. *Urban and Community Fisheries Programs: Development, Management, and Evaluation.* American Fisheries Society, Symposium 67, 2008.

Engle, Carole and Ganesh Kumar. "Ictalurus Punctatus (Channel Catfish)." *CABI Compendium*. February 2023. https://doi.org/10.1079/cabicompendium.79127.

Finney, Carolyn. *Black Faces, White Spaces: Reimagining the Relationship of African Americans to the Great Outdoors.* University of North Carolina Press, 2014.

Fisheries, NOAA. "How Removing Dams Changes River Channels." NOAA, March 24, 2017. www.fisheries.noaa.gov/feature-story/how-removing-dams-changes-river-channels#:~:text=At%20the%20same%20time%2C%20rivers.

Fitzgerald, Des. *The Living City: Why Cities Don't Need to Be Green to Be Great.* Basic Books, 2023.

Gerald E. Galloway, Lewis E. Link Jr., and Gregory B. Baecher, "How Civil Engineers Must Adapt to the New Risks of Flooding." *Civil Engineering Magazine*, July 2024. https://www.asce.org/publications-and-news/civil-engineering-source/civil-engineering-magazine/issues/magazine-issue/article/2024/07/how-civil-engineers-must-adapt-to-the-new-risks-of-flooding.

Gersonius, Berry, Richard Ashley, Assela Pathirana, and Chris Zevenbergen. 2012. "Climate Change Uncertainty: Building Flexibility into Water and Flood Risk Infrastructure." *Climatic Change* 116 (2): 411–23. https://doi.org/10.1007/s10584-012-0494-5.

Gordon, Greg, editor. *Rewilding the Urban Frontier: River Conservation in the Anthropocene.* University of Nebraska Press, 2024.

Hawley, Steven. *Cracked: The Future of Dams in a Hot, Chaotic World*. Patagonia Works, 2023.

Henry, Michael, et al. "Impact of Chemical Fertilizer and Pesticides on Aquatic Microcosms." *Journal of the Pennsylvania Academy of Science* 87, no. 1 (2013): 42–49. https://doi.org/10.5325/jpennacadscie.87.1.0042.

"Home—Trinity Flyfest." *Trinity Flyfest*. December 2023. https://trinityflyfest.com/. Accessed August 6, 2024.

Houghtalen, Robert J., A. Osman Akan, and Ned H. C. Hwang. *Fundamentals of Hydraulic Engineering Systems*, 5th ed. Pearson, 2015.

HR&A. "Panther Island Real Estate Economic Development and Implementation Strategy." *Panther Island*, March 5, 2024. https://pantherisland.com/assets/documents/Panther%2520Island_Real%2520Estate%2520Economic%2520Development%2520and%2520Implementation%2520Strategy_%252003052024-compressed.pdf. Accessed August 6, 2024.

Jackson, Donald C., editor. *The First International Smallmouth Bass Symposium*. Mississippi Agricultural and Forestry Experiment Station, Mississippi State University, 1991.

Joosse, Sofie, et al. "Fishing in the City for Food—a Paradigmatic Case of Sustainability in Urban Blue Space." *NPJ Urban Sustainability* 1, no. 41 (2021). https://doi.org/10.1038/s42949-021-00043-9.

Jordan, Philipp, and Peter Fröhle. "Bridging the Gap between Coastal Engineering and Nature Conservation?" *Journal of Coastal Conservation* 26, no. 4 (February 2022). https://doi.org/10.1007/s11852-021-00848-x.

Katopodis, Christos. "Ecohydraulic Approaches in Aquatic Ecosystems: Integration of Ecological and Hydraulic Aspects of Fish Habitat Connectivity and Suitability." *Ecological Engineering* 48

(November 2012): 1–7. https://doi.org/10.1016/j.ecoleng.2012.07.007.

Kennedy, Victor S. "Thermal Pollution—An Overview." *ScienceDirect Topics*, 2004. https://www.sciencedirect.com/topics/earth-and-planetary-sciences/thermal-pollution.

Klein, Ezra, and Derek Thompson. *Abundance*. Avid Reader Press, 2025.

Kumari, Dipty, and Dilip Kumar Paul. "Assessing the Role of Bioindicators in Freshwater Ecosystem." *Journal of Interdisciplinary Cycle Research* XII, no. IX (September 2020): 58–65.

Lake Flato, et al. "Panther Island Strategic Vision Update Final Report." *Panther Island*, February 29, 2024. https://pantherisland.com/assets/documents/Panther%2520Island_Strategic%2520Vision%2520Update_Final%2520Report_03052024-compressed.pdf. Accessed August 6, 2024.

Massey, William, et al. "Impacts of River Bank Stabilization Using Riprap on Fish Habitat in Two Contrasting Environments." *Earth Surface Processes and Landforms,* vol. 42, no. 4 (July 28, 2016): 635–46. https://doi.org/10.1002/esp.4010.

"Mid-South Climate Action Plan Priority Reduction Measures." February 2024. https://www.epa.gov/system/files/documents/2024-02/memphis-tn-pcap.pdf.

Miller, Matt. "A Sucker (Myth) Is Born Every Minute." *Cool Green Science*. March 2, 2015. https://blog.nature.org/2015/03/02/a-sucker-myth-is-born-every-minute/.

Miltner, Robert, Dale White, and Chris Yoder. "The Biotic Integrity of Streams in Urban and Suburbanizing Landscapes." *Landscape and Urban Planning* 69, no. 1 (2004): 87–100. https://doi.org/10.1016/j.landurbplan.2003.10.032.

Momota, Kyosuke, and Shinya Hosokawa. "Potential Impacts of Marine Urbanization on Benthic Macrofaunal Diversity." *Scientific Reports* 11, February 2021. https://doi.org/10.1038/s41598-021-83597-z.

Neal, J. Wesley, and David W. Willis, editors. *Small Impoundment Management in North America*. American Fisheries Society, 2012.

Nielsen-Gammon, John, and Savannah Jorgensen. *Climate Change Recommendations for Regional Flood Planning*. OSC Report 2021-01. Office of the Texas State Climatologist, Department of Atmospheric Sciences, Texas A&M University, April 16, 2021. https://climatexas.tamu.edu/files/CliChFlood.pdf.

Nussbaum, Martha C. *Justice for Animals: Our Collective Responsibility*. Simon & Schuster, 2024.

Paul, Michael J., and Judy L. Meyer. "Streams in the Urban Landscape." *Annual Review of Ecology and Systematics* 32 (2001): 333–65. https://www.jstor.org/stable/2678644.

Reeve, Dominic, Andrew Chadwick, and Christopher Fleming. *Coastal Engineering: Processes, Theory and Design Practice*, 3rd ed. CRC Press, 2018.

Reynolds, Julian, and Catherine Souty-Grosset. *Management of Freshwater Biodiversity: Crayfish as Bioindicators*. Cambridge University Press, 2012.

Russell, James. 2023. "A Watchdog in the Water Wars." *The Texas Observer*. June 5, 2023. https://www.texasobserver.org/mary-kelleher-tarrant-regional-water-board/.

Rypel, Andrew L., et al. "Goodbye to 'Rough Fish': Paradigm Shift in the Conservation of Native Fishes." *Fisheries* 46, no. 12 (2021): 605–16. https://doi.org/10.1002/fsh.10660.

Salena, Matthew. "It's a Trap! The Allure of Wastewater for Freshwater Fish." *Habitat Fisheries*. December 1, 2020. https://habitat.fisheries.org/its-a-trap-the-allure-of-wastewater-for-freshwater-fish/.

Samsel, Haley. "How Will Panther Island Impact Fort Worth's Northside? Neighbors Have Their Say." *Fort Worth Report*. September 3, 2023. https://fortworthreport.org/2023/09/03/how-will-panther-island

-impact-fort-worths-northside-neighbors-have-their-say/.

Samsel, Haley and Rachel Behrndt. "What Is Panther Island? Tracing the $1.16 Billion Project's Complex Past, Present, and Future." *Fort Worth Report,* June 14, 2023. fortworthreport.org/2023/06/14/what-is-panther-island-tracing-the-1-16-billion-projects-complex-past-present-and-future/.

Schellenberg, Greg, et al. "Dealing with Sediment: Effects on Dams and Hydropower Generation." *Hydro Review*. February 22, 2017. https://www.hydroreview.com/world-regions/north-america/dealing-with-sediment-effects-on-dams-and-hydropower-generation/.

Shahady, Thomas D. "Degradation and Improvement of Urban River Water Quality." In *Water Quality—Factors and Impacts*, edited by Daniel Dunea. IntechOpen, 2021. https://doi.org/10.5772/intechopen.89694.

Siepker, Michael J., and Jeffrey W. Quinn, editors. *Managing Centrarchid Fisheries in Rivers and Streams*. Symposium 87. American Fisheries Society, 2019.

Streams & Valleys, Inc. *Confluence: Optimized*. Streams & Valleys, Inc., November 2018. https://streamsandvalleys.org/wp-content/uploads/2018/11/Confluence_Optimized.pdf. Accessed August 6, 2024.

Stevens, Andrew L., et al. "Differences in Mercury Exposure among Wisconsin Anglers Arising from Fish Consumption Preferences and Advisory Awareness." *Fisheries* 43, no. 1 (December 2017): 31–41. https://doi.org/10.1002/fsh.10013.

Tibbetts, John. "Combined Sewer Systems: Down, Dirty, and out of Date." *Environmental Health Perspectives* 113, no. 7 (July 2005): A464–67. https://www.ncbi.nlm.nih.gov/pmc/articles/PMC1257666/.

Universal Angling Access Design Guide: Focused on the Denver South Platte River. Produced by Current Creative LLC and River Works LTD., published by Denver Trout Unlimited, 2021.

U.S. Army Corps of Engineers. *Upper Trinity River Central City Fort Worth, Texas, Final Supplement No. 1 to the Final Environmental Impact Statement*. March 2008. https://media.defense.gov/2024/Jan/03/2003367594/-1/-1/1/FSEIS_FORTWORTHCENTRALCITY.PDF.

U.S. Army Corps of Engineers, Omaha District. *Southern Platte Valley Denver, Colorado Section 1135 Study Feasibility Report Appendix C Hydraulic Engineering & Stability Analysis*. September 2018.

U.S. Global Change Research Program. *Climate Science Special Report: Fourth National Climate Assessment, Volume I*. 2017. https://science2017.globalchange.gov/downloads/CSSR2017_FullReport.pdf.

Ward, Andy D., et al. *Environmental Hydrology*, 3rd ed. CRC Press, 2016.

Waters, Thomas F. *Sediment in Streams: Sources, Biological Effects, and Control*. American Fisheries Society, 1995.

INDEX

Note: Page numbers in *italics* indicate photographs. Page numbers followed by *t* indicate tables.

A

agricultural fertilizers, eutrophication from, 117–19
Airflo, 17, 19
algae, 117–19
All-Rounder recommended setup, 16–19, *18*, 26
American Carp Society, 67
American Fisheries Society, 142
American Whitewater, 53
ancient water control infrastructure, 94–95
angler harassment laws, 55–56
anglers, use of term, 2
Apple Maps, 44, 50
apps
  Creek Critters app, 104–5
  onWater Fish app, xii, 53, 54, 202
  for scouting fishing spots, 42, 43–44
  Tides Near Me app, 172
  See also online resources
aquarium nets, for observing food sources, 90
aquatic plants, tips for fishing around, 118–19
aquifers, over-extraction of, 199
Armand Bayou Nature Center, 174
armored shorelines, 179–180, *181*
armored waterways, 153–55, *154*, *155*
Atlantic killifish, 136

B

Backcountry Hunters & Anglers (BHA), 54
backing, for reels, 18–19, 20
Backstabber patterns, 30
banks of waterways, fishing from, 149–150
barbless hooks, 33
Barry's Carp Fly patterns, 30
Bartlett, Robert, *72*, 105
bass, profile of, 128–130, *129*, 134–35
beaches, urban, 174–77, *176*
beadhead flies, 86
behavior of fish, observing, *80*, 81, 86–90, *88*, *89*, 98
bends, in armored waterways, 155
BHA (Backcountry Hunters & Anglers), 54
bicycle trails, for fishing spot access, 44, 46, *46*
Bing Maps, 44, 50
Birringer, Ryan
  bow-and-arrow casting, *50*
  creek fishing, 212–13, *212–13*
  golf course fishing, 174
  smallmouth bass catch, *129*
  streamers use, *112*
  turbulent eddy fishing, *155*
bluefish, profile of, 139
bluegill, 128, 129–130
blue-tinted ponds, 119
bobbers. *See* indicators (bobbers)
Boeser, Josh, *21*, *44*, 70
book resources, 225–26
Boston Harbor shoreline, *171*
bottom dweller patterns, *27*, 30
bottom feeding behaviors, 88
bottom of water bodies
  channelized waterways, 150, 154
  fly patterns for, *27*, 30
  investigating food sources in, 90
  sedimentation effects on, 116
bow-and-arrow casts, *50*, *85*
bowfin, profile of, 131–32
breakwaters, 183–87, *184–87*
bridges, fishing from, *143*, 149, *152*
Brown, Emma, *58*, 59, *115*
Brown Folks Fishing, 67
brown trout, profile of, 133–34
bubbles in water, decoding, 118
Buffalo Bayou (Houston), 102
bullhead catfish, profile of, 130–31

C

calm waters, 84, *84*
Carmichael, Ben, 47, *187*
carp
  competitions for, 76
  excitement of fishing for, xi–xii, xvi
  feeding behaviors, *88*, *89*, *91*, 119, 127, *197*
  fly patterns for, 30, 32
  jumping behaviors, 87
  Los Angeles River fishery, *48*, 49
  as nonnative species, 141
  profile of, 126–28, *126*
  resources on fishing for, 67, 70, *71*
  in Salt River canals, 199
  scales of, *140*
  sight casting for, 36, *205*
Carp In The Park NYC, 70
Carp Nasty patterns, 30
casting
  bow-and-arrow casts, *50*, *85*
  clinics for, *21*, 22
  dapping, 6, *7*
  diversity of techniques, 6–7
  fly-fishing leader role in, 22–23
  pitch casting, 182–83
  practice for, 26
  roll casting, 18, 177
  sight casting, 36, 133, 187, *205*
  skills vs. gear, 20–22, *21*
catching and releasing, 6, 34
catfish, profile of, 130–31
Central Park, fishing in, xiv, 41, 77, *84*, 86, 119
changing conditions of urban waters, 193–216
  "flashy" urban waterways, 209–14, *210*, *212*, *213*
  frequency and intensity of fluctuations, *192*, 193, *193*
  "hoses" and "straws," 195–200, *197*, *200*
  nonurban waterway fluctuations vs., 208–9, *209*
  revitalization efforts, *214–15*, 215–16

changing conditions of urban waters (*continued*)
seasonal changes, 193–95
streamgage use, 200–208, *201–6*
traditional infrastructure stressed by, 214
channel catfish, profile of, 130–31
channelized waterways
basic information for fishing in, 147–153, *148*, *151*, *152*
impacts on habitats, 211
children, fishing with, 52
chironomids (midges), 29, 198
Chubby Chernobyl floating flies, 28
citizen-based groups, 69–70
cleaning fly lines, 22
Clean Water Act (1972), 97, 101, 102, 110, 113, 121
Clean Water Act Owner's Manual, 122
climate change impacts
CSO health risks, 113
disruption of seasonal cues, 194
increased flooding, 213–14
weather conditions, 113, 214
Clouser Minnow streamers, 27, 86, 183
Clouser Swimming Nymph patterns, 29
Coastal Conservation Association, 142
Coldwater River, water level fluctuations in, 208–9, *209*
Colorado Carp, 70
combined sewer overflows (CSOs), 110–13, *110–12*
combos. *See* fly-fishing setups
communal waters, 77–79
communities, 61–79
building and promoting, xiv–xvi, 74–76, *75*
communal waters, 77–79, *78*
fishing groups, 67–74, *68*, *69*, *71–73*
giving back to, *21*
overview, 61–62, *61*
skills and safety enhanced by, 62–66, *62–65*
social aspects of fishing, 66–67, *66*, 218–19
urban fly fishing benefits, 3
Community Fly Fishing, 74
competitions, 76
concrete surfaces
for armoring waterways, 153, 154–55, *154*
history of, 96–97, 98–99
walkways along ponds and lakes, 179, 180
Conservation Fisheries, 141
convergence of waters, 84, *98*, 149
cooking fish, 108
cover and structure, 84–86, *85*
covering water, 62–63
crappie, 130
Craven, Caroline, *48*, 78, *93*, 176
Crawford, Carl
beach fishing, 77, *77*, 172, 176–77
breakwaters fishing, 183
jetty and groin fishing, 189
Crawford, Ethan, *194*, 195
crayfish, 27–28, 129
Creek Critters app, 104–5

D

Dale, Brandon
bow-and-arrow casts, *85*
calm waters, 84, *84*
carp fishing, 119
Central Park fishing, 41, 77
creative problem-solving, *7*
guide services, 70, *71*
preface by, xiv–xvi
structure and cover utilization, 86
trail fishing, *46*
traveling by bus, *47*
dams, 157–163, 159*t*, *161*, *162*
dapping, 6, *7*, 18
DataStream Learning Centre, 104
David, Solomon R., 141
dechlorinated treated water, 197
deep release dams, 159
DEET insect repellents, avoiding, 22
Del Razo, Rafael, 55, 172, 180
del Rosario, Analiza
beach fishing, *2*, 176
Los Angeles River fishing, 78, 101, *151*, *200*
promotion of urban fly fishing, 74–75
Denver Carp Slam and Sucker Slam, 76
Denver Trout Unlimited, 108
deposition and erosion, 145–46
desalination facilities, 199
detached breakwaters, 186–87
detritivores, defined, 132
diet of fish, fly patterns based on, 88–90, *89*
DigIndy project, 214
digital mapping tools, 43–44, 46–50, 52–53, 94
discharge, of rivers and streams, 202–7, *203*, *204*
docks, marinas, and piers, 182–83
drag, of reels, 20
drag and drop technique, 90–91, *91*
drainage basins, defined, 208
dredging operations, 184–85, *185*
drop nets, 173
drop-offs, 84
dry-dropper rigs, 86, 119, 178
dry flies, 28–29

E

eating fish, 8, 107–8
eddies
in armored waterways, 155, *155*
in director-modified waterways, 165
egg patterns, *27*, 30–31, 86
elevated vantage points
channelized waterways, 150, *152*, 153
levees, 156
emerger fly patterns, 29–30
Enforcement and Compliance History Online (ECHO), 122, 196
environmental considerations
biodiversity of species, 139–141, *140*
sharp object disposal, 121
sustainability of urban fisheries, 124–25, 219–220, *219*
See also water quality concerns
Environmental Protection Agency, website resources, 103, 104, 112, 122, 196
epilimnion layers, 159
equity concerns
alternative water control structures, 168
homelessness, 79
revitalization of water management systems, 216
Equity in Every Drop podcast, 105
erosion and deposition, 145–46, 153
estuaries, 174, *175*
eutrophication, from agricultural fertilizers, 117–19

F

feeding behaviors, 87–90, *88*, *89*

fenced-off waters, 51, *51*
fertilizers, eutrophication from, 117–19
fighting butts, 18, *18*
financial considerations
  affordability of urban fly fishing, 3, 5
  budget for gear, 14
  buying tips, 15–16
fish consumption advisories, 107
Fishing For All, 70, 71
fishing groups, 67–74, *68*, *69*, *71–73*
fishing licenses, 42
fishing spots. *See* scouting for fishing spots
fish stocking programs. *See* stocking programs
flashiness, defined, 210
flashing behaviors, 88
"flashy" urban waterways, 209–14, *210*, *212*, *213*
floating breakwaters, 185–86
floating flies, 28–29
floating lines
  all-purpose, 25
  All-Rounder setup, 17
  Heavy Hitter setup, 19
  for walkway fishing, 180
  for WWTP fishing, 198
flood hazards, 211–13, *213*
floodplains, defined, 146
flounders, profile of, 136, *136*
flow alterations
  by dams, 160, 163
  by directors, 164–66, *164*, *166*
  in nonurban waterways, 208–9, *209*
fluorocarbon leaders, 25
fly boxes, *27*
Fly Fishers International, 224
fly fishing
  conventional perceptions of, 1
  other fishing methods vs., 5
  See also urban fly fishing
fly-fishing leaders, 22–25
fly-fishing setups
  All-Rounder, 16–19
  buying tips, 15–16
  defined, 14
  factors in choosing, 14–15
  Heavy Hitter, 19–20
  order of choosing equipment, 16
Fly Fish Instruct, 224
fly lines
  All-Rounder setup, 17
  cleaning, 22
  factors in choosing, 16
fly patterns
  choosing based on diet of fish, 88–90, *89*
  defined, 5
  presenting to fish, 90–91, *91*
  recommendations for, 26–31, *27*, 86
  tying your own, 31–32, *32*
  versatility of, 5–6, *5*, 31
fly rods
  All-Rounder setup, 17–18
  factors in choosing, 16
  Heavy Hitter setup, 20
  lack of industry standards for, 20
  maintenance of, 22
fly shops
  advantages of, 15–16
  community aspects of, 70
foam beetle floating flies, 28, 86
Food & Drug Administration, 107
footwear, 36
forceps, for removing hooks, 33
fountains, in ponds and small lakes, 178
freshwater drum, profile of, 133

G

gar, profile of, 131–32, *131*
Gar Lab, 141
gear, 13–29
  All-Rounder setup, 16–19, *18*, 26
  buying tips, 15–16
  customizing your kit, 35–39, *37*, *38*, *39*
  fly-fishing leaders, 22–25
  fly patterns, 26–32, *27*, *32*
  Heavy Hitter setup, 19–20
  importance of casting skills vs., 20–22, *21*, 26
  maintenance of, 22
  minimizing fish injury and mortality, 32–35, *33*, *34*
  overview, 13–15
  Tenkara rods, *24*, 25–26
George Daniel's Spark Plug streamers, 182
getting in the water
  at urban shorelines, 172–74, *173*
  wading considerations, 105–7, *105*, *106*
getting skunked, as term, 11
getting started, encouragement for, *9*, 58–60, *58*, *60*, 217, 220, *220*
Google Earth Pro, for finding fishing spots, 49–50
Google Maps
  finding parks using, 52
  layers in, 44, 46, 48
  Street view, 50, 52
grass carp, 127–28
Green Eggs and Ham fly pattern, 32
green sunfish, 128, 129–130
Griggs, Evan, 70, 98, *98*, *100*
groins, 187–89, *188*
groundwater, 199, *200*
groups, 67–74, *68*, *69*, *71–73*
guide services, community aspects of, 70

H

habitats
  along shorelines, 174, *175*
  by artifacts and debris, *98*, 150, *151*
  channelization effects on, *144*, 148–49, 154
  by dams, 163
  by detached breakwaters, 186
  by directors, 165
  "flashy" urban waterway impacts on, 211
  hybrid water control infrastructure benefits, 216
  at marinas, docks, and piers, 182
  sedimentation effects on, 116–17
  in winding waterways, 146–47, *146*
halibut, profile of, 136, *136*
Hall, Nic
  advocacy work, 108
  bridge fishing, 11, *11*
  carp fishing, xi
  fishing during runoff events, 115, *115*
  South Platte River fishing, 46, *47*, *63*, *80*
  streamgages use, 206
  use of elevated vantage points, 153
handling fish, 34, *34*
hand washing, 103
Hangman Creek (Spokane), *117*
Hare's Ear Nymph patterns, 29
harmful algal blooms (HABs), 117–19, 165–66
hatcheries. *See* stocking programs
heads, of fly lines, 19
Heavy Hitter recommended setup, 19–20

hemostats, for removing flies, 33
history of urban waters, 93–99
homelessness concerns, 79
Hook, Line, and Supper (Shaw), 108
hooks, modifying barbs of, 32–33, *33*, 34
"hoses" and "straws," 195–200, *197*, *200*
Houdyshell, L. J., *5*
How's My Waterway web page, 103
Hsia, Jennifer
  evolving skills of, 12, *12*
  fenced-off water fishing, 51, *51*
  pond fishing, 179
  smallmouth buffalo catch, *102*
Hunters of Color, 67, 69, 75
The Hybrid patterns, 30
hypolimnion layers, 159

I

iFishiBelong, 72, 73, 75
impervious surfaces
  flow alterations from, 208, 209–14, *210*, *212*, *213*
  pollution from, 96–97, 98–99, 109–10
impoundments, 158
indicators (bobbers)
  for ponds and small lakes, 118, 177–78
  for seams, *82*, 115
  types of, 38–39
industrial waste-related pollution, 121–22, *122*
injury to fish, minimizing, 32–35, *33*, *34*
inlets and outlets, of ponds and lakes, 178–79
insect repellents, avoiding, 22
Izaak Walton League of America, 104–5

J

James, Davis, xi
jetties, 189–190, *190*, *191*
jig streamers, 28, 114, 182
Jubilado, Lino
  advocacy work, *60*, 69–70, 75, *75*
  Green Eggs and Ham fly pattern, 32
  Surf and Turf Slam, 76
jumping behaviors, 87

K

Kamata, Shuhei "Shu," *66*, 67
killing fish, 108
knot tying, 23

L

large arbor reels, 20
largemouth bass, profile of, 128–130
large woody debris, fish attracted to, 150
Larry the Lunker, 70
leaders, 22–25
leaping behaviors, 87
lefteye flounders, 136
Lefty's Deceiver streamers, 27, 183
legal concerns. *See* rights to fish; trespassing concerns
levees, 156–57, *156*, *157*
light levels, 175
Lindsay Mlynarek, *24*
lines. *See* fly lines
lining the fish, 90
Los Angeles River
  carp fishing in, *48*, 49
  channelization of, 148
  cleanup of, 101
  groundwater infiltration, *200*
  objects in the water of, *151*
  Surf and Turf Slam at, 76
  water control infrastructure in, 96
low-head dams, 162, *162*
low-light conditions, 175

M

Mad River Outfitters, 16, 224
maps, interactive, 42
marinas, docks, and piers
  for accessing the water, 173–74
  tips for fishing near, 182–83
marshes, defined, 174
Mayfly Project, 73–74
McCord, Colton, *64*, *65*, 66
McCord, Nate
  bridge fishing, 66, *143*, 153
  large fish catch, *18*
  observing seams, *82*, 83
  scanning a stretch of water, *40*
  South Platte River fishing, 46, *47*, *63*, *64*, *65*, *197*
  streamer use, *83*
  streamgages use, 206
Medina, Mike, *91*
mending line, 18
mentors, benefits of, 21
microplastics, 121
mid-column feeding behaviors, 88
midges (chironomids), 29, 198
Mikesell, Rick
  bridge fishing, 153
  carp fishing, xi, *89*
  guide services, 70
  shoreline fishing, 180
  South Platte River fishing, 46, *63*
  streamgages use, 206
Miller, Jane, *60*, 65, 73, *73*
Milton, Quincy, *46*, *68*
Minneapolis Carp Angler's Potluck and Fly Fishing Tournament, 76
Mississippi River
  lock-and-dam system, 84, 158
  meandering path of, *147*
Missouri River
  armoring of, *154*
  directors in, *166*
Mlynarek, Lindsay, *191*
monofilament
  for fishing along walkways, 180
  for leaders, 22–23
  tying knots in, 103
  as weed guards, 118
moored boats, habitat created by, 182
mooring cells, as structure and cover, *85*
mortality of fish, minimizing, 32–35, *33*, *34*
municipal separate storm sewer systems (MS4s), 110, 113–14, *113*
municipal wastewater treatment plants
  pollution from, 121–22
  tips for fishing near, 196–99, *197*

N

Nanaimo River estuary, *175*
National Inventory of Dams, 158
National Water Dashboard, 201, 206, 207
Native Fish Bill (Minnesota), 141
Native Fish for Tomorrow, 141
native species, historical links provided by, 139
Near-Nuff Crayfish streamers, 27–28
needle-nose pliers, for modifying and removing hooks, 33, *33*, 37
nets
  for catching fish, 37–38, *38*
  for observing food sources, 90
New York City, fishing in, 41, *42*, *47*

Nonconnah Creek, water level fluctuations in, 210–11, *210*
nonnative species, varying perspectives on, 140–41
nonurban waterways
  fishing in, 76–77
  water level fluctuations in, 208–9, *209*
Northern pike, sharp teeth of, *33*
nylon leaders, 25
nymph patterns
  description of, *27*, 29–30
  for pond and small lake fishing, 177–78
  for runoff event fishing, 114–15
  in two-fly rigs, 86

O

observing fish behavior, *80*, 81, 86–90, *88*, *89*, 98
obstacles in the water, fish attracted to, 150, *151*
Olentangy River, discharge from, 203–5, *203*, *204*, *205*
online resources, 223–25
  CSOs, 112
  digital mapping tools, 43–44, 46–50, 52–53
  dry-dropper rig instructions, 86
  ECHO database, 122, 196
  for handling fish, 34
  harmful algal blooms, 117–18
  levee database, 155
  National Inventory of Dams, 158
  Orvis Fly Fishing Learning Center, 23, 223
  saltwater shoreline fishing, 172
  scouting for fishing spots, 42–43
  streamgages data, 201–3, *201–3*, 206
  water pollutants, 122
  water quality information, 103–5, 107
  See also apps
onWater Fish app, xii, 53, 54, 202
onX Hunt app, 53
Oros indicators, 38–39
Orvis
  fly boxes, 27
  fly lines, 17, 19
Orvis Fly Fishing Learning Center, 23, 223
outfalls, of combined sewer overflows, 111–12, *111*
outfits. *See* fly-fishing setups
outlets and inlets, of ponds and lakes, 178–79
outside the city fishing, 76–77
oxygen levels of water
  harmful algal bloom effects on, 117, 118
  near municipal wastewater treatment plants, 198
  water temperature effects on, 109

P

Pacific halibut, *136*
Parachute Adams floating flies, 29, 199
parks, scouting fishing spots at, 52–53
partners, fishing with, 62–63, 65–66, 175
Pearl Riverkeeper, 69, 104
pedestrian trails, for fishing spot access, 44, 46, *46*
Perdigon patterns, 29–30
perfection loops, 23, 25
Phetsavong, Rick
  drop-off fishing, 84
  guide services, *8*, 12, *71*
  lock-and-dam system fishing, 158
  outfall fishing, *113*
  structure and cover utilization, *85*
photography
  of anglers, 78
  of fish, *3*, 34, *34*, *37*
piers, marinas, and docks, 182–83
pilings, habitat created by, 182
Pillsbury Mill (Minneapolis), 97–98, *98*
pitch casting, 182–83
plastic debris, in urban waters, 119–121, *120*
pleco catfish, 37
pliers, for modifying and removing hooks, 33, *33*, 37
podcasts, 226
point source pollution, defined, 121
  See also water quality concerns
polarized sunglasses, 36, 37
ponds and small lakes, *169*, 177–79, *178*, *179*
poppers, 28–29
presenting the fly to the fish, 90–91, *91*
Prince Nymph patterns, 29
public transportation, to fishing spots, 46–47, *47*

R

rainbow trout, profile of, 133–34, *134*
ramp-like structures, for accessing the water, 173
reading the water
  channelized waterways, 149
  decoding bubbles, 118
  directors, 165–66
  at the former Pillsbury Mill, 98
  principles of, *80*, 81–86, *82–85*
  saltwater shoreline fishing, 172
Recreational Boating and Fishing Foundation, 224
redband trout, *134*, *194*, 195
reels
  All-Rounder setup, 18–19
  factors in choosing, 16
  Heavy Hitter setup, 20
  maintenance of, 22
resources
  books, 225–26
  podcasts, 226
  saltwater shoreline fishing, 170–72
  species of fish, 141–42
  water quality information, 102–5, *103*
  See also online resources
riffles, 149, *151*, *152*
righteye flounders, 136
rights to fish, 41, 53–56, *54*, *55*
Rio, OutBound Short series, 20
riparian zones, 146, 208
riprap, for armoring waterways, 153, 154–55, *154*
River Network, 122
rock ramps, *167*
rods. *See* fly rods
roll casting, 18, 177
roly-poly retrieves, *187*
Rosenbauer, Tom, xi–xiii
rough fish, as term, 140, 141
running lines, defined, 19
runoff
  combined sewer overflows for, 110–13, *110–12*
  effects of, 109–10, *192*, *193*
  fishing during runoff events, 114–15, *115*
  municipal separate storm sewer systems for, 110, 113–14, *113*
run-of-the-river dams, 160

S

safety considerations
beach fishing, 177
benefits of community, 62–66, *62–65*
casting near boats and docks, 183
dams, 162, *162*, 163
directors, 166
eating fish, 8, 107–8
"flashy" urban waterways, 211–13
groin fishing, 189
hand washing, 103
homelessness impacts on urban waters, 79
jetty fishing, *190*
proximity of CSO outfalls, 111, 112, 113
runoff event fishing, 114
sharp object disposal, 121
saltwater, desalination of, 199
saltwater fly fishing
along shorelines, 170–72, *171*
flies for, 86
reels for, 20
saltwater species profiles, 135–39, *136–38*
San Juan worm patterns, 30
Santa Monica Beach, *2*, *76*, *176*
satellite imagery
for finding fishing spots, 48–49, 94
for tracing "hoses," 196
scavenger hunts, 76
Schultz, Jule, 104
Scientific Anglers, 17, 19
scouting for fishing spots, 41–60
best time of day for fishing, 43
channelized waterways, 149–150
digital mapping tools for, 43–44, 46–50, 52–53
in fenced-off waters, 51, *51*
getting out there, 58–60, *59*, *60*
key resources for, 42–43
overview, *40*, 41–42
rights to fish, 41, 53–56, *54*, *55*
secret spots, 57–58
in smaller urban waters, 45, *45*
trespassing concerns, 56–57, *56*
seams, looking for, 82–83, *82*
seasonal changes in urban waters, 193–95
secret fishing spots, 57–58
sedimentation
dam trapping of, 159–160
defined, 116
in dirty waters, 115–17, *116*
dredging operations for, 184–85, *185*
tombolos formed by, *186*
setups. *See* fly-fishing setups
shallow waters
channelized waterways, *152*
checking before getting in the water, 173
drag and drop technique for, 90
sharp objects, disposing of, 121
Shaw, Hank, 108
sheepshead, profile of, 133
shooting-taper (ST) lines, 19–20, 189
shorelines. *See* urban shorelines
sight casting/fishing, 36, 133, 187, *205*
Simpson, Elizabeth, *21*
sinking lines
all-purpose, 25
All-Rounder setup, 17
Heavy Hitter setup, 19–20
for jetty fishing, 189, *191*
for walkway fishing, 180
for WWTP fishing, 198
skills
building through community, 62–66, *62–65*
for encountering new species, 142, *143*
observing fish behavior, *80*, 81, 86–90, *88*, *89*, 98
presenting the fly to the fish, 90–91, *91*
reading the water, *80*, 81–86, *82–85*, 98, 118, 149, 165–66, 172
See also casting
skunked, as term, 11
slack-water pools, 165
sliders, 28–29
small lakes and ponds, 177–79, *178*, *179*
smallmouth bass, profile of, 128–130, *129*
smallmouth buffalo, *102*
Sneaky Pete poppers, 28
social aspects of fishing, 66–67, *66*, 218–19
See also communities
soft hackles (wet flies), 29
South Platte River
channelization of, 148
Chatfield Dam on, 163
Clear Creek confluence with, 196
pedestrian paths along, 46
ramp-like structures in, 168
shoreline of, *170*
streamgage data for, 206
water quality concerns, *57*
species found in urban waters, 123–142
biodiversity of, 139–141, *140*
downstream of dams, 159*t*
generalist freshwater species, 125–131, *126*, *129*
learning about local species, 141–42
other freshwater species, 131–35, *131*, *132*, *134*
overview, 123–25, *123*
ponds and small lakes, 177
saltwater species, 135–39, *136–38*
speckled trout, profile of, 136–37, *137*
spey rods, *21*
split shot, 38–39
Spokane River
cleanup of, *69*
failure of hybrid water management system, *214–15*
redband trout fishing on, *134*, *194*, 195
sediments from Hangman Creek, *117*
sucker caught on, *132*
Spokane River Forum, 78
Spokane Riverkeeper, 69, 104, 207
spots for fishing. *See* scouting for fishing spots
spotted seatrout, profile of, 136–37, *137*
spotting fish, 87
See also observing fish behavior
state fisheries management agencies, 42
steady risers, 87–88
stilling basins, 160–61, *161*
stocking programs
catching your first fish, 42
eating stocked fish, 107
environmental considerations, 125
rainbow trout, 134
white bass-striper hybrids, 135
storage-release dams, 160

"straws" and "hoses," 195–200, *197*, *200*
streamers, 27–28, *27*, *112*, 114
streamgages, 200–208, *201–5*
Street View (Google Maps), 50, 52
strike indicators. *See* indicators
striped bass
freshwater behaviors, 134–35
saltwater behaviors, 138–39, *138*
Stripers Forever, 142
stripping baskets, 39, *39*, *191*
stripping lines, 155, *155*, 182
stripping streamers, *112*
strip sets, 155, *155*
structure and cover utilization, 84–86, *85*, 114
substrate. *See* bottom of water bodies
suckers, profile of, 132–33, *132*
sunfish, xii, 128–130
sunglasses, 36, 37
super gages, 207
surface activity, spotting fish by, 87
surface feeding behaviors, 87–88
surface release dams, 159
Surf and Turf Slam, 76
surfcasting, 76, 77, *77*
surfperch, profile of, 137–38
sustainability of urban fisheries, 124–25, 219–220, *219*

T

tailing behaviors, 87
tailwaters, 158
Take Me Fishing online resource, 224
Tall Bull, William, *99*
temperate bass, profile of, 134–35
temperature, water. *See* water temperature
Tenkara rods, *24*, 25–26
Terrain layer, Google Maps, 48
thermal stratification, 158–59
thermometers, for measuring water temperature, 109, 159
tide changes
checking before getting in the water, 173, *173*
reading the water of, 170–72, *171*
Tides Near Me app, 172
time of day for fishing, 43
tombolos, *186*
topography, digital mapping of, 48
tournaments, 76
trails, for fishing spot access, 44, 46, *46*
trash, in urban waters, 119–121, *120*
trespassing concerns, 56–57, *56*, 173
The Triple Haul website, 224–25
trout, profile of, 133–34, *134*
Trout Unlimited, 74, 142
turbulent waters
beyond breakwaters, 183
channelized waterways, 149
reading the water of, 83, *83*, *160*
rod position for, *155*
two-fly rigs, 86
tying knots, 23

U

Ubuntu Fly Anglers Network, 72
unaltered waterways, 145–47
United Women on the Fly, 73
urban fly fishing
accessibility of, 2–6, *4*
overcoming perceptions of, 1–2, 11–12
rewarding nature of, *10*, 217–19, *218*
urbanization, as term, 125
urban shorelines, 169–191
armored, 179–180, *181*
breakwaters, 183–87, *184–87*
critically important shorelines, 174–77, *175*, *176*
getting in the water, 105–7, *105*, *106*, 172–74, *173*
groins, 187–89, *188*
jetties, 189–190, *190*, *191*
marinas, docks, and piers, 182–83
overview, 169–170, *170*
ponds and small lakes, *169*, 177–79, *178*, *179*
saltwater fishing resources, 170–72, *171*
urban waterscape
built environment impacts, 98–99
defined, 94
formation of, 94–97, *96*, *98*
urban waterways, 145–168
alternative water control infrastructure, 167–68, *167*
armored, 153–55, *154*, *155*
channelization impacts, 147–153, *148*, *151*, *152*
dams, 157–163, 159*t*, *161*, *162*
directors, 164–66, *164*, *166*
exploring new waters, *92*
exploring smaller water bodies, 45, *45*
fenced-off waters, 51, *51*
habitat changes in, *144*, 146, *146*, 148, 154, 163, 165
history of, 93–99
levees, 156–57, *156*, *157*
unaltered waterways, 145–47
See also changing conditions of urban waters; reading the water; water quality concerns
US Army Corps of Engineers National Levee Database, 155
US Geological Survey, 160, 200

V

vegetation, observing food sources in, *89*

W

waders, 35–36, 106
wading, considerations for, 105–7, *105*, *106*
wading boots, 36
wastewater treatment plants. *See* municipal wastewater treatment plants
water access laws, 53–54, 173
water conditions, variable nature of, 50
water control infrastructure
history of, 94–96, *96*
impacts of, 98–99, *98*
revitalization efforts, *214–15*, 215–16
stresses on, 214
See also channelized waterways
water depth changes, 84
Waterkeeper Alliance, 69, 105
water level fluctuations
dam release levels, 159–160, 159*t*
"flashy" urban waterways, 209–14, *210*, *212*, *213*
by levees, 156, 157
nonurban waterways, 208–9, *209*
runoff events, 114–15, *192–93*
tide changes, 170–72, *171*
water quality, defined, 101
water quality concerns, 101–22
checking before getting in the water, 173
cleanup and restoration efforts, 102, *102*

water quality concerns (*continued*)
common pollutants and water quality issues, 97, 98–99, 108–15, *110–13*
dam effects, 158–160, 159*t*
dirty waters, 115–122, *116*, *120*, *122*
eating fish, 8, 107–8
entering the water, 35
hybrid water control infrastructure benefits, 216
indicators of water and habitat health, *104*
overview, 101–2
resources for information on, 102–5, *103*, 107
super gages for monitoring, 207
wading decisions and, 105–7, *105*, *106*
watersheds, defined, 208
water temperature
near municipal wastewater treatment plants, 197–98
seasonal changes, 195
water quality concerns, 108–9, 158–59
waterways, defined, 145
See also urban waterways
weather conditions
at beaches, 175
climate change impacts, 113, 214
for spotting fish, 87
Weberian apparatus, 127, 130
website resources. *See* online resources
weed guards, 118
welded loops, for swapping leaders, 23
wet flies, 29–30
wet wading, 106
white flashes, 88
white perch, profile of, 134–35
Winter, Tyler, 141, 198
wipers (white bass-striper hybrids), 135
woody debris, fish attracted to, 150
Woolly Bugger streamers, 27, 86
worm patterns, *27*, 30–31

ABOUT THE AUTHOR

MARC FRYT is an urban fly-fishing guide, writer, and photographer whose work has appeared in multiple fishing and outdoor magazines. While serving in the army, he discovered a passion for fly fishing—a spark that ultimately revealed how much adventure awaits beneath our city skylines. By highlighting overlooked waters, Marc's stories and photographs show how casting a line close to home can inspire genuine discovery and a deeper bond with the places we live. Marc currently resides in Spokane, Washington, with his wife, Lindsay, and their dog, Windsor "the Bugaboo." You can explore more of his work at www.TheTripleHaul.com.

Lindsay Mlynarek